KOREA

PEOPLE, COUNTRY and CULTURE

Edited by
Keith Howard

with
Susan Pares and Tessa English

The School of Oriental and African Studies
LONDON

Cover photograph, of *Ogwangdae* masked dancer, by Keith Howard

First published in 1996

ISBN 0 7286 0266 0

This publication, and the research and preparation thereof, has been funded by the Korea Press Center and the Korean Overseas Information Service, Seoul, and the School of Oriental and African Studies, London.

Published by The School of Oriental and African Studies, The University of London, Thornhaugh Street, Russell Square, London WC1H 0XG.

Printed in the United Kingdom by Hobbs the Printers Ltd, Brunel Road, Totton, Hampshire SO40 3WX

CONTENTS

THE BOOK

CONTENTS

FACTSHEETS

CONTRIBUTORS

Don Baker. Chapter 8.1, 8.2, 8.3. Canada-Korea Business Council Chair in Korean Studies in the Department of Asian Studies, University of British Columbia, Vancouver. An editor of *Sourcebook of Korean Civilization*, vol.2 (New York, Columbia University Press, 1996). Author of many articles on the history of Korean religion, philosophy, and traditional science, most recently 'Morality and Metaphysics in Chosŏn Neo-Confucianism' in *Journal of Korean Thought, 1* (Spring 1996).

Katherine and Eckart Dege. Chapters 9, 10, 11. Eckart Dege is a professor of geography at the University of Kiel, Germany; Katherine Dege is a freelance translator. Eckart is the author of *Kleiner Reiseführer: Nordkorea* (Kiel, Verein zur Förderung regionalwissenschaftlicher Analysen e.V., 1989), *Korea: Eine landeskundliche Einführung* (Kiel, Verein zur Förderung regionalwissenschaftlicher Analysen e.V., 1992) and *Entwicklungsdisparitäten der Agrarregionen Südkoreas* (Kiel, Der Universität Kiel, 1982). Katherine Dege is translator of *Korea: Scenic Beauty and Religious Landmarks* (text by Fritz Vos and photographs by Mark de Fraeye; Freiberg, Schillinger Verlach, 1995). Katherine and Eckart co-edited and translated Hermann Lautensach's *Korea: A Geography Based on the Author's Travels and Literature* (Berlin, Springer-Verlag, 1988).

Martina Deuchler. Chapter 7.1. Professor of Korean Studies, School of Oriental and African Studies, London. Author of *Confucian Gentlemen and Barbarian Envoys: The Opening of Korea, 1875-1885* (Seattle, University of Washington Press) and *The Confucian Transformation of Korea: A Study of Society and Ideology* (Cambridge MA, Harvard University Press, 1992).

Tessa English. Co-writer of factsheets. Research Officer, Korea Schools Project, 1993-5. Currently, Programmes Administrator in Continuing Vocational Education at Bath College of Higher Education; previously project officer on 'Thinking Futures' for Worldwide Fund for Nature, a technical vocational education project with Avon Local Education Authority, and a flexible learning project for the Department of State for Employment and Education.

Ruth Grayson. Chapters 12, 13, 14. Honorary lecturer in Korean Studies, University of Sheffield. Author of *Knife-making in Sheffield* (Sheffield, Hallam University, 1995) and 'More myth than reality: the independent artisan in 19th-century Sheffield', *Journal of Historical Sociology* (1996).

James Hoare. Chapters 4, 15.2, 15.3. Researcher on East Asian affairs since 1964. PhD from the School of Oriental and African Studies, London. Author of *The British Embassy Compound, Seoul, 1884-1984* (Seoul, Korean-British Society, 1984), *Japan's Treaty Ports and Foreign Settlements: Uninvited Guests in Meiji Japan* (Folkestone, Japan Library, 1988), and with Susan Pares *Korea: An Introduction* (London, KPI, 1988).

Keith Howard. Writer and co-writer of all factsheets, Chapters 2, 3, 6.2, 7.3, 7.5, 8.4, 8.5. Director, Korea Schools Project. Chairman of Music Studies and lecturer in Korean Studies at the School of Oriental and African Studies, London. Author of *Korean Musical Instruments: A Practical Guide* (Seoul, Se-kwang, 1988), *Bands, Songs and Shamanistic Rituals* (Seoul, Royal Asiatic Society, 1989), *Sounds of Korea* (Seoul, Korean Overseas Information Service, 1990), *Korean Musical Instruments* (Hong Kong, Oxford University Press, 1995), *True Stories of the Korean Comfort Women* (London, Cassell, 1995), co-translator of Hahn Man-young's *Kugak: Essays in Korean Traditional Music* (Seoul, Tamgu Dang, 1991), editor of *Papers of the British Association for Korean Studies*, vol.1-6 (1991-1996).

Beth McKillop. Chapter 6.1. Curator, China and Korea Section, British Library. Previously, curator of the Samsung Gallery of Korean Art, Victoria and Albert Museum, London, and author of *Korean Art and Design: The Samsung Gallery of Korean Art* (London, Victoria and Albert Museum, 1992).

Kevin O'Rourke. Chapter 5.2. Professor of English Literature at Kyung Hee University, Seoul. Editor and translator of *The Sijo Tradition* (Seoul, Jung Eum Sa, 1987), Yi Mun-yol's *Our Twisted Hero* (Seoul, Minumsa, 1987), *Tilting the Jar, Spilling the Moon: Poems from Koryŏ, Chosŏn, and Contemporary Korea* (Seoul, Universal Publications Agency, 1988), *Singing Like a Cricket, Hooting Like an Owl: Selected Poems of Yi Kyu-bo* (Ithaca, Cornell East Asia Program, 1995), and Midang So Chong-ju's *Poems of a Wanderer* (Dublin, Dedalus, 1995).

Susan Pares. Chapters 1, 5.1, 6.3, 7.2, 7.4, 8.6, 8.7, 15.1, 15.4 and co-writer of factsheets. Research Officer, Korea Schools Project, 1995-6. Freelance editor and writer. Author of *Crosscurrents* (Seoul, Seoul International Publishing House, 1985) and co-author with James Hoare of *Korea: An Introduction* (London, KPI, 1988).

ACKNOWLEDGEMENTS

We express our gratitude to the following for their assistance:

Korea Press Center and The School of Oriental and African Studies for funding the project; Korean Overseas Information Service for supplying CD-Roms; Korean National Tourism Corporation for supplying maps.

Steve Davy and Juliet Coombe, La Belle Aurore Media Agency, London, for the design and layout of the factsheets and the cover design, and Andrew Mowat, graphic designer, for the factsheet line drawings; Jeon Myung-ok, for calligraphy (factsheet 2.2); Eckart and Katherine Dege, for geographical and geological maps (factsheets 3.1, 3.3, 3.5); Catherine Lawrence, SOAS, for maps (factsheets 3.2, 4.2, 4.4); James Hoare, for Korean war map (factsheet 4.3).

Tina Waight, for typing assistance and patience.

We also gratefully acknowledge the following credits and appropriate permissions to reproduce:

The line drawings on factsheet 1.2 are after J. H. Kim, *Prehistory of Korea*, figure 12 and figure 65 (Honolulu, Hawaii University Press, 1978), W. Y. Kim, *Recent Archaeological Discoveries in the ROK*, figure 17 (Paris/Tokyo, UNESCO/Centre of East Asian Studies, 1983), and Sahara Makoto, *Nihon no Genshi Bijitsu 7: Dotaku*, page 74 (Tokyo, Kodansha, 1979). The line drawing on factsheet 2.3 is after Paul Crane, *Korean Patterns*, page 127 (Seoul, Korea Branch of the Royal Asiatic Society, 1978). The poster on factsheet 3.2 was prepared for Seoul Metropolitan Government and provided for use here by the Korea Press Center. The map and graphic on factsheet 5.2 was originally prepared by Zeno Vassiliades, Cheil Communications UK. The notations on p.4 of factsheet 6.3 were prepared by Kim Kisu and first published in *Haegŭm chŏngak* (Seoul, Han'guk kugak kodŭng hakkyo, 1979); other notations are by Keith Howard and were first published in *Sounds of Korea* (Seoul, Korean Overseas Information Service, 1990) and *Korean Musical Instruments* (Seoul, Se-kwang, 1988). The paintings by Shin Yunbok and Kim Hongdo used in factsheets 6.1 and 6.2 are housed in the Kansŏng Art Gallery, Seoul; the two ink paintings on factsheet 2.7 are kept at the British Museum. The *maedŭp* pictured on factsheet 2.6 is by Kim Hŭijin.

The cartoon on factsheet 4.4 first appeared in *The Economist* on 28 May 1994 and is used with permission of the copyright holder. The two drawings of room layouts on factsheet 2.4 first appeared in Beth McKillop's *Korean Art and Design: The Samsung Gallery of Korean Art* (London, Victoria and Albert Museum, 1992), pages 150 and 152, and are used with permission. The map of Cheju on factsheet 5.3 is used with permission from the Korean National Tourism Corporation.

Photo credits: Keith Howard and Korean Ministry of Information *EXCEPT*: Dorrit Wegner (Songgwang temple, factsheet 2.3), James Hoare (plaque at Solma-ri, factsheet 4.3), Korea National Tourism Corporation (*Tol harubang*, factsheet 5.3), The Deep-Rooted Tree, Seoul (*hanbok*, factsheet 2.6). Two Korean war photographs on factsheet 4.3 are reproduced from *Korea: 1951-53* (Washington, Department of the Army, c.1953), pages 32-3 and 40.

We have attempted to record and thank all those who have helped us with this project and to acknowledge all credits and permissions to reproduce. We apologise for any oversights and should be glad to have them brought to our attention.

PREFACE

Korea: People, Country and Culture consists of photocopiable factsheets, a book, and a separate map. The book contains a directory of Resources and reading lists for each topic, while maps, statistics, illustrations and graphs are incorporated on the factsheets. Taken together, it is envisaged that the pack will act as a useful resource bank of information and ideas on Korea. We hope it will be used for project work, class work, group discussion and individual research. The materials are designed primarily for use with students at Key Stage 4 of the (British) National Curriculum, but we hope that they will also be of interest to teachers delivering post-sixteen Liberal/General Studies programes. The potential audience is, of course, substantially wider.

The relevant curriculum areas include geography, history, religious education, creative arts (there are sections on music, dance, literature, and fine arts), business studies and economics, tourism, and education for citizenship (particularly in respect to international understanding and global issues).

The *FACTSHEETS* are illustrated and are meant primarily for class use. Each explores a single topic of potential interest, divided into six groups: profiles, the people, land, politics, economy and culture. The factsheets may stand alone, or be used to supplement other texts which include information on Korea. A separate *MAP* is included. Additional tourist information, and maps and brochures, can be obtained from the Korean National Tourism Corporation; Korean Overseas Information Service has also published a CD-Rom which may be requested from the Embassy of the Republic of Korea: the directory of Resources includes the appropriate addresses.

The *BOOK* offers a much more in-depth look at each topic introduced in the factsheets, and adds sections covering matters and issues of interest. It is hoped that the text can be used to prepare material prior to class teaching, and should also serve as a resource for individual and group student research. The 15 chapters in the book are written by a group of internationally known scholars and teachers. In many cases, the choice of material presented in these chapters is personal to the authors concerned. There is some overlapping of material between sections, and between parts of the book and particular factsheets. This is intentional, since we anticipate that the materials may be used by teachers in a number of different disciplines. Issues such as economic and social development and demographic changes, for example, fit into a number of contexts. Cross referencing is given in the book, both to different sections of the book and between book and factsheets, in an attempt to cut down the necessity for searching for information.

A Resources section, at the end of the book, offers a starting point for locating additional information on Korea. The annotation given for books and other materials which are more generally available is meant to be neither judgemental nor comprehensive. In the book, at the end of each chapter, and often at the end of each section, a list of readings is given. The lists are again not comprehensive and, since they are designed to help teachers and students locate additional information, do not venture beyond titles which can be found or ordered in Britain. The reading lists do not attempt to provide a bibliography, and hence do not summarise the texts used by authors in the preparation of the text.

In both book and factsheets, we have used the McCune-Reischauer romanisation system for Korean. In the spelling of Chinese names, dynasties, places and other words, the *pinyin* romanisation system is used, with the exception of personal names where an alternative spelling is better known. McCune-Reischauer is the most commonly used system for Korean amongst scholars, and has since 1984 been the preferred system of the South Korean Ministry of Education (although a number of other systems are still employed by some in South Korea, for example *kimchi* and *kimchee* in place of the McCune-Reischauer *kimch'i* for Korea's pickled cabbage dish). McCune-Reischauer differs from the system used in North Korea mainly through the addition of two diacritical marks. We have, as is normal practice, retained the preferred spellings of people's names, and the common spelling of well-known terms. Readers should also remember that 'n', 'r', and 'l' are in some cases used interchangeably.

The table below gives a simplified guide to the Korean (*han'gŭl*) script, with McCune-Reischauer romanisations. More information is given in chapter 5 and factsheet 2.2. The pronunciation of consonants varies depending on where they occur in a lexical unit, and here they are listed in the three possible positions as initial/middle/final.

LETTER	ROMAN--ISATION	PRONUN--CIATION	LETTER	ROMAN--ISATION	PRONUN--CIATION
ㅏ	a	ah	ㅞ	we	wei (as in *weight*)
ㅑ	ya	ya	ㅟ	wi	wee
ㅓ	ŏ	o (as in *dog*)	ㅢ	ŭi	(close to the French, *oui*)
ㅕ	yŏ	yaw (as in *yawn*)	ㄱ	k/g/k	*unaspirated* k/g/k
ㅗ	o	oh	ㄴ	n/n/n	n/n/n
ㅛ	yo	yo (as in *yo-yo*)	ㄷ	t/d/t	*unasp.* t/d/t
ㅜ	u	u (as in *Susan*)	ㄹ	l or r/r/l	l *or* r/r/l
ㅠ	yu	you	ㅁ	m/m/m	m/m/m
ㅡ	ŭ	oo (as in *good*)	ㅂ	p/b/p	*unasp.* p/b/p
ㅣ	i	ee (as in *see*)	ㅅ	s/s/t	*as in spring*, s/s/t
ㅐ	ae	e (as in *peck*)	ㅇ	(*silent*)/ng/ng	(*silent initial*)/ng/ng
ㅔ	e	e (as in *hen*)	ㅈ	ch/j/t	*unasp.* ch/j/t
ㅖ	ye	ye (as in *yen*)	ㅊ	ch'/ch'/t	*aspirated* ch/ch/*unasp.* t
ㅚ	oe	way	ㅋ	k'/k'/k	*asp.* k/k/*unasp.* k
ㅘ	wa	wa (close to *water*)	ㅌ	t'/t'/t	*asp.* t/*asp.* t *or* ch/t
ㅝ	wŏ	wo/wa (as in *wand*)	ㅍ	p'/p'/p	*asp.* p/p/*unasp.* p
ㅙ	wae	wea (as in *weather*)	ㅎ	h/h/t	h/h/t

INTRODUCTORY PORTRAIT

Images

What do we know about Korea? Situated to the east of the Asian landmass, between China and Japan, it seems distant to us sitting way to the west of that same landmass, 5500 miles away in Britain. It briefly emerges onto our television screens and the inside pages of our national broadsheets only when some attention-grabbing headline is facilitated by disaster or politics. It could be that our lack of knowledge reflects a national penchant for ignorance, or it could even be—but surely not—that we prefer negative images. MASH showed us a war-ravaged, poverty-stricken nation: Korea is no longer anything like that. Korean industry has found it hard to shake off its old image of sweat shops achieving profits because of cheap labour, but the reality is very different, particularly in the major conglomerates—Hyundai, Samsung, Daewoo, Lucky Goldstar (LG), and so on—which dominate South Korea. Actually, many South Korean products are now well known: cars from Hyundai, Daewoo, Kia and Ssangyong, home electronics from TVs to microwaves and fax machines from Samsung and Goldstar, training shoes, computers, and so on.

Yet the images remain:

1996. Elections for the National Assembly are held in South Korea in April. The New Korea Party of President Kim Young Sam is expected to lose its majority, but he has become a statesman, and surprisingly manages to garner sufficient support to stay in office. The two previous presidents are on trial for amassing slush funds from business donations, and for the way they came to power through a military coup in 1979. Kim is the first civilian president for over three decades. Opposition parties claim he received some of the slush funds of his predecessors to finance his own 1992 election campaign, but he manages to ride above the storm. Meanwhile, TV screens show pictures of student demonstrations: a student suffered a heart attack in a recent rally, and his body has since been guarded on campus by students armed with batons, to prevent the police removing and cremating it (without a body, there can be no funeral).

President Clinton is about to visit. In North Korea, food shortages are becoming critical, and the UNDP reports widespread hunger. In the North, the economic situation looks dire and, possibly in an attempt to divert domestic attention from home, the North has pulled out of the armistice treaty that ended the Korean war in 1953. Could a new war erupt? Watch this space.

1994. North Korea is suspected of developing a nuclear weapon. Seoul, less than 30 miles from the border separating the two halves of Korea, could be an easy target. Atomic inspectors report that nuclear material is missing from the reactor sites they have been allowed to visit. To the world, a crisis looms, since North Korea is considered unstable and is known as a major exporter of arms. North Korea bargains, finally achieving some international assistance and a potential for diplomatic recognition with the establishment of KEDO, a Japanese, US and South and North Korean body charged with building two new nuclear reactors for the North.

In the midst of the bargaining, Kim Il Sung, the 'Great Leader', founder of the Northern state in 1948 and its ruler ever since, dies. The Northern nation mourns, uncontrollably, for days on end.

1988. Seoul successfully hosts the Olympic Games. The slogan is "Seoul to the World, the World to Seoul". Seoul has built magnificent new facilities, its way of saying that South Korea has matured and can ably take its place amongst developed nations. Two years earlier, when Seoul was the site for the Asian Games, overtures were made to restore friendly relations with China. The Seoul Olympics see many more countries attending than had been expected (and more than in Los Angeles in 1984): the Cold War stand-off between the Soviet Union and its comrades and the US and its capitalist allies seems to be drawing to an end. China and the Soviet Union both send athletes, despite the fact that at this time neither had diplomatic relations with South Korea. North Korea, which had hoped to co-host the games, is left isolated. Soon, South Korea will enter into full diplomatic relations with the Soviet Union, China and many other socialist states.

1987. "Phut, phut, phut". Tear gas canisters explode in front of students. The students sing songs and chant slogans: "Yankee, go home!" "Give power to the people!" They have rags tied around their mouths in an effort to prevent the searing pepper reaching their throats. But every eye begins to water. Only the shock troops can breathe comfortably, cosseted beneath proper masks. The troops block escape and, eventually, charge, forcing the students to retreat back into the safety of their university campus. Demonstrations have become a way of life. They are rituals, cleverly choreographed through repetition. Students join with workers; strikes grow. In June, the government of Chun Doo Hwan is forced to cave in: his chosen successor (and earlier, his fellow military general), Roh Tae Woo, announces sweeping reforms to government and a free and democratic election process. The streets fall quiet.

1960-1980. These were two decades of dramatic growth, when industry rapidly grew, a transport infrastructure was built, and when the foundations for prosperity were laid. Perhaps there was too little to grab the headlines, but through the whole period South Korean GNP growth averaged a mighty impressive 8.4%.

1950-3. Some still remember the Korean war. The British government dispatched troops and resources to support a United Nations' force as what had begun as a civil dispute spiralled into a stand-off between the superpowers. This was where the Cold War turned hot, where it was feared that nuclear weapons might be used. In the fighting, something like four million people died. After the North pushed to the southern tip of the peninsula and the South with its UN allies pushed them back to the Chinese border in the north, the war stalemated. Eventually, an armistice agreement was signed; there was never a peace treaty. Nobody really won. The Demilitarized Zone (the DMZ, the most heavily fortified place on earth) separating the two halves of the peninsula became a permanent fixture. In the North, where isolation is so complete as to prevent knowledge of the world outside seeping in, dogma demands they see things differently and somewhat unbelievably: "Under the sagacious guidance of the Supreme Commander of the Korean People's Army Marshal Kim Il Sung, the all-triumphant, resolute and incomparable commander and outstanding military strategist, the heroic Korean people defeated the US imperialist aggressors and succeeded in victory." Everyone outside the North would disagree.

Discussion

Today, South Korea is a major economic power, the 12th largest economy in the world, pushing at the heels of a number of European states. Several South Korean companies are listed by *Fortune* as major global players. Samsung, a major investor in Britain, is one of the top 15 global companies. South Korea is one of the Asian tigers, and a massive success story: per capita GNP increased from less than $100 per year in 1960 to over $10,000 in 1995. South Korea has come of age: thirty years under presidents who began as military generals ended with the election of the civilian Kim Young Sam at the end of 1992.

North Korea is one of the last socialist states, trying steadfastly to maintain a virtually unreformed Stalinist system although it has lost most of the support (and the barter trade) it once enjoyed from China and the former Soviet Union. Until the early 1970s, development in North Korea outstripped that south of the Demilitarized Zone. It built up heavy industry, starting from the almost total destruction of the Korean war; it collectivised farms, and got rid of private property. By the 1990s, the economy was shrinking. Output was down, and factories were operating at partial capacity due to a shortage of oil and raw materials caused by transportation problems and the lack of foreign currency.

The Korean peninsula sits between Japan and China, and has a short northeastern border with Russia. In history, links with China have been strong. Much of the Korean heritage originated in China, from Confucianism to court culture, but in Korea met an indigenous heritage with roots further north amongst the Manchurian and Siberian groups whom Koreans claim as their ancient ancestors. Much of the cultural heritage passed from Korea to Japan.

The area around Korea has always been a dodgy neighbourhood, and Korea has suffered a number of invasions. Koreans call themselves the "shrimps between whales", and this is precisely what they became at the end of the 19th century, with wars between Japan and China and Russia. But, a strong will to survive and nationalism has maintained a strong and unique identity to today.

The location of Korea ensures that the peninsula continues to be of major strategic importance. As industry and finance in the world moves to the Asia-Pacific region, so Korea sits bang in the middle, between what is currently the most successful global economy and the largest, most dynamic. Unified under Shilla in the 7th century and painfully divided only at the end of World War II, (re)unification in the next few years now looks like a real possibility. A unified Korea would combine the undoubted strengths of the South with the raw materials, energy sources, and cheap labour of the North. It would balance China and Japan. Suddenly, it would also be able to ship its products by land northwards into Russia and westwards to Europe, and by sea to the rest of the world.

Korea, though, is far more that just politics and economics. It is a country of stunning physical beauty and memorable extremes of climate. It has a rich history spanning some 5000 years, with a succession of dynasties under which literature and the arts flourished (Chosŏn, 1392-1910, was the longest-lasting dynasty anywhere in East Asia). It still boasts a rich culture, with unique music, dance, literature and fine arts. It has a fascinating language—written either with Chinese characters or an indigenous phonetic alphabet— and a distinctive cuisine best known through the fiery hot pickled cabbage, *kimch'i*. It is a country that is changing rapidly, where the old can still be seen alongside the new, and where urban sprawls meet age-old rural scenes that seem frozen in time. It is a land of mountains and rivers, of animist spirits, Buddhas, Confucian scholars and Christians. It is now a tourist destination.

Korea, then, is of interest to us all, geographers, historians, religious studies' specialists, economists, political scientists, musicians, dancers, linguists, and more. We hope that this book, together with the enclosed factsheets and CD-Rom, will aid teachers and students alike to study the richness of this important but neglected land.

1
HISTORICAL OVERVIEW

1.1 Early history

Ancient period

Archaeological excavations show that in the early centuries of the first millennium BC the original population, which possessed a Neolithic culture (characterised by the use of stone implements), was being displaced and absorbed by immigrants from the north. These people, whose origin may have been in northeastern Asia, belonged to the Tungusic group and spoke a language which today is considered as belonging to the Altaic languages. They were familiar with the production of bronze. Possession of this metal may have given them social and economic superiority. Evidence of their culture is provided by the stone dolmens built as burial repositories, which are scattered over what is now the northeast part of China and the whole of the Korean peninsula. Some of these graves have yielded fine weapons, mirrors and horse trappings in bronze. These newcomers amalgamated with others to become the forefathers of present-day Koreans.

The use of bronze continued up to the end of the first millennium BC. Overlapping with the Late Bronze Age came the introduction of a new metal—iron—from China, permitting the production of more effective weapons and agricultural implements.

Social and political organisation during the Bronze Age was along tribal lines, each group or chiefdom occupying a small area of territory. Gradually, loose federations of tribes formed under leaders, some of whom were elected. One such powerful league emerged in the area between the Liao river in what is now northeast China and the Taedong river in the central northwestern part of the peninsula. By the end of the 2nd century BC this primitive state, known from the name of its leader as Wiman Chosŏn, had become so strong that the Chinese Han dynasty (206BC-AD220), regarding it as a major threat to the eastern flank of its empire, invaded and established four military colonies or commanderies in its territory. Of these only the one at Nangnang (in Chinese Lelang), established in 108BC in the region of present-day P'yŏngyang, survived as a military and trading post from where Chinese goods and ideas spread through the country. Eventually, in AD 313, Nangnang fell to attack from a new Korean state: Koguryŏ.

The Nangnang commandery functioned as the most important centre in the peninsula. The southern part of the country was occupied by the Samhan (the Three Han), a loose grouping of small tribes held in check by the Chinese, the eastern section by the Okchŏ and the Yemaek, while in the northeast of the peninsula and the areas north of it the Koguryŏ were gaining in strength. The period from about AD 0 to about AD 300 is describe as the Proto-Three Kingdoms period, when three states coalesced. The Chinese presence tended to inhibit political growth in other parts of the peninsula, but with its removal local groupings began to develop forms of government that eventually led to the emergence of three separate states.

Political development in the north of the peninsula came early. This area faced unsettled and often disputed regions to its north and northwest, from which local populations, displaced by fighting and conquest, might spill over in to the peninsula. The Chinese extended their presence in to the north to secure this flank of their empire. The result was to make the northern area a point of entry for both new people and new cultures and the Chinese presence may have served to stimulate neighbouring tribes to some kind of unity.

The Three Kingdoms

The Koguryŏ, who ousted the Chinese in 313, created the most northerly of the Three Kingdoms. This came to cover a large area extending from the fertile plains of the Liao river to the banks of the Taedong river, with its early capital situated on the middle stretch of the Yalu river. To its south the kingdom of Paekche emerged, with its capital initially in the Han river basin, in the area of present-day Seoul. It seems likely that the people of the southwest corner of the peninsular, the Mahan (one of the Three Han), were augmented by one, possibly two, influxes of refugees in the 3rd and 4th centuries. These new people came from the Puyŏ tribe far to the north in what is now Chinese territory, and were driven out of their lands. They went on to assimilate with the indigenous Mahan to form the state of Paekche. In the 5th century, Koguryŏ expansion forced the Paekche kings to remove their capital further south to the Kŭm river basin, to present-day Puyŏ and Kongju.

The third kingdom, Shilla, in the southeast of the country, was based on the area around the modern city of Kyŏngju. Out of the various small entities that had made up Chinhan—another of the Three Han—one group, Saro, subdued the others and by the middle of the 4th century had established itself under a king. From the beginning of the 6th century this kingdom was known as Shilla. The third of the Three Han, Pyŏnhan, which occupied the basin of the Naktong river in the south, never consolidated itself as a state but survived as a federation of small groups better known as Kaya, until in 562 it was absorbed by Shilla.

Developments inside the peninsula

The period from the 4th century to the mid-7th was not a time of peace, as the three states fought and manoeuvred for control of the peninsula. It was, however, a time of intensive political and social maturing for all three, as well as of increasing international contacts and cultural growth. A common feature of all three kingdoms was the emergence of a strong aristocracy within a strongly hierarchical, land-owning, status-oriented society.

Two extremely important influences entered the Korean peninsula from China in the second half of the 4th century: Buddhist religion and Confucian doctrine (see chapter 8, sections 1-2, for a discussion of these teachings). Until then, animist belief in the power of natural forces and of good and evil spirits had prevailed. Buddhism was brought first to Koguryŏ by missionary monks from northern China. The new teaching spread quickly to Paekche, aided by the kingdom's direct links with China across the Yellow Sea. In both states the new religion's support for royal rule smoothed the way for its adoption. Shilla resisted the new faith for nearly two centuries longer, but by the mid-6th century it had been accepted by the king, who again saw its value as a means of strengthening royal authority.

While Buddhism had the profounder impact, Confucian teaching on good principles of state administration was also absorbed. Chinese models were further used in drawing up laws in the Three Kingdoms. In the absence of a native system of writing, the Chinese system of characters was adopted, even though it was not really suited to expression of the spoken language. Other systems, for example *idu* (see chapter 5.1) were developed.

Little has survived in the way of cultural relics, but architecture, painting and sculpture all flourished in the Three Kingdoms. Much artistic output was intended to enhance the new Buddhist teaching. Temples and pagodas were constructed. Stone sculptures and exquisite statues in bronze gilt from all three kingdoms portrayed the Buddha in one or other of his aspects. Wall paintings in Koguryŏ tombs in the north of the peninsula depicted lively scenes of hunting and banquets, guardian creatures and sometimes Buddhist symbols. Shilla royal tombs have yielded superb examples of gold crowns, belts and jewellery.

External contacts

Manoeuvring for supremacy within the peninsula took place against a wider backdrop of relations with China and, to a lesser extent, Japan. Each of the three states agreed to pay tribute to China and received gifts in return. Chinese luxury goods such as ceramics and glassware were also imported. Korea had absorbed Buddhism from China but in turn helped to pass it on to Japan. The kingdom of Paekche in particular, linked by sea routes with Japan, sent missionaries there in the 6th century, and its artisans travelled to work on the decoration of Japanese Buddhist temples. The federation of Kaya states also had close connections across the sea with Japan.

The political and military struggles between the Three Kingdoms frequently drew in China and sometimes alliances would be formed by two of the three states against the third and by one or other state with a foreign partner. Koguryŏ, bordering China, was on occasion in open conflict with its neighbour. China was a dangerous ally because it tried to incorporate any territories it had helped to win into its own empire. With the aid of Tang China (AD618-907), Shilla defeated first Paekche in 660, then Koguryŏ in 668, but then, in 676, had to beat off Tang attempts to take control of the whole peninsula. From that point on Korea was, for the next thirteen centuries, a united country.

1.2 Unified Shilla

A time of glory

The newly united kingdom, Unified Shilla (AD668-935), was able to enjoy a great period of prosperity and achievement in the first century of its existence. Many present-day Koreans like to look back on this time as proof of their country's talent and capability. Once the Chinese had withdrawn, the threat of hostile external attack largely receded. On the northern border beyond the Yalu and Tuman rivers, a new state called Parhae was formed by refugees from the defeated Koguryŏ. This state, which lasted until 926, assimilated much of the Chinese Tang culture and appears to have co-existed politically with both China and Unified Shilla.

The splendour of Tang China, exemplified in the magnificence of its capital at Chang'an (near modern Xi'an), was something that Unified Shilla wished to emulate. Its capital, Kyŏngju, was laid out on a grid pattern, following the model of Chang'an, and was described as a place of great luxury, with fine houses and many Buddhist temples. The practice of delegations bearing tribute from Korea to China and gifts from China back into Korea continued, supplemented by private trade in the hands of Korean merchants, who established bases on the east coast of China and dominated trade across the Yellow Sea between the two countries and as far afield as the Ryukyu islands between Taiwan and Japan. Goods imported into Korea were largely luxury items such as textiles and goods destined for personal use in aristocratic households.

Trade was not the only area of communication between Korea and China. Buddhist monks returning from study in China brought back new doctrines and new styles of Buddhist statues and paintings. Books and works of art were imported. Chinese concepts of government organisation were introduced and in 788 a state examination system on the Chinese pattern for selecting entrants to the civil service was instituted.

While Confucianism provided many of the ideas in matters of government, Buddhism functioned as the state religion. Though much influenced by doctrines prevalent in China, Korean monks developed their own schools of teaching. As marks of devotion temples and monasteries were built. Some of the finest art that has survived from the Unified Shilla period is of Buddhist inspiration. Best known is the Sŏkkuram, dated to the mid-8th century, a manmade stone shrine in the hills above Kyŏngju, which contains superb carvings of disciples and attendants flanking an enormous statue of the Buddha. Buddhist and Confucian text were reproduced in woodblock printing (the oldest example in the world of such printing is from Korea). Other skills, such as astronomy, were active, as seen in the construction of Ch'ŏmsŏngdae observatory in Kyŏngju even before the establishment of Unified Shilla.

The political system that developed within Korea in the Unified Shilla period helped to sustain achievements through concentrating wealth in the hands of a few, who in turn could commission works of art; although a peaceful environment and extensive international contacts undoubtedly also contributed. The system was centred on the king, around whom flourished a powerful aristocracy organised in a complicated hierarchy based on lines of descent. The monarchy created and encouraged government institutions, such as an executive council, that would respond to its needs. The military were made responsible to the king. Unification meant that the territories of the three former kingdoms had to be brought under one authority, so a system of provincial government was established.

The prominent noble families and government officials gained their wealth through grants of land from the state. They were entitled to the taxes paid by the farmers—free commoners—who worked the land. Many aristocratic households and state institutions owned great numbers of slaves, drawn from the ranks of prisoners of war or criminals. Craftsmen were obliged to remain in the service of royal palaces or official agencies, for whom they produced a whole range of goods. No other forms of economic organisation existed, apart from a number of markets which were tolerated, though not encouraged, because Confucian teaching disdained economic activities. By the early 8th century four government markets served the capital, while rural areas had their own markets.

Decline of the dynasty

The king had constantly to exert his authority over the ambitions of powerful aristocratic families. From the late 8th century, aristocratic resistance to his authority increased, as these same families challenged each other in bids to secure the throne. During the last 150 years of Unified Shilla the country had around 20 kings and queens. Further source of discontent lay with local land-owning families who, even though they had come up through the state examination system, could not secure promotion to the highest political posts reserved for those of recognised aristocratic birth. Such men developed local power bases, sometimes financed through seaborne trade with China and Japan. Chang Pogo, for instance, in 828 established his own garrison on the island of Wando, off the southern coast of Korea, to suppress activities of Chinese pirates. Within their regions, such families fortified local towns and controlled the economy, including the payment of taxes by the farmers, thereby further undermining state power and wealth. Attempts by the government to raise revenue by enforcing the collection of state taxes drove the peasantry to rebel against double taxation. The first revolt in 889 led to disturbances at many levels throughout the country and eventually to attempts to form new kingdoms in the old areas of Paekche and Koguryŏ. In 918, Wang Kŏn, leader of the northern ex-Koguryŏ region, with his base at Kaesŏng, emerged to dominate the struggle. With Shilla rendered powerless, the fight was between 'Koguryŏ' and 'Paekche' factions. By 935 Wang Kŏn had defeated his opponents and accepted the formal surrender of Shilla. He named his new kingdom Koryŏ, a shortened version of Koguryŏ.

1.3 Koryŏ

The Koryŏ era (918-1392) was one of mixed fortunes for Korea. A strong state bureaucracy developed, but promotion still depended largely on birth. The Buddhist faith still functioned as the national religion, with different schools gaining support among the various sections of society. Buddhist monasteries acquired extensive lands and wealth. Koryŏ ceramics and painting, the latter often of Buddhist inspiration, are considered some of the finest products of Korean art. The country, however, did not always prosper. The struggle between monarchy and aristocracy and factionalism between rival families continued to weaken the state; and Korea suffered hostility and invasion from the north and attacks from Japanese pirates.

Problems for the new dynasty

Wang Kŏn, who ruled the new kingdom under the name of T'aejo from 918 to 943, had to secure the support of powerful families in the old Paekche and Shilla areas whom he had recently defeated. After 926 he also had to accommodate refugees from the northern kingdom of Parhae when it was overrun by Mongols. By gifts of land and office and by taking wives from among these families he managed to gain some co-operation. At this same time he endeavoured unsuccessfully to break the old lineage patterns of the former Shilla aristocracy. The 'castle lords', who had built up local power bases in the late Shilla period, continued to defy royal authority. Reforms introduced by King Kwangjong (r. 949-974) aimed to control such opposition by reducing the numbers of slaves privately owned, by developing a strong central bureaucracy and, where necessary, by liquidating his critics.

Building a powerful state

During the 10th and 11th centuries the structure of central and local administration, both civilian and military, was strengthened, generally following Chinese models. Two central secretariats were responsible for formulating policy and a third was charged with carrying it out through six boards of offices. In addition, a Royal Secretariat transmitted royal commands and handled urgent military matters. The heads of these various secretariats formed a kind of privy council. Their activities were scrutinised by another organisation, the Censorate, which kept a check on the performance of officials.

The country was divided into regions and border zones and further subdivided into eight provinces (which formed the basis of the modern provinces) and smaller administrative units. Three regional capitals were established. Government officers were sent from the capital Kaesông to the regions, where local officials working under them dealt with the local population. The army was similarly organised on a regional basis. Society itself was still locked into a hierarchy of classes, led by the aristocracy, some of whom originated in the old Shilla nobility, while others represented powerful local families. Membership of these social classes was often determined by occupation. Careers in higher government posts were regarded as the right and obligation of sons of men already holding these same jobs. Military officials expected to hand on their duties to their sons. At a lower level, craftsmen often worked in hereditary professions. Farmers were not eligible to hold official posts, though they were in theory free to take the examinations that would lead to such appointments and their entry into the ranks of officials.

Such social rigidity was broken to some extent by a new state examination system introduced in 958, which offered lower provincial officials an opportunity for promotion, as well as allowing selection among candidates from the hereditary aristocratic families. Soldiers commended for meritorious service could also hope to move upwards in the ranks. At the same time an arrangement of protected appointments, permitting one son of an official at or above a specified grade to secure a government post, ensured that the interests of the upper classes were safeguarded.

Two different examinations tested candidates in the knowledge of the Confucian classics or in their skill at composing in set Chinese literary forms. A less prestigious set of examinations tested for ability in a range of professional and technical skills, such as medicine, law and accounting. To prepare candidates, a national university was established in 992, divided more than a century later into six colleges offering courses in the Chinese classics and in technical subjects. Entry to college was determined by the official ranking of the candidates' families. A network of rural schools was in place by the first half of the 12th century to train boys for the examinations. Clearly, modern Korean zeal for education and pre-occupation with the relative merits of differing schools and universities have deep roots.

Funds for the state

As under Unified Shilla, the source of wealth for the state and the aristocracy in the Koryŏ period continued to be land, which, through being worked by tenant farmers, provided revenue. Although in principle all land belonged to the king, in practice it was divided between public and private holdings. Public land, managed by the state, yielded funds for public expenditure. It also included 'stipend land', that is, land allocated to officials. The rents collected on this land formed the official's salary. When he died, the land reverted to the state. Private land was often awarded to both civilian and military officials in recognition of merit. It was generally regarded as support for a family in return for the fulfilment of hereditary government or military duties. The family collected rents on such land, which in time became hereditary property.

The peasant class, which provided labour and rents on the land it worked, was not itself eligible for any grants of land. Instead, freeborn farmers could cultivate public areas known as 'people's land', on which they paid rent to the state. Rents to private landowners were heavier. Farmers were moreover subject to taxes, and had to give their labour free at certain times. A more lowly class of peasants was employed in mining and working with metals, in the manufacture of silk, paper or pottery, and in transport. Slaves often worked as domestic servants. A class of outcasts worked in despised occupations such as butchering and entertainment.

Although coins were minted during the Koryŏ period, not many were in circulation. Instead, grain and cloth were generally used in local transactions and for the payment of taxes. Exports continued to flow to Song China (960-1279) and Japan until the early part of the 13th century, when the Mongol invasions from the north caused disruption. Diplomatic missions often conveyed goods destined for China, while private trade also flourished. Principal exports were textiles, precious metals, ginseng root and pine-nuts and manufactured goods such as paper, brushes and ink. Imports from China included porcelain, silk, books, medicines and spices. Celadon, the fine glazed stoneware for which Koryŏ was famous, was also exported. The recovered wreck of a boat carrying a cargo of 30,000 pieces of celadon from a kiln in the southwest corner of Korea, which sank off the south coast in the late 11th century, suggests the scale of the trade. The principal harbour for international trade was Yesŏng in Hwanghae Province, the port for Kaesŏng, which was even visited by Arab ships trading with China.

Buddhism, the national religion

Ever since it had entered the Korean peninsula in the second half of the 4th century, Buddhism had actively supported royal authority and in return it enjoyed considerable favour from the rulers of first Koguryŏ and Paekche, then later Shilla. In each state the new religion spread from the royal family downwards. Links were particularly close in Shilla, where Buddhism was closely related to affairs of state, and monks served as officials. Faith in Buddhism came to be regarded as a guarantee of the safety of the nation. This combination of political and religious matters culminated in a mission in Shilla to unify the peninsula under one rule, a feat that it achieved in 668.

For a long time Buddhism remained the creed of the upper class. It not only satisfied the religious needs of individuals, but also justified the hierarchical organisation of society. To be born as a Shilla aristocrat was interpreted as a reward for merit in a previous life. In the following Unified Shilla period Buddhism consolidated its hold. Monks travelling to China (one, Hech'o, even journeyed to India) returned with a range of new interpretations, which they had absorbed through study with the various sects proliferating in Tang times. These varying doctrines, as developed and preached by Korean monks, appealed to different sections of society, from the aristocracy down to the common people.

Towards the end of Unified Shilla, Sŏn Buddhism (also known by its Japanese name, Zen) began to flourish and became one of the principal schools of thought in the succeeding Koryŏ period. This meditative form, with its search for sudden enlightenment, rejected both the prevailing close connection with state affairs and the emphasis on textual learning of the established schools. The two approaches did not coexist easily. In an attempt to defuse conflict the Ch'ŏnt'ae sect, introduced from China, sought to unify the two traditions. Eventually, by the 13th century, the Chogye school emerged from the Sŏn stream of Buddhism. It advocated that the search for sudden enlightenment through meditation should be accompanied by continual cultivation of the mind through study. The Chogye approach has prevailed ever since in Korea.

The identification not only of personal salvation but also of national security with Buddhism remained very strong in the Koryŏ period. Buddhist festivals were celebrated and temples and monasteries founded as signs of piety and in the hope of strengthening the state. In the course of the 11th century the complete collection of Buddhist scriptures, known as the Tripitaka, was engraved on wooden blocks, from which printings were made. One purpose of this task was to systematise Buddhist doctrines; another was to implore divine protection for the country against invasion. The first set of woodblocks was destroyed by Mongol invaders in the first half of the 13th century. Immediately, work started to carve a second set of woodblocks. Completed in 1251, these have survived and are now kept in Haein temple in the south of the peninsula.

Personal and state devotion to Buddhism led to a privileged status for Buddhist monks, who received grants of land and were permitted to take over one of the state civil service examinations. This awarded them clerical ranks. Monasteries expanded their land holdings, on which they enjoyed tax exemption.

Painting and ceramics

Buddhist devotion provided the inspiration for paintings surviving from the Koryŏ period, many of them executed by artist-monks. The various aspects of Buddha and large numbers of attendants attributed to him supplied a wide range of models. Some of the most exquisite of these paintings depict the 'Water Moon Kwanseŭm', which shows Buddha as a figure of compassion. Koryŏ art was much appreciated by the Japanese, who managed to acquire many fine examples.

Ceramics, in particular those known as celadons, are the other prized product of Koryŏ art. These are vases, flasks, bowls, dishes, boxes, incense burners, ornaments and other objects made from clay, decorated in a variety of ways and coated with one of a range of transparent glazes before being fired at high temperatures. The term 'celadon', which denotes a greyish-green colour, applies strictly to only one of the glazes used, but is often employed to describe this type of ceramic product as a whole. China again supplied the original models, but the Korean products came to be acknowledged as superior in craftsmanship and taste. Such valuable objects were found only in wealthy households, particularly in scholars' studies, where celadon water droppers might be used, and in temples as altar accessories. Those who actually produced these precious goods, the potters, were despised as lowborn artisans.

Aggression from outside and inside the country

From the end of the 10th century, the state of Koryŏ suffered repeated hostilities from the tribes living to the north and northwest of the peninsula. These same tribes, bent on expansion, were also harassing the Chinese empire along its northern borders; and Koryŏ found itself at times drawn into a three-way relationship with China and the enemy, confronting them both.

First on the scene were the Khitan, a nomadic people occupying the region of the Yalu river, where they established their own dynasty, the Liao (907-1125). In 926, they had overrun the state of Parhae (see above). Between 993 and 1018 they launched three attacks against Koryŏ, but in 1018 were heavily defeated. They were in turn defeated by the Jürchen, who set themselves up as the Jin dynasty (1115-1234) in north China. The Jürchen had once come under Parhae rule. Their base extended to the area of the Tuman (Tuman in Korean) river, and eventually they came into conflict with Koryŏ. As they gained the upper hand in China, they insisted that Koryŏ should accept them as overlords. For the sake of peace this was agreed to.

Pressure from beyond the country's borders was matched during the 12th century by disturbances within the country, sparked by the ambitions of powerful aristocratic families ready to challenge the king and each other. Landless peasants and slaves, driven to revolt by taxes and demands for forced labour, added to the unrest. A further resentful group was the military, angered by what it saw as civilian disregard. In the end this last group proved the most dangerous. In 1170, a revolt of military officers led to a period of bloodshed and confusion in the country as one leader succeeded another. Eventually, in 1196, Ch'oe Ch'unghŏn, a soldier, seized effective power. He suppressed all opposition, including the Buddhist clergy, whom he banished from the capital. Although the monarchy was never toppled, its authority was undermined as the Ch'oe family exercised real control for the next sixty years, back by its own private army.

The country's woes increased as in 1231 it faced invasion by a Mongol army. The ultimate intention of this nomadic tribe from the steppe of north central Asia was to crush the Southern Song empire in China (the Song dynasty, ousted in the north of the country, had re-established itself in 1127 in southern China). Korean co-operation was judged important in achieving this. In the first quarter of the 13th century Koryŏ temporarily joined forces with the Mongols to repel Khitan incursions. The Mongols then represented themselves as benefactors of Koryŏ and demanded tribute. The killing of a Mongol envoy was taken as justification for invasion. In face of danger the Koryŏ court fled to

Kanghwa, a large island about 50 km northwest of Seoul, facing the Han river estuary. Though Kanghwa is separated by only a narrow strip of water from the mainland, it was enough to defeat the Mongols, who had a dread of crossing the sea. The common people were ordered to take refuge in mountain fortresses—areas of land surrounded by fortified walls—or on offshore islands. From these points such resistance as was possible was launched against the invaders, but the country and the population suffered terribly. In all, the Mongols mounted six invasions of the Korean peninsula over a period of nearly thirty years, but the Koreans fiercely resisted.

In the end Koryǒ was obliged to give in. The grip of the Ch'oe clan was loosened with the assassination of the head of the family in 1258, and the king was eventually able to reassert some authority. In 1270, he returned the capital to Kaesǒng and made peace with the Mongols or Yuan, the dynastic name they chose when in 1271 they established themselves in China. The next eighty years were a time of enforced acceptance of Yuan control, though not occupation. Through successive marriages with Yuan princesses, Korean kings had to accept the inferior status of 'sons-in-law' to the Yuan emperor. The country had to participate in Yuan military expeditions against Japan and was obliged to supply tribute that included falcons—much prized by the hunting Mongols—eunuchs and young women. The burden of meeting these levies fell, as ever, on the peasantry.

Powerful families saw it was in their interests to keep the needs of the Yuan supplied, and thus a pro-Yuan tendency arose in the country. Only when the authority of the Yuan themselves was challenged in the mid-14th century by new forces in China did it become possible for King Kongmin (r.1351-1374) to loosen the Yuan stranglehold on his country and to seek to reduce the power of his nobles. Kongmin gave his support to the new dynasty, the Ming, which in 1368 assumed control of China. His attempts at internal reform, however, met with resistance, and in the end he was assassinated. To the turmoil inside Korea was added attack from outside, from Chinese brigands and Japanese pirates. The latter had been devastating the coasts of Korea for over a century. They were subdued, but a fresh threat then came from the Ming emperor to intervene in the northeast of the peninsula. Disagreement flared between military leaders. One of them, Yi Sǒnggye, saw his chance, turned south and in 1388 seized power. Four years later, in 1392, he proclaimed a new dynasty, the Chosǒn.

1.4 Chosǒn

The Chosǒn dynasty (1392-1910), the name selected by the Yi family (some older sources still refer to the Yi dynasty), spans the long period that in Europe went from late medieval times to the pre-World War I years. Although moving primarily in rhythm with Ming (1368-1644) and Qing (1644-1911) China and in reaction against Japan, Korea grew gradually aware of the wider world beyond East Asia. The Confucian principles promoted by Yi Sŏnggye became firmly embedded in Chosŏn society, and Buddhism descended to the level of a personal faith. Christianity, which is now accepted by a quarter of the population in South Korea, first entered the peninsula at the end of the 18th century, but had to fight for a century for its place. Towards the beginning of the dynasty Korea devised and adopted its own alphabet, *han'gŭl*. Later, in the relatively peaceful years of the 18th century, the sciences and arts flourished anew. In the course of the 19th century, however, Korea, in common with its East Asian neighbours, had to face the challenges of Western expansion into the region. Reluctantly it had to open the country to European and American influences and to submit to increasing Japanese intervention in its affairs. Eventually, in 1910, the dynasty came to an end as Japan annexed the whole of the peninsula as a colony. This period of subservience ceased only in 1945.

Neo-Confucianism–the ideological underpinning of the new regime

The philosophy that inspired Yi Sŏnggye was a reinvigorated form of Confucianism, which had developed in China during the Northern Song period (960-1127). Through close association with Chinese scholars during the years of Yuan domination of the Korean court, Korean philosophers absorbed the new ideas. Whereas in the past the Confucian classics had been studied as a means of passing the state examinations, Neo-Confucian texts were now taken as sources of a far more rigorous approach to society and its management. The metaphysical and political applications of Neo-Confucianism were a strong force undermining Buddhism in the final century of the Koryŏ period. The Chosŏn dynasty took them as the basis for a new order in Korea.

The new teaching cultivated the vision of a utopian society that had to be realised in the present. The model for this society lay in the past or rather in the idealised version conveyed through Chinese classical literature of how feudal society in China had operated. The principle guiding this vision was that of harmony, between ruler and subject and between the various sections of society ranged in hierarchical order. In the hands of the ruling elite the new teaching provided the intellectual basis for far-reaching social reforms. The scholar-officials trained in Confucian precepts who assisted Yi Sŏnggye saw themselves as perfect bureaucrats fit to take charge of both government affairs and the moral condition of the people. For them, governing meant primarily reforming unformed human nature and bringing it into harmony with state and society. In the process such officials also strove to secure for themselves foremost positions in the social hierarchy. The earlier state religion, Buddhism, was discredited, its institutions were weakened and restrictions placed on the construction of new temples and on recruitment into the priesthood.

Changes in government and society

The ideal society of the Neo-Confucians remained often just that—an ideal. In the political sphere, long-established tendencies towards factionalism and challenge of central authority frequently made it difficult to secure any kind of harmony. Central government, if it felt it was strong enough, generally did not seek compromise, but expected to rule through a strong bureaucracy enforcing a set of procedures.

One of the first moves of the new regime was to attempt reform in the administration of land. In theory ownership of all land lay with the king, who distributed portions of it as reward to meritorious subjects, while trying to strengthen his own holdings. In practice the aristocrats' control over land ceded to them, on which they had the right to collect rent, tended to grow as hereditary rights to raise income on such land turned into virtual private ownership. As with the dynasty before, pressure on land was a continuing source of contention in the Chosŏn period.

The new dynasty retained many of the features of central and regional government of the earlier Koryŏ period: that is, a State Council, Royal Secretariat and Six Ministries in the capital and a network of governors and county magistrates operating within the eight provinces into which the country was divided. Care was taken to incorporate a system of checks on government through the bodies of inspectors and censors.

The most powerful section of Chosŏn society, drawn from the literati or scholar-officials, was known as the *yangban,* literally the 'two orders' of civil and military officers. Preference was given to the civil order. The *yangban* rested on a wider base than the earlier aristocracy, recruiting their members, both military and civil, through a rigorous set of examinations. Success led on to official ranking in a society where for the upper classes the holding of public office was the sole profession tolerated. Although in theory the examinations were open to young male scholars from all social classes, in practice opportunities for schooling and thus success in the tests were largely the privilege of families that were already well established. The system encouraged the elitist tone and aspirations to hereditary status of the *yangban* class. They had no interest in, and indeed much disdain for, other occupations, such as agriculture, commerce or manufacturing; nor would they follow such professions as law, medicine, interpreting, painting or astronomy, which they left to the *chungin* or 'middle people', who filled these technical posts. Regional discrimination also showed itself in a bias against promotion for officials from the northernmost provinces.

Supporting the *yangban* and *chungin* classes through their labour and taxes were, as ever, the peasant farmers, who, although freeborn, led closely supervised lives. Artisans, generally also of commoner status, often worked in government workshops. A lowborn class of slaves and outcasts continued to exist. Commerce was still little developed and geared towards meeting official requirements through government-sponsored shops in the capital. Private shops, periodic markets and itinerant peddlers served the rest of the population. Paper and bronze currency were mainly used to pay taxes, and cotton cloth continued as the chief medium of exchange. As in the Koryŏ period luxury goods were imported under cover of the diplomatic missions to China.

A new alphabet

Among the most respected of Chosŏn kings was Sejong (r.1418-1450). His greatest achievement was the promulgation of a new alphabet for the Korean people—*han'gŭl*. The use of Chinese characters to write Korean had become increasingly unsatisfactory. The grammar and structure of Korean diverged widely from those of Chinese and demanded a more flexible and representative writing system. King Sejong put a committee of scholars to work. Drawing on a number of sources, they devised the new alphabet, which the king introduced in 1446. Despite royal patronage, *han'gŭl* was long scorned by scholars and officials of the upper classes, who were anxious to keep their monopoly on literature and learning through their mastery of Chinese characters. They considered the new alphabet the preserve of women and the ill-educated. Nonetheless, *han'gŭl* came to be used in calligraphy alongside the traditional Chinese scripts (see chapter 5.1 and Factsheet 2.2 for a fuller discussion of *han'gŭl* and examples of *han'gŭl* script).

The 15th century was a period of expansion in scholarship, much of it directed by the government and intended to explain and strengthen the new Confucian order. Many manuals were published on branches of science, along with histories of the Koryŏ dynasty and annals of the reigns of preceding kings. The use of movable metal type was already known in the late Koryŏ period and was further developed under the early Chosŏn kings. Among other practical inventions were a rain gauge, water clock, astronomical instruments and surveying tools.

A troubled century

The 16th century in Korea was marked by continuing struggles between rival leading groups and family clans for influence and state positions. Members of the scholar-official classes, often based on provincial family estates, vied with the 'meritorious elite', holders of hereditary land. Between 1498 and 1545, members of the literati suffered four purges. Meanwhile, the burden of taxation on the farming class was at times so heavy as to drive peasants from the land and into a wandering life of brigandage.

At the very end of the century Korea found itself pitted against its neighbour Japan. After a long period of instability, Japan was united under a military leader, General Toyotomi Hideyoshi. Anxious to expand his authority and absorb his soldiers' energies, he planned the invasion of Ming China, using Korea as a stepping stone to the Asian continent. Korea was unwilling to be drawn into this expedition, regarding itself as an ally of China. Hideyoshi forced the issue by landing in 1592 at Pusan in the south of the peninsula and marching north. King Sŏnjo (r.1567-1608) panicked and fled Seoul with his court, leaving the population to face the Japanese onslaught. The situation was only reversed when Admiral Yi Sunshin routed Japanese warships at sea off the southern coast of Korea, using armed, heavily protected vessels known as his 'turtle boats'. Guerrilla attacks on the Japanese land troops and the arrival of Chinese forces in the north of the country brought the invasion to a halt. Truce talks ensued but broke down, and Hideyoshi launched a second invasion of Korea in 1597. The attack only ended with his death in mid-1598.

Korea suffered terribly in the Imjin war, seven years of Japanese invasion. Temples were destroyed and many Korean artisans were taken captive to Japan, where their skills in pottery had great influence on the development of Japanese ceramics.

A new threat to Korea emerged as it became pulled into the conflict that erupted in the early decades of the 17th century between Ming China and the Manchu tribe pressing on its northeast border. The pro-Ming policy of King Injo (r.1623-49) so angered the Manchu that they invaded the Korean peninsula twice, in 1627 and 1636, and forced him to accept their suzerainty or overlordship. In 1644, the Manchu established themselves in Beijing as the Qing dynasty, but it was long before Korea abandoned its hostility to the new Chinese regime.

A changing society

In the two and a half centuries of peace that followed the Manchu invasions, Korean society lost some of its social and intellectual rigidity. Political life continued to be dominated by those sections of the *yangban* eligible for office, but among the middle and lower social classes signs of independence and prosperity were emerging. Improvements in agricultural techniques during the 17th century benefited a number of farmers. A merchant class was establishing itself, able to buy the products of craftsmen, who had previously been bound by government controls but were achieving some independence. The use of coins and money transactions grew more widespread. Reforms in the system of taxation which included taxes to cover the annual tribute to China and to support the army, allowed for payment in rice, cotton cloth or coins. Gradually an equalised standard of taxation was applied to the peasantry over the whole country. The *yangban* as ever remained exempt from taxes.

Not all *yangban* men could hope for an official position. The sons of secondary wives were excluded, while factional struggle or misdemeanours might result in office-holders being exiled from court. Those excluded from power had time to reflect on the functioning and shortcomings of society. They took a pragmatic view, examining the reality of a situation or process and looking for factual evidence. Their field of interest included agricultural techniques and management, scientific and technical matters, economic issues and history and geography, all aspects of 'practical learning' or *shirhak,* by which term their approach was summed up. The acceptance of reality was reflected in the 'true-view' landscapes of artists such as Chŏng Sŏn (1676-1759) and the genre paintings of Kim Hongdo (1745-?) and Shin Yunbok (1758-?), who both flourished in the second half of the 18th century (see Factsheets 6.1 and 6.2). Literature was marked by a growing volume of works written in *han'gŭl.*

As with scholars in the past, proponents of *shirhak* looked to China for information and ideas. Through contact in the first half of the 17th century with European Jesuit missionaries at the Qing court, Korean envoys and others brought back Western artefacts and books on scientific subjects and saw their first maps of Europe. (Firsthand knowledge came when Dutch seamen were shipwrecked on the coasts of Korea in 1628 and 1653.) The Christian Catholic teaching of these missionaries also interested the Korean visitors to Beijing. At first such interest was purely intellectual; but in 1784 a young Korean man, baptised in Beijing by a Western Catholic priest, returned to Korea as the first Christian convert. Korea has the distinction of having introduced Christianity not through foreign missionary activity but through its own initiative.

1.5 The final century of Chosŏn

The 19th century was a time of growing stress for Korea. From 1800, the weakness of succeeding kings allowed power to pass to the families of their queens, with consequent bitter rivalry. Continuing social change led to cracks in the old class system, as those members of the *yangban* who had lost or never held office grew in numbers and discontent. In 1801, government slaves were accorded their freedom, thought private slavery was still tolerated. Heavy taxation continued to alienate the farmers, some of whom became brigands or joined in popular uprisings. The gradual spread of the new religion, Catholicism, was a further unsettling factor. Official policy swung between tolerance and persecution of Korean converts and the French missionaries who began to arrive from 1836. Christianity had its largest following in the towns. In the countryside peasants were drawn to a new sect, *Tonghak* (Eastern learning as opposed to *Sŏhak,* the

Western learning of Catholicism), attracted by its doctrine of equality. Eventually, in 1864, strong authority was re-imposed when the father of the twelve-year-old king Kojong assumed power on behalf of his son.

The Taewŏn'gun, as he was called, permitted no challenge to his authority. He applied taxes to the *yangban* class for the first time. In foreign policy he embarked on a course of isolation for Korea, rejecting requests for trade with Western states, which were already penetrating China, and turning against native and foreign Catholics inside Korea. Attempts by Western nations, notably France in 1866 and the US in 1871, to force Korea to open up, were routed. The Taewŏn'gun was equally suspicious of Japanese intentions. After he was ousted from power in 1873, Japan was indeed the first to impose a 'treaty of friendship' on Korea, the Treaty of Kanghwa in 1876. This led to the opening up of Korean ports to Japanese trade. Western nations followed and treaties were signed with the US (1882), Britain (1884) and with other European powers.

Support was growing for foreign trade and access to Western technology and ideas, and fact-finding visits were made to China and Japan. Exposure to new concepts and practices encouraged the evolution of 'enlightenment policies' and of new administrative organs to cope with social changes. Ranged against such developments were Confucian scholars and officials, who saw in these new trends a threat to Korea's security and traditions. China still claimed suzerainty over Korea, but it was increasingly challenged by Japan. Attempts by these two countries to involve Korea in their own struggle for domination in the region further complicated the situation and gave scope for pro-Chinese and pro-Japanese factions within Korea. Russian expansion into East Asia introduced another destabilising factor. In 1884, Korean 'progressives' attempted a coup d'état, in which they hoped for Japanese support, but failed.

By the last decade of the 20th century, old institutions were coming under challenge, often from Japanese pressure for reforms. The traditional style of schooling was displaced by new academies offering Western-type courses. Some of these were run by the Western Protestant missionaries who started to arrive in large numbers after the treaties of the early 1880s and who helped to put Christianity on a firm footing in Korea. The influx of foreigners, however, roused not only the Confucianists but also the peasantry, who resented in particular Japanese penetration of the economy. They were, moreover, forced as ever to bear the brunt of taxation in support of government expenditure. The revival of the *Tonghak* movement, suppressed in 1864, rallied many disaffected farmers, who saw it as a means to turn on both their *yangban* masters and the foreigners. In 1894, revolt broke out in the southwest of the peninsula as supporters established an administrative network and a *Tonghak* army sought to march north. In alarm the government called on China for support, and Chinese troops landed in Korea. There they were confronted by Japanese soldiers, ostensibly sent to protect Japanese civilians in

Korea. By July 1894, China and Japan were at war. Japan's victory the following year left it in an even stronger position in the region.

In Korea a reform-minded government of pro-Japanese sympathies was installed in 1894. The changes it introduced, known as the Kabo reforms, reached into central and local government, into the administration of justice and the functioning of the police, the management of national financial affairs, class structure and social practices. The system of recruitment by state examination was abolished, the former pre-eminence of the *yangban* classes was undermined, slavery was forbidden and family law was liberalised. The spirit of modernism spread to the organisation of trade, industry and agriculture and to an interest in Western technology. Such challenges to orthodox Confucianist thought aroused the anger of traditionalists and set off questioning on the relative merits of Korean and foreign values that persists to this day.

Administrative and social change together with an awareness of Korea's weak position led to experimentation in political forms. Knowledge of Western liberal political doctrine and practice encouraged the formation of the Independence Club in 1896, the first appearance of a national press, some of it in *han'gŭl* and English versions, and attempts in 1898 to form a new political party. National independence was as much an issue as political reform and education. Korea, however, was not to have much say in the matter. Although King Kojong refused, after 1897, to recognise Chinese suzerainty and declared Korea an empire in its own right, his authority in his own country was diminished and Korea was being gradually being brought under Japanese control. Japan's encroachment was recognised but not checked by other states. In the 1902 Anglo-Japanese Alliance and again in 1905, when the alliance was renegotiated, Britain acknowledged Japan's special interests in Korea, in return for Japanese recognition of Britain's interests in China. In 1905, Japan forced the Protectorate Treaty on Korea, assuming all responsibility for Korea's foreign affairs, and in 1910 proceeded to annex the peninsula. King Kojong had been obliged to abdicate in 1907. His son, King Sunjong, reigned only until 1910, when he too abdicated. When Korea regained its independence in 1945, other forms of government were to take over.

Readings

Gina L. Barnes, 1993. *China Korea and Japan: The Rise of Civilization in East Asia*. London: Thames and Hudson

Carter J. Eckert, Ki-baik Lee *et al.*, 1990. *Korea Old and New: A History*. Seoul: Ilchokak Publishers

Ki-baik Lee, 1961. *Han'guksa sillon*. Trans. Edward W. Wagner and Edward J. Shultz, 1984, as *A New History of Korea*. Cambridge, MA: Harvard University Press

Sarah Milledge Nelson, 1993. *The Archaeology of Korea*. Cambridge: Cambridge University Press

James B. Palais, 1975. *Politics and Policy in Traditional Korea*. Cambridge, MA: Harvard University Press

2

FOREIGN INTERVENTION AND JAPANESE COLONIAL RULE: 1864-1945

2.1 Stirrings within the kingdom

The world knew little of Korea until the late 19th century: it was often called the 'Hermit Kingdom'. Relations were mainly confined to its two mighty neighbours, China and Japan. Korea had a tributary relationship with the former, using the term *sadae* (to serve a superior), and between 1645 and 1894 twice-yearly missions were sent to Beijing. Japan was a neighbour, as the term *kyorin* implied, distrusted after invasions in the 1590s, with trade confined to the *wegwan*, the so-called Japan House, in the port city of Pusan, and channelled through the Japanese island of Tsushima. From the 18th century onwards, fishermen were not allowed to move beyond coastal waters, and a law made disclosures about Korea to foreigners punishable by death. In 1871, as foreign ships were increasingly sighted offshore, steles were erected throughout the land, warning of the death penalty for anybody talking peace to such barbarians.

Isabella Bird Bishop, an early travel writer, who visited at the end of the century, wrote in 1898:

> Into this archaic...unspeakable grooviness, this irredeemable, unreformed Orientalism, this parody of China without the robustness of race which helps to hold China together, the ferment of the Western leaven has fallen, and this feeblest of kingdoms, rudely shaken out of her sleep of centuries, half frightened and wholly dazed, finds herself confronted with an array of powerful [Western nations]...ringing with rude hands the knell of time-honoured custom, clamouring for concessions, and bewildering her with reforms, suggestions, and panaceas, of which she sees neither the meaning nor the necessity.

This was a country "stifled intellectually by Confucianism, stagnant economically, and politically bound to the decaying Chinese empire" (Martina Deuchler, *Confucian Gentlemen and Barbarian Envoys*, p.1). Social stratification was strangling the people. Control was vested in the court and *yangban* (aristocracy), who by 1910 accounted for around 3% of the population. The majority of government revenues (in 1905 and 1906, 65% and 69% of total receipts) came from a land tax imposed on commoners, the *sangmin*, some 75% of whom were tenant farmers working an average holding of about

2.5 acres. Change was inevitable. China, as an old ally, was declining, particularly after defeat in the opium wars of 1840-42 and 1856-58. Japan was increasingly powerful after the 1860s Meiji restoration had opened the country to foreign ideas, to modern education and Western economic systems. Korean scholars were already aware of new ideas in scholarship, which countered the totalitarian hierarchy of Confucianism with ideas of justice and the rights of man learnt partly from foreign Christian missionaries in Beijing.

Discontent was controlled well for a long time, with rebellion ruthlessly repressed. Yet the holders of power remained remote from the populace. The *yangban* were seen as exploiters: they demanded taxes but gave little in return. Villagers, however, had considerable local autonomy and lived within a family, lineage and clan structure based on reciprocity. Local loyalty was to this clan structure, and to the soil they worked. Seoul, or Hanyang as it was known, was the seat of government, but it was a distant and alien place.

The potential for rebellion grew as new ideas filtered down to the populace. Persecutions of Christian converts during the 19th century reflected official fear over these new ideas, which pitted *Sŏhak* (Western learning) against Confucian orthodoxy. The persecution of 1801, as much against a faction of scholars known as the *Namin*, came because Catholic converts opposed rites: if people failed to honour their ancestors, then they might soon question other rules designed for ordering society. Converts who escaped sought refuge in the countryside, introducing Christian ideas of equality and the afterlife which appealed to hungry, poverty-stricken commoners.

It was within this milieu that *Tonghak* (Eastern learning) emerged. Founded by Ch'oe Che-u around 1860, *Tonghak* mixed elements from Catholicism, Buddhism, Taoism and Confucianism, arguing equality above social status and placing man's spirit on a par with the godhead. Ch'oe suffered through the social system. Since his mother was concubine to an impoverished local aristocrat, he was able to receive education but was ineligible for any civil service position. In a dream, while suffering from an unspecified illness (this is rather like the characteristic calling of a shaman), he was given magical powers to heal. *Tonghak* spread through the south, spawning a minor rebellion in Kyŏngsang Province in 1864. Ch'oe was executed in 1866.

The 'Prince of the Great Court'

In 1864, Kojong, the adopted son of the king, acceded to power. He was 12, and his father, Yi Ha-ŭng, a little-known distant royal prince, took effective power as regent. Known as the Taewŏn'gun ('Prince of the Great Court'), he began a restoration much along the lines of the Tongzhi Restoration in China. To subjugate the factions that had gradually usurped power during the previous years, he curbed rights to inherit positions based on lineage and began to appoint officials on merit. He abolished tax-exempt private academies, because these he considered to be controlled by aristocrats outside the Seoul circles of officialdom. He extended taxes to the previously exempt aristocracy. In an attempt to restore Confucian propriety, he authorised further persecutions of Christians, and reinforced the state policy of isolation. To restore the king's power, he rebuilt the royal palace, but to do so he used irregular conscription and imposed additional taxes. This last was a step too far: the Taewŏn'gun had become unpopular amongst both aristocracy and commoners. He was forced into semi-retirement, but not before he had chosen a consort for the king, who as Queen Min soon allowed a new and corrupt family to take control once the king came of age in 1874.

The Taewŏn'gun's view of foreign relations was unsustainable. When the American ship, the *General Sherman*, sailed up the Taedong river towards P'yŏngyang in 1866, it was set on fire—North Korean state hagiography nowadays claims that Kim Il Sung's grandfather was the responsible party. The United States retaliated in 1871, leading to a brief battle near the island of Kanghwa to the west of Seoul. Five years earlier, Kanghwa had been sacked by seven French ships in retaliation for the murder of French missionaries. That same year, 1866, after being told that imperial rule had been restored with the overthrow of the Tokugawa family, Korea had broken off relations with Japan, declaring that this was the "behaviour of a country without law". Korean refusal two years later to consider the establishment of a 'modern' form of relations with Japan in accordance with international practice further tried Japanese patience.

2.2 Japan and China wrestle

In 1875, Japan provoked an incident, claiming Koreans had attacked a Japanese vessel after it entered the Han river downstream of Seoul. A large Japanese force returned. Simultaneously, a Japanese diplomat in Beijing asked China to relinquish suzerainty over Korea. Despite an official rebuff, which stated Korea was independent in terms of government but subordinate to China, the Korean government was advised to consider Japanese demands. The result was a treaty, signed in 1876, which allowed two Korean ports to be opened to Japanese vessels in addition to Pusan, agreed to the exchange of diplomats, and granted rights of residence.

1880 saw Japan establish a permanent mission, but there was local alarm at Japanese activity, which first surfaced in 1881 when a putsch against the king was uncovered. A year later, the king's life was threatened and the Japanese legation attacked in a mutiny by soldiers. The Taewŏn'gun was recalled to restore calm. He once more re-imposed the formal Confucian order. Hearing that its legation had been attacked, Japan sent a punitive force which landed in August and marched on Seoul, seeking an apology and the right to station troops to protect its legation. China reacted by sending its own troops, who arrested the Taewŏn'gun, claimed he had been behind the mutiny and led him to exile in China. This restored Chinese control and left 3000 Chinese troops stationed in Korea, together with 2000 Korean soldiers under Chinese command. Other treaties were soon signed, all with Chinese guidance and co-operation, first with the United States, then, by 1893, with Britain, France, Germany, Italy, Russia and Austria. All the treaties were similar, in that they established diplomatic and trade links, stipulated tariffs and offered extraterritorial rights which typically favoured the other nation over Korea.

Not every Korean wanted to see a continuation of Chinese control. A group of young officials, seeking for independence and domestic reform, formed themselves into the *Kaehwa tang* (Civilisation Party). Kim Okkyun, the most active member, had been sent to study in Japan in 1881 along with Pak Yŏnghyo and Sŏ Kwangbŏm and later returned to Tokyo, as China proposed devaluing the Korean coinage to negotiate— unsuccessfully—a 3 million yen loan. The group enlisted Sŏ Chaep'il on his return from military training in Japan (Sô later took the name Philip Jaisohn). On 4 December 1884, as a banquet was in progress to celebrate the opening of a new postal service, a coup was mounted, supported by the Japanese, in an attempt to overthrow the pro-Chinese government. The Japanese had promised assistance, yet had only 200 troops in Seoul; the Chinese, still with 1500 men, acted on behalf of the government, and within three days the coup failed. The Japanese legation was burned by its own minister, and conspirators fled to Japan. The setback was felt in Korea as much as in Japan. Throughout the next decade the Korean government vacillated towards Russia as China weakened; at times, other countries jousted for influence. Britain, for example, occupied Kŏmundo, an island off the southern coast, for two years, renaming it Port Arthur.

Kim Okkyun was murdered in a Shanghai hotel in March 1894. By then the peasants had revolted. *Tonghak* grew, as persecution continued, under the leadership of Chŏn Pongjun. Members petitioned for Ch'oe Che-u, its executed founder, to be posthumously pardoned, in rallies that turned into a rebellion in February 1894. Starting in Kobu, in the southwestern Chŏlla province, the uprising spread rapidly as the focus shifted from a plea for pardon to anger at government excesses. The rebels seized government granaries and returned taxes to the peasants. Four months later, now centred around the city of Chŏnju and controlling 53 administrative counties, they began to march northwards towards the capital. They were defeated. Three things conspired against them. First, they lacked unity and co-ordination. Second, local aristocrats, who controlled much of the land they farmed, saw the uprising as the beginning of a class war and threw in their lot with the government. Third, and most decisively, government forces were joined by Chinese troops. The government had requested assistance on 1 June, and China sent in 1500 troops and two warships.

2.3 Japan takes control

Chinese action to quell the disturbances provided an excuse for Japan to re-enter the fray. Back in 1890, the Japanese foreign minister, Aoki Shuzo, had written: "Korea should be made part of the Japanese map." On 10 June 1894, 400 Japanese marines arrived, ostensibly to counter the Chinese forces. The troops soon numbered 8000, in a show of force. Japan confronted China: this was the beginning of the Sino-Japanese War. Japan convincingly won naval battles, and by October China had withdrawn all troops from Korea. Humiliated and defeated, China signed a peace treaty in the Japanese port of Shimonoseki on 17 April 1895, in which it repudiated all tributary ties with Korea and gave the peninsula unconditional independence.

But independence would always be a mirage. Back on 23 July 1894, Japanese troops had marched into Kojong's royal palace in Seoul. The minister at the Japanese legation, Otori Keisuke, forced the king to commit the Koreans to accept Japanese advice on internal reforms. Count Inoue arrived from Japan in late October to prepare a more extensive programme of reform. In January 1895, King Kojong, escorted by Japanese police, swore before the spirits of his ancestors at their shrine in central Seoul to terminate the relationship with China and to reform the Korean legal and administrative system.

The reform programme, known as the *Kabo kyŏngjang*, continued until February 1896. Some Koreans who have gone down in history as independence thinkers, such as Philip Jaisohn and Yun Ch'iho (the latter a Methodist whose diary, in English, has been published), were involved, but Koreans today consider the reforms are witness to Japan's attempt to make Korea its colony. One decree is often given as evidence, though from the other side of the world the significance is hard to grasp: Korean men were forced to cut off their topknots, their distinctive uncut locks of hair gathered and pinned underneath wide-brimmed hats, which had marked their status as mature men.

The reforms were financed partly with 3 million yen from Japan. In outline, they dealt with:

— *independence*. Chinese privileges in Korea were abolished, the king was elevated to emperor, and the Chinese calendar was abandoned.

— *education*. Confucian-style education, and the Chinese-style examination system for entry into the civil service, were abandoned. New schools were opened, from elementary to college, some operated by missionaries.

— *politics*. The king renounced his right to intervene in government. A constitutional monarchy and a cabinet system were introduced. Central power was increased and regional leadership downgraded.

— *money*. The tax system was modernised and banks were established.

— *judiciary*. The need for a modern judiciary followed on from restrictions to the king's power and the downgrading of local authority (which had formerly administered justice regionally).

— *social system*. Legally, all distinctions between the *yangban* aristocracy and *sangmin* commoners were abandoned, along with the stigma attaching to certain occupations. Slavery was outlawed.

Things did not go smoothly. Queen Min was assassinated on 9 October 1895, officially by disaffected Korean troops, but clearly in an action planned and supported by the Japanese. The king was held captive and forced to appoint pro-Japanese cabinet members. The American and Russian legations announced they would not work with the new regime; America offered asylum to the king. Russia landed 150 marines when, in February 1896, the king was smuggled out of the palace to the Russian legation. In May, the situation resolved itself, when a memorandum was signed by Japan and Russia, allowing both to station troops in the capital and to have a say in cabinet appointments. The king was free to return to his palace. Japan and Russia continued to be rivals for Korean influence until 1904, when the two went to war. Japan routed Russian naval vessels off Inch'ŏn, sealing the fate of Korea.

The period 1904-1910 was a time of transition. Korea became a protectorate once the new war forced negotiations between Tokyo and Seoul. In return for guaranteeing the safety of the royal household, the king agreed to follow Japanese advice on administrative matters. On 22 August 1904, Japan introduced financial and diplomatic advisers and on 9 November announced it would take control of Korea's foreign relations. On 17 November, the king was forced to sign a convention to this effect: Japanese troops surrounded the palace and held his prime minister in a side room. Kojong sent a request for assistance to the United States; politely accepted, nothing was done. In 1907, Kojong sent letters to the International Peace Conference in The Hague. Japan successfully argued that since Korea had ceded its diplomatic rights of representation to Japan, it could have no separate delegation. This second attempt to gain international backing made Japan retaliate back in Seoul. On 16 July 1907, Kojong was asked by the government to abdicate in favour of his son, Sunjong. He refused. On 19 July, the government denounced Kojong, saying he had lost the trust of his people and disgraced his position. This time he yielded. Sunjong, portrayed in accounts as a half-wit, ascended the throne but was never allowed to become a leader. Indeed, Koreans recall that he was forced to marry a Japanese, thereby polluting the royal blood line. Public opposition to the Japanese was initially significant, but soon declined. At the height of opposition, in 1908, Japanese figures claim 69,832 insurgents were encountered and 11,562 killed; in 1910, only 1891 were encountered, of whom 125 were killed.

2.4 Colonial rule

Korea was a colony of Japan from 1910 to 1945. The Japanese Director of Foreign Affairs reported to the Korea Branch of the Royal Asiatic Society in Seoul in 1911 that "Japan has now made the country [Korea] an integral part of her dominion and has set upon herself the work not [only] of improvement but of rejuvenescence of territory." The Korean perspective remains rather different. They would prefer to emphasise the harshness of colonial rule, their exclusion from government, the arbitrary abuses of the Japanese police, forced labour, and so on. During the later years of control, Koreans were expected to speak Japanese, to take Japanese names and to practice the Japanese state religion of Shintoism. Koreans today still feel that their colonial experience was unique. Bitterness remains. Perhaps the experience is too recent for many. Enmity between Japan and Korea dates back many centuries, and perhaps this too informs the collective memory.

Looking from outside, we have to consider four aspects of colonial rule:

— the *Korean industrial base,* and built on this the economic miracle of recent times, was developed during the colonial period. Nearly 60% of the founders of South Korea's conglomerates had business experience before 1945. Park Chung Hee, the president of South Korea who presided over the rapid expansion of the 1960s and 1970s, was a colonial product, trained in Japan, as was Kim Yŏnsu, the chairman of the Federation of Korean Industries during the same period.

— the colonial period brought much *suffering* to Koreans, but not uniformly throughout the 35 years.

— by the end of the 19th century, the lethargic *administration* had reduced Korea to a pitiful state. Poverty was rife and starvation was commonplace. The tax burden was inequitable, and hit hardest those who struggled to produce the nation's food. There was virtually no industry, and little except agricultural products that could be traded. Japan introduced more vigorous patterns of administration, a new tax system and legal reforms. Although intended to facilitate the government of Korea as a colony, these changes brought modern forms of administration to the country.

— the changes imposed by the Japanese regime brought Korea abruptly into the *modern world*. Urban dwellers grew from 3% of the population in 1910 to 13% in 1945. This encouraged and supported the growth of banking and a cash economy, accompanied by trading and manufacturing. Construction of a road and railway system eased the transport of both goods and people. Although most of the profits and the production itself went to Japan, between 1910 and 1940 agricultural output doubled, and mining and manufacturing output increased by 1500%.

The changes brought by Japan were tangible. According to one Korean scholar, Kang Man-gil, writing in 1963:

During the 36 years annexation, Koreans were never allowed to participate in any political activities in the modern sense. However, in the fields of thought, literature and religion, they had access to the trends of the times to some extent; in economics, although they lived under a capitalistic system, the Japanese had complete control over the Korean economy. And in the social aspect, Korean society, whether compulsorily or spontaneously, was gradually growing into a modern society.

Carter Eckert, an American historian writing in 1991 (*Offspring of Empire*, p. 1), adds a graphic illustration of the change:

> In 1876, on the eve of the Kanghwa treaty, Min Tuho and Pak Munhoe were roughly the same age and both were residents of Kyŏnggi province. Their relative positions in society however, were starkly different. Min was a member of one of the wealthiest and most powerful families in the country. His uncle, Min Ch'igu, was the maternal grandfather of the king, and before his assassination in 1874, Tuho's first cousin had been both the reputed leader of the clan and the adoptive brother of the queen. Pak, on the other hand, was a poor peasant eking out a meagre existence on land that was not even his own but which belonged to the Min family. There was little opportunity for two such men to meet on a social basis...but even if they had found themselves in the same room, there would hardly have been much common ground for discourse.

> By 1945—and indeed, long before—things had changed. By then, the sons and grandsons of these same two men were members of the same exclusive social club in Seoul. Unlike their fathers, who had been separated by a chasm of land and lineage, the younger Mins and Paks had been brought together in a burgeoning new class where possession of capital (or shares) had become a common bond. The Mins had become bankers, the Paks merchants, and both were investors in industrial enterprise.

1910-1919

Japan began with a four-pronged approach:

> — from the outset, Japan took a harsh line. It had taken control of Taiwan in 1895. There it had encountered tribal people, largely illiterate and supposedly unsophisticated, who mounted considerable opposition to its rule. Japan would make no similar mistake in Korea.

> — Japanese legend had it that Japan had a divine mission in which Korea was to be exploited for the benefit of the motherland.

> — Japan was increasingly self-confident. It had thrashed both China, the repository of old tradition, and Russia, a major world power. Who could stop its expansion?

> — Japan was further convinced its plan was right because it met no real opposition. The United States and European powers seemed little concerned.

The first period was one for restructuring and cementing control. The Japanese governor-general, always a military officer, was answerable only to the Japanese emperor in Tokyo. He issued decrees and appointed governors. The pyramid of power was biased towards urban districts, where the Japanese were concentrated, and had Japanese at the top and Koreans only near the bottom. The police force was trebled from 7700 men in 1910 to 21,000 in 1937. Land registration by 1918 brought in a new and fairer tax system that encouraged a more efficient use of land. Education and industry developed gradually through the whole 35-year period. The Japanese put in place a six-year elementary school system. This was complemented by six years of secondary and four years of college training, to which few Koreans were admitted. Education was meant primarily to turn Koreans into useful members of the labour force, hence there was initially little enforcement of school attendance. Thus, in 1930, only 13% of Koreans went through the whole of the six years' elementary school; by 1940, less than 40% attended. Until 1923, there was no university, and no girls were ever admitted to this. Industry, like agriculture, was developed for Japan's benefit, particularly after the agricultural slump of 1929-1930. Rice production doubled during the 35 years, yet Korean consumption actually fell, as the surplus was shipped to Japan. Manufactured goods were for the Japanese market. Transport was improved accordingly, with roads and railways built primarily along an axis from Seoul southeastwards to Pusan, the major port for Japan, and northwestwards towards Manchuria as the empire expanded its territory.

1920-1931

The second period began after the March 1919 Declaration of Independence, a key point in the years of colonisation (see chapter 7.5 Nationalism). The Japanese were caught by surprise at the success of the declaration and the nationwide meetings held to discuss and disseminate it, and shifted to a stance less intolerant towards Korean sentiments. A new governor-general was appointed to "pursue harmony between Korea and Japan" (*Nissen yuwa*), and reforms were made as part of a cultural policy (*bunka seiji*). These included permission to publish two daily newspapers, both of which survive to this day, the *Tonga ilbo* (East Asia Daily News) and *Chosŏn ilbo* (Korea Daily News), as well as a variety of journals. This new freedom of discussion in turn encouraged Korean nationalism to move down two distinct paths, one leading, on the right, to the moderate *munhwa undong* ('cultural nationalist') grouping. Members established a new Korean literature and stressed myths such as the Tan'gun foundation legend (see Factsheet 2.1 for an explanation) and indigenous culture to separate Korea from both China and Japan in its historical development. Their campaign for the use of *han'gŭl* , the Korean alphabet, finally led to the 1933 *Match'umbŏp t'ongiran* (Unified Orthography). They also tried to encourage self-sufficiency based on Korean production. They argued for gradual reform, for increases in education and capitalism amongst the populace. But as part of this approach they were prepared to tolerate Japanese rule. This was their downfall. The mantle of nationalism fell increasingly over those leaning more to the left, who preferred overt resistance to the colonial power. More radical socialist and Communist groups developed, which as time went on split into a number of factions.

A provisional government, set up in Shanghai, continued to argue for independence, with associated people such as Syngman Rhee (who was briefly elected president) campaigning in Washington. But opposition mounted from outside a country is rarely successful, and the 1930s were marked by incursions across the borders by guerrilla groups in Manchuria, Siberia and China proper (see chapter 15.4). (Many of these were Communist groups with links to the growing Chinese Communist Party and were later important in setting up the North Korean state.) They enjoyed some limited success: in North Korea, battles at places such as Poch'ŏnbo and Wangjaesan are remembered, and Kim Il Sung is considered the major independence fighter. But such incursions presented no major obstacle to the Japanese, who by now were concerned with a larger empire.

1931-1945

In September 1931, the Japanese army attacked Chinese troops in Manchuria. Korea quickly assumed critical importance to Japanese plans as the Pacific War began in 1937. It was a keystone, producing goods and food for the war effort, and providing labour which could be (and was) taken to Japan and Manchuria to work. Korean industry, along a southeast-northwest corridor marked by the Pusan-Seoul-Ŭiju railway, effectively linked Japan to Manchuria. Korean students were compelled to join 'volunteer' forces, and all students were ordered to wear military uniforms. Women were enlisted to repair roads and maintain the transport infrastructure. Young women were taken to work in factories at home and abroad, replacing men who had been force-drafted into the military. As a 'women's volunteer corps', women became factory girls and, in the tragic story which has only unfolded in the 1990s, many thousands were coerced into becoming prostitutes for the Japanese military, euphemistically known as 'comfort girls' (*ianfu* in Japanese, *wianbu* in Korean). As Japan shifted to a war footing, so any hint of tolerance was lost: Koreans were to be made Japanese.

One thing needs to be stated: independence in Korea came, not as the result of nationalist struggle, but because of the defeat of Japan by the Allies in August 1945. Before Japan fell, the conferences of Allied leaders held in Cairo and Tehran in 1943 had agreed on trusteeship for Korea. The United States knew that Soviet troops would be on the spot when the war ended (US forces arrived only in September 1945), and in 1945 two young Washington officers—one was later to become Secretary of State, Dean Rusk—were asked to propose a temporary partition. They did so, drawing a line along the 38th parallel, arbitrary but roughly equal in terms of territory. The line had one advantage to the United States, since Seoul was to the South, but it left the bulk of industry and raw materials in the North.

Readings

Isabella Bird Bishop, 1897. *Korea and her Neighbours: A Narrative of Travel, with an Account of the Recent Vicissitudes and Present Position of the Country,* 2 vols. London: John Murray. Reprinted in one vol., 1970, Seoul: Yonsei University Press; 1985, London: KPI

Martina Deuchler, 1977. *Confucian Gentlemen and Barbarian Envoys.* Seattle: University of Washington Press

Carter J. Eckert, 1991. *Offspring of Empire: The Koch'ang Kims and the Colonial Origins of Korean Capitalism 1876-1945.* Seattle: University of Washington Press

Carter J. Eckert, Ki-baik Lee *et al.,* 1990. *Korea Old And New: A History.* Seoul: Ilchokak Publishers

C. I. Eugene Kim and Dorothea Mortimore (eds), 1977. *Korea's Response to Japan: The Colonial Period 1910-1945.* Kalamazoo: Western Michigan University

Stewart Lone and Gavan Mc Cormack, 1993. *Korea Since 1850.* New York: St Martin's Press

Andrew Nahm (ed.), 1973. *Korea under Japanese Colonial Rule.* Kalamazoo: Western Michigan University

Michael E. Robinson, 1988. *Cultural Nationalism in Colonial Korea, 1920-1925.* Seattle: University of Washington Press

3

DEVELOPMENT IN PARALLEL

3.1 Rival leaders

The collapse of Japan was catastrophic for Korea. In the initial period of fluid politics, the two controlling powers, Soviet in the North and American in the South, found political allies. In the North it was inexpedient to be a former landlord, a collaborator with the Japanese, to be Christian or anti-Communist. In the South, it was not sensible to be left of centre. As rival governments were declared in 1948, so two leaders emerged.

In the South, Syngman Rhee was 70 when Japan was defeated. He came from an aristocratic but poor family who were distantly related to the royal household. He had consequently begun with a Confucian education, but continued with Western training, achieving a PhD at Princeton University. He had been in exile since 1911. He had suitable credentials: he had been active in the Independence Club, and in 1919 had become president of the Provisional Government in Shanghai. He visited China in 1920-1921, but gave up the presidency and returned to the United States, where he began to act as the government's Washington representative. After the Japanese attack at Pearl Harbour, records show he badgered the State Department about Korea, realising that independence would follow if Japan lost the war.

In the North, Kim Il Sung was much younger. Born Kim Sŏngju to a peasant family in 1912, he had been a minor guerrilla fighter (North Korean texts suggest he was the *major* figure) in Manchuria during the 1930s. He may have been at Yen'an with the Chinese Communist Party for some time, but he retreated from the Japanese into Siberia, probably in 1941, where his son Kim Jong Il was born in Khabarovsk. In 1945, he returned to P'yŏngyang, now the capital of the North, in Soviet uniform. There is no record that Kim Il Sung had any contact with the Communist groups in Korea itself. In 1945, the four main communist factions jostled for power. There were some 200,000 Koreans in the Soviet Union loyal to Moscow, and 430,000 Koreans in Manchuria, some of whom had carried out guerrilla attacks on the Japanese. Many Koreans had worked with the Chinese Communists, still fighting to wrest control from Chiang Kai-shek; many others had stayed in Korea. Pak Hanyŏng, in Korea, was the best known leader. He re-established the Korean Communist Party in September 1945, but was outmanoeuvred by Kim Il Sung and purged after the war as Kim moved to assume total control.

3.2 Descent into war

War was the wellnigh inevitable consequence of the establishment of two rival states, each with a strong leader claiming to represent the whole Korean peninsula. Let's look at what happened, starting with what became **The Republic of Korea (South Korea)**:

In 1945, people's committees emerged in about half of the South Korean counties. These were locally rooted, and shunned any Japanese collaborators. The US military occupation force saw these as a threat since, because they represented the 'have-nots', they were radical. General Hodge, a poor-man-come-good, was appointed to head the US military occupation force. He was not a politician, and believed that the only way to avoid a Communist take-over was to cultivate those with right-wing leanings. He accordingly used the authority structures left by the Japanese, allowing collaborators to remain in place.

By August, the left-wing Committee for the Preparation of Korean Independence had been founded. This proposed the release of political prisoners and argued for workers to organise themselves. Within it was a Communist faction.

Hodge tried to control the emerging radicals. In September 1945, a provisional cabinet of a so-called Korean People's Republic included the right-wing Syngman Rhee and the left-wing Kim Ku. These two struggled for power. In December, Kim organised strikes and sought to establish a government. In Moscow, meanwhile, a Soviet-American commission to advise on a provisional government was proposed. Hodge allied himself against Kim with Rhee and Rhee's Korean Democratic Party. In February 1946, Rhee set up a right-wing Representative Democratic Council. Hodge supported this until October, when Rhee's speeches about setting up a government were complemented by the announcement of an Interim Legislature. Rhee's supporters stirred up demonstrations, keeping Hodge talking.

Elections for the Interim Legislature made use of the revived Japanese election system, allowing landlords and leaders (the former aristocracy) to vote, while many poor farmers found themselves left out. Rhee and the right were victorious. Whipped up by Rhee, demonstrations against Communism increased in early 1947, with unrest shifting focus in June and July to the trusteeship of Korea by the US.

As the US sought to reduce involvement, noting that it would not be able to counter the spread of Communism indefinitely, so it began to consult on setting up UNTCOK, the United Nations' Temporary Commission on Korea. Elections were proposed for a Korean government, with US and Soviet troops to be withdrawn within three months of them. UNTCOK found itself with an impossible task: not allowed to observe anything in North Korea, in February 1948 it agreed to supervise elections only on South Korean territory. In the run-up to the election, Rhee censured rivals and criticised Hodge. Hodge, worn down, asked to be withdrawn. Elections were held in May, in South Korea only. Despite claims of widespread corruption, Rhee was victorious. A new constitution, approved on 12 July, enshrined Rhee's claim to represent 'all Korea'. He became president on 15 July.

Rhee was never really popular. Inflation rocketed in 1948, and after several years of poor harvests, unrest began to flare. US figures of 1949 suggest that over 3000 guerrilla groups were operating in opposition to Rhee's government. Rhee suppressed these and, seeing North Korean infiltration behind many of them, increased his forces on the border with the North, where there was intermittent fighting. The US wanted to build up South Korea's forces, but its Senate refused. A Korean Military Advisory Group (KMAG) was set up. In May 1949, Northern and Southern forces were involved in incidents in Kaesŏng and Ongjin. The US produced a White Paper, indicating its withdrawal of support for Taiwan and suggesting that Korea had little strategic value.

The KMAG still tried to improve South Korean strength. Actions against guerrillas by the police left a reasonable standing force, which by May 1950 numbered 100,000 men. These would fight for Rhee, but were not yet sufficient to fight for the nation. Weapon stocks were moreover low, based on leftovers: the South had just 14 obsolete planes.

The situation was also developing in what became **The Democratic Republic of Korea (North Korea)**:

People's committees functioned in virtually every county in the Northern territory. They were, though, indistinct and lacking in clear command structures, and they were distrusted by the Soviet forces. Kim Il Sung became leader of the North Korean Communist Party in December 1945. He mixed Leninism with Maoism in a centralised, tightly-organised party.

Mirroring developments in the South, he formed and headed an Interim People's Committee. Autonomous organisations were gradually brought under the Communist Party umbrella. An army began to be assembled, lightly armed, using Koreans who had been in China and guerrillas migrating back from Soviet territory. Korean communists who had been in Yen'an had formed a New Democratic Party. In July 1946, Kim merged this with his party, creating the North Korean Workers Party.

By the beginning of 1948, the Soviet forces considered that Communist rule was sufficiently established to begin a withdrawal. A constitution was approved in September, copying some of the Soviet constitution, thereby creating a state. Pak Hanyŏng was at this point foreign minister of this new North Korean state and leader of the South Korean Workers Party. As Rhee tackled insurgency in the South, so Pak's power declined.

Kim and Pak visited Moscow in March 1949. Some have claimed that this was when Stalin approved an attack on the South. By now, there was a 36-plane regiment in P'yŏngyang. Pak was a threat to Kim's power, so Kim merged the North and South Korean Workers Parties, effectively sidelining Pak. By early 1950, the centralised pyramid structure of the Korean Workers Party was firmly established. Agricultural reform was being pushed through, and considerable economic progress had already been made, using plant left by the Japanese and new equipment supplied by the Soviet Union.

(See chapter 4 for an account of the Korean War.)

3.3 A divided peninsula

The division of the peninsula survived the Korean War, a result of the armistice signed on 27 July 1953. Control, decision making and planning for economic development were centralised in both states. North Korea began well, and until around 1973, North Korean GNP exceeded that of South Korea. The state soared on the back of rapid economic growth and industrial expansion. But decline set in, as the tight authoritarian rule of Kim Il Sung refused to reform what was essentially a Stalinist state. South Korea began with right-wing rule that, in maintaining some social stratification, left corruption unchecked. After Rhee, it took 30 years of military rule to develop a vibrant economy before democracy was ushered in in the early 1990s.

3.4 North Korea

Reconstruction

In the North, the Sixth Plenum of the Central Committee of the New Korean Workers Party, held in August 1953, approved an ambitious three-year economic plan that would return the state to pre-war levels of production. Based on Soviet models, it gave priority to heavy industry. The Soviet Union pledged $250 million in grant aid, and China waived war debts and promised $325.2 million over the next four years. Quotas were reached ahead of schedule, averaging an annual industrial growth rate of 41.8%, with corresponding improvements in wages and food supply. 1954 saw the beginnings of a collectivisation of agriculture. In this, mutual aid teams were first established, which pooled land but shared profits on the basis of input of land and labour, before all land was collectivised. By 1958 all private farms had been abolished. Private industry was phased out by introducing prohibitive taxes on commerce. Thus was laid what began as a remarkable story: people worked hard, and saw the benefits of the new system.

North Korea accepted aid from both China and the Soviet Union. Initial loyalty to the USSR reflected the fact that in 1945 it had brought liberation. The Sino-Soviet split after the death of Stalin in 1953 allowed the North to move closer to China, and assistance from Beijing during the 1950s seemed to cement these ties. But Kim proved to be no lackey of either power. He spoke against the 'revisionism' of the Soviet Communists and the 'dogmatism' of the Chinese. He signed treaties of friendship with both, perceiving that this would strengthen national security against a potential Southern attack. Kim denounced Khruschev after the Soviet Union agreed a peaceful coexistence policy with the West and capitulated in the Cuban missile crisis. But then, after Khruschev's demise, he moved back to the Soviet orbit, denouncing China over Vietnam in October 1965. Cultural policy, likewise, gradually shifted from Soviet Socialist Realism to a copy of Chinese practice during the Cultural Revolution.

Consolidation

In a speech dated 4 April 1955, Kim called for a 'confession movement'. Aimed at corruption in commerce, it would soon permeate all areas of life. Pak Hanyŏng had been sentenced to death at the end of the war along with six others for claimed espionage. Uneasy after Khruschev's denunciation of Stalin in February 1956, Kim abolished the politburo during the Third Congress of the Korea Workers Party in April, replacing it with a standing committee. In an attempt to consolidate the different Communist factions, the eleven committee members were a mix of the North Korean, Manchurian, Chinese and Soviet factions. At the end of August, six opponents moved against Kim, claiming he was 'anti-people'. Kim imprisoned them and expelled them from the party, but pressure from the Soviet and Chinese governments forced their release. In February 1957, under the banner of "the party's concentrated guidance", factions loyal to both the Soviet and Chinese parties were isolated. Within a year, 80 high officials were purged, and the Korean Workers Party could announce it was free of factionalism. Kim was now the paramount leader. But consolidation of power came at a cost, and the North still has a system of gulags confining an estimated 100,000 or more people judged undesirable.

Kim's legitimacy was also enshrined through a new philosophy, *juche*. First mentioned in a 1955 speech, and later backdated to the 1930s (the wonders of hindsight!), *juche*, which survives until today, is often glossed as 'self-reliance'. As an ideology, it argues that the Party is solely responsible for reconstruction since it alone has full understanding. Independence is maintained in diplomacy, wherein each country is treated as an equal, thus explaining the shifting relationships with the Soviet Union and China. In domestic policy, *juche* has it that human resources and individual efforts must maintain self-sufficiency and self-defence.

A five-year plan was announced in April 1956. The aim was no longer recovery, but growth. The lack of sufficient outside aid meant that mass mobilisation became the tool: a plenum of the Central Committee in December 1956 announced the *Ch'ŏllima undong*, a movement based on the legend of a flying horse which could take its rider 300 miles in one day. Workteams vied for ever greater production, and targets were completed one year in advance of the schedule. On the surface, this was impressive. A 36% annual industrial growth was recorded, but there were signs of over-centralisation and an unresponsive bureaucracy. The state reacted by stimulating activity. To the west of P'yŏngyang, Kim visited the village of Ch'ŏngsan in February 1960. He told leaders and farmers to co-operate. Farmers were to be given a say in decision making, and profit-sharing was introduced amongst work teams. In December 1961, the experiment was repeated when Kim visited the electric appliance factory in T'aean; party committees were introduced onto the shop floor.

A seven-year plan was announced in 1961. The target for growth was an annual 18%, but only 12% was achieved. A three-year extension was announced, taking the plan through to 1970, after Kim in October 1966 blamed matters on insufficient aid and the crippling effect of needing to keep military preparedness for a potential attack. Economists beyond Korea suggest the real problems were in inefficient management, centralisation, and an unwillingness to move beyond heavy industry to increase technical expertise.

Decline

Juche, as much as it remains trumpeted in the North, created problems. It balanced alliances between China and the Soviet Union, hence limiting potential aid receipts, and appealed to poorer states in the non-aligned movement, particularly those in the Third World. It preached self-sufficiency, without creating flexible management structures or accepting the need to develop competitive technology. And *juche*, together with the related concept of *yuil sasang* ('one mind ideology'), meant Kim, as leader of the party, was infallible. No criticism was tolerated. There was no mechanism for feedback, no way to stimulate change and development in industry. The rhetoric of mass mobilisation chimed 'unity' and 'loyalty', but 'speed drives' had become so routine that they seemed now to achieve little. The initial success was tremendous, but until the mid-1960s the impressive development partially reflected massive aid and the two advantages North Korea set out with: the remnants of industrial complexes, and abundant raw materials and energy sources.

The Northern economy stagnated in the 1970s and 1980s largely because nothing changed. A six-year plan from 1971 to 1976 concluded with a year's 'adjustment'. This plan began well, with imports of advanced technology from Japan and Europe. But drought and an unexpected drop in exports left the North unable to pay its debts. The oil crisis led to a readjustment of international trade, with the cost of Korean imports—the technologically superior finished goods—rising as the main exports, raw materials, declined in value. Europe has never been paid, hence to this day an international consortium of banks monitors and tries to withhold further credit to the North. The next seven-year plan (1978-1984) ended with two planless years. The targets were set lower, with an annual growth rate predicted at 12.1%. The 1987-1993 plan rolled over targets from the previous period, scaling down some (for example, steel output) and predicting large increases in others.

This last plan was thwarted for many reasons. The collapse of the Soviet Union left the North unable to barter. It could not pay hard currency, and lost much of its oil imports. China, too, has moved to a cash-based trading structure. The lack of capital, and the need to pay for imports, means that the North cannot invest in industry. This leads to more inefficiency, in power, transportation and the availability of raw materials. In the early 1990s, GNP contracted severely. Today, factories are reported to be working at far below capacity, and there are frequent power cuts. Production is down: official reports state proudly that 10% of consumer goods are recycled, and that tractors are being reassembled from 1950-vintage parts. Indeed, the trumpeted mechanisation of agriculture has come to a grinding halt, and fields are once again tilled by men and occasional oxen. Self-sufficiency in food has always presented a challenge, since 80% of the territory is mountainous, and perhaps self-sufficiency was never achieved. Despite continuing to claim bountiful harvests, grain was imported from China until 1991, then from Thailand through 1993, and from South Korea and Japan in early 1995, until devastating floods led the regime to appeal for international food aid. For a number of years there have been rumours of food shortages, fuelled by food riots near the border with China. There have been reports of a campaign to get Koreans to eat two not three meals daily, and by late 1995 there was considerable evidence that many in the countryside were suffering advanced malnutrition.

The future

Kim Il Sung died in July 1994. From the mid-1970s, the son from his first marriage, Kim Jong Il, had been groomed to take the reins of power. By the end of 1995, there was no evidence of a power struggle, although, even if effectively in control, the son had not officially taken over as head of state. Much of the world expected Kim the elder, 'Great Wise President for Life Dearly Beloved and Sagacious Leader' (to give him his official state title), to bequeath a power vacuum. There were two main reasons for this. First, his authority to rule came as a revolutionary leader, and his history was tied to the state. His people credited him with the defeat of both the Japanese in 1945 and the Americans—'Yankee aggressors'—in the Korean War, and with the development of the 'Socialist paradise' in which they lived. His son had none of his credentials, and his lack of military experience was thought likely to damn him in the eyes of the large standing army.

Second, there were other potential leaders. In the 1960s, the elder Kim's brother, Kim Yŏngju, was prominent amongst these. Once Jong Il was appointed to the secretariat of the Korean Workers Party in 1973, Yŏngju dropped out of the same body. In 1977 he lost the post of deputy premier. He disappeared from sight, only reappearing in 1994; it is assumed that he, with the elder Kim's second wife, opposed Jong Il. When Jong Il disappeared from public view in 1977, a Japanese report suggested he had been involved in a road accident planned as an assassination attempt. Jong Il reappeared in early 1979, and at the Sixth Congress of the Party was nominated successor and elected to high political posts. Next he became Supreme Commander of the armed forces. But evidence of resistance continued. Several high-ranking military fled to China in 1982, and according to the Japanese press, 1000 party members were purged in 1983. Jong Il is still rarely seen in public, photographs are few, and he virtually never speaks. Tied to his father's legacy—he has preached the doctrine of *juche* for many years—it is unclear how he can make substantial changes to the state and its management. But, without such changes, it is hard to see how North Korea can survive.

3.5 South Korea

The First Republic

Syngman Rhee remained in power until 1960. His regime was characterised by the promotion of his own interests. He initially thrived because of the war. His state became the frontline between capitalism and Communism; this was where the Cold War turned hot. Rhee did not sign the armistice agreement, and on 15 August 1953, he declared bitterly that the war could have been won had the United Nations not decided against victory. With the war behind them, he found in the US a dependable and wealthy ally. Indeed, US aid became the fulcrum for reconstruction and development.

Rhee's regime was kept afloat by a motley assortment of political allies. To appease these he left many of the nation's economic problems unresolved, channelling aid elsewhere than into reconstruction. Corruption and inefficiency chipped away at his prestige, leaving shortages of food and fuel coupled to massive inflation. To remain in power, he became increasingly authoritarian. Prior to elections in 1952—the war was still going on—Rhee removed his presidential mandate from legislative control, so that he could be elected by popular vote rather than by fellow politicians. He was elected for a four-year term. He then formed the Liberal Party, which enjoyed a majority in the National Assembly after elections in 1954. He abolished the post of prime minister, increasing his personal power, then changed the constitution to allow a president to serve indefinitely. The result of all this was that the opposition united—a rare event in South Korean politics—as the Democratic Party. In 1956, aged 81, Rhee announced he would stand down. But supporters encouraged him to "bow to popular opinion", so he stood and again won, partly because the main opposition candidate, Shin Ikhŭi, died of a heart attack during the campaign. The only serious remaining opposition candidate was Cho Pongam, who still managed to get 30% of the vote. Threatened, Rhee's regime alleged Cho had Communist connections: he was charged under the National Security Law and executed eight months before the next presidential elections in 1960.

Rhee, as he increased his iron rule, failed to comprehend social changes that were marked by increasing urbanisation, rising literacy, better education and a widely read press. There was much greater dissemination of information amongst a knowledgeable, educated population than ever before. As the elections loomed in 1960, Myŏn Chang, a Catholic with the baptismal name John, who had been elected Vice-President in the previous elections above Rhee's candidate, emerged as the main opposition contender. The election, held on 18 March, was described as 'terrorised'. There was widespread violence against the opposition, and observers were forced to withdraw. Official results gave Rhee an astonishing 92% of the vote, 9.6 million, when he had only achieved 55% in 1956. His Vice-President, Lee Ki Poong, was declared to have over eight million votes, two million more than the opposition candidate. Demonstrations against this obvious rigging broke out in Seoul, Pusan and Kwangju, initially led by students. In Masan, the police station was burnt, and seven people were killed by the police. When on 11 March the body of a student was found, suggesting more people had died, fresh demonstrations broke out; the police shot two to death and injured many more. By 19 April, 30,000 workers had joined students in Seoul to march on the presidential palace. The police opened fire as they breached the perimeter fence, leaving more than 20 killed. Rhee imposed martial law, moving thousands of troops from the Demilitarized Zone

(DMZ)—the heavily fortified corridor that separates North and South Korea—to patrol Seoul's streets. Yet demonstrations continued, and on 24 April Rhee announced he might be willing to resign. However, he clung to power. In the face of political defections and by 26 April reports that the army and police had begun to take the side of student demonstrators, Rhee finally announced the elections had been 'illegal' and, a day later, resigned. His Vice-President, Lee, was shot by his son, and at the end of May Rhee slipped away to exile in Hawaii.

The Second Republic

...was not a success. Rhee's Liberal Party quickly disintegrated. What had been the opposition, the Democratic Party, came to power on 29 July 1960 with 206 seats in the National Assembly. Yun Posŏn was elected president on 12 August. By this time, much of the repressive legislature had been repealed. In June, a revised constitution had moved power away from the president back to a two-tier National Assembly. The president remained head of state, but now had a more ceremonial role.

Failure came because of factionalism, a lack of commitment to change, and perhaps an ambivalence to democracy, of which Korea had had no experience. Rather, politicians returned to the better understood principle of autocracy: they were quick to censure debate and restrict any activity they felt threatened security. Factionalism within the government was soon apparent, with an uneasy alliance between 'old' Democrats led by their founder, Yun, and a 'new' group under Myŏn Chang. Yun was, like Rhee, from aristocratic stock with links to the royal family, and he had served the Shanghai Provisional Government. Rhee had appointed him mayor of Seoul, and for a couple of years he had been a minister before becoming one of Rhee's critics. Chang had more revolutionary credentials. He had been educated in the US, returned to liberated Korea and became a teacher. Elected to the National Assembly in 1948, he served briefly as Prime Minister during the Korean war and was elected Vice-President in 1956. Rhee had excluded him from all state affairs, and kept him under virtual house arrest until 1960.

Rivalry between the two camps was soon apparent, as followers of Yun and Chang blocked any appointments the other tried to make. Both camps were also compromised by dealing too lightly with the abusers of power, often releasing them with reprimands. Tougher legislation had little effect. Students had by this time become extremely radical, hardly surprising among those who had recently brought down a government. Cries for reform and demonstrations continued. To appease the clamour for justice, the government announced it would cut 30,000 troops from the standing forces, and this spurred the military to intervene.

An army of 5000 in 1945 had grown to 600,000 by the end of the Korean War. The war, and the continued threat of invasion, meant it was well armed and well trained. On 16 May 1961, paratroopers and marines under General Park Chung Hee marched into Seoul. The architect of the coup was Kim Jong Pil, a graduate of the officers' academy in 1948; Park was his uncle by marriage. Martial law was imposed, public gatherings were banned and a curfew imposed. The government was dissolved, and arrest warrants were issued for all its members. President Yun was placed under house arrest. The following day, senior military leaders announced their support for the coup. A day later, the now-dissolved cabinet met for the last time, announcing martial law retroactively. This, in effect, legalised the coup. Yun stayed on as president, ensuring that international recognition would not be rescinded, but transferred legal authority to a Supreme Council for National Reconstruction. The Council was military in make-up, as was a cabinet proclaimed on 21 May. By July, following purges among the military, Park was effectively in control, with Kim Jong Pil supporting him as head of a new organisation, the Korean CIA.

The Third and Fourth Republics

Park Chung Hee's rule marks the moment when Korean economic development took off. His regime was oppressive, tolerated little opposition or unrest, and used martial law and curfews as regular control mechanisms. In some ways Park's junta appeared like a European fascist dictatorship. It was non-partisan, non-class based, it offered gestures of support to workers through co-operative unions and it enshrined legal rights. As a stabilising force, it was welcomed by the US, which issued a statement to this effect from the State Department in July 1961.

To become legitimate, Park first had to become president. A provisional constitution, approved in December 1962, allowed for an elected president as head of state and head of government. In August 1963, Park resigned from the military to run in elections held on 15 October. He received 4.7 million votes, narrowly beating Yun Posŏn's 4.5 million. In later elections for the National Assembly, Park's Democratic Republican Party (DRP) got 110 of the 175 available seats on receipt of just 34% of votes. Military rule was officially over on 17 December, when Park was sworn in as president, but was re-imposed in the summer of 1964 to deal with student demonstrations. A cycle had begun: martial law meant public meetings were banned, newspapers closely censored and universities closed. More demonstrations greeted the signing in spring 1965 of a normalisation treaty with Japan (accepting $800 million, of which $300 million came as straight aid) and the committal of Korean troops to Vietnam.

Support for Park increased as economic change began to be felt. He inherited an economy with total exports worth less than $50 million annually, 80% of which were of primary goods. The first five-year plan aimed to change this, channelling aid into rapid industrialisation (America, between 1945 and 1976, provided $5.7 billion in economic and $6.8 billion in military aid). Average GNP growth during the first plan was 8.5%. Exports increased by a massive annual 40%, reaching $180 million in 1965. Textiles, from serving domestic needs, generated $100 million in exports in 1968. Private industry was encouraged to support the government plan, but with tax concessions and loans at favourable rates channelled to a few trusty companies. These companies developed into the conglomerates, known in Korean as *chaebŏl*. Hyundai, for example, moved into heavy industry, construction, civil engineering, motor manufacturing and cement.

The government took on long-term capital intensive projects such as the development of the P'ohang steel mill, now the second largest in the world. Korea became an attractive place for foreign investment, since tight control of labour kept unions weak and wages a fraction of those in Japan. The whole plan echoed what had happened in post-war Japan, with central management favouring a few large companies to encourage exports above local development. The major difference was that, unlike Japan where American involvement prevented abuses of power, Park was sole arbiter in Korea. The conglomerates had a vested interest in retaining Park's presidency. Businessmen implicated in corruption during Syngman Rhee's rule went unpunished; and companies which now received loans could control their competition as they grew, effectively endangering small businessmen and stunting the development of small and medium companies.

Park entered the next presidential elections, in May 1967, duly strengthened, and received 51.4% of the vote. In June elections to the National Assembly, Park's Democratic Republican Party increased its representation to 130. The second five-year plan (1967-1971) saw an acceleration in the annual growth rate to an average 10.5%. The peak came in 1969, with 15.9%, dropping to 9.8% in 1971. By now, the people took economic growth for granted.

Irregularities in the 1967 elections had resulted in some demonstrations, but by 1969 it was clear that Park intended to stay in power beyond the constitutional two-term limit. Despite unrest, but using his large majority, he pushed a bill through the Assembly removing the constitutional bar in September 1969. The presidential elections, on 27 April 1971, were surprisingly calm. Park got 51% of the vote; in place of Yun, Kim Dae Jung was the New Democratic Party (NDP) nomination. Elections for an enlarged Assembly on 25 May weakened the DRP: they got 113 seats to the NDP's 89. Stability was further undermined at the beginning of 1972 by the world beyond Korea. The American gold standard broke down, the US and its allies suffered setbacks in Vietnam, and rapprochement between China and the US was looming: all ominous signs of a possible end to American aid. Park began to seek a rapprochement with North Korea, a move, he argued, which would permit cuts in the hugely expensive armed forces and give the South access to raw materials and power supplies. But the legitimacy of South Korea rested on its anti-Communist stance, and local reaction to the plan was ferocious opposition. Park's reaction was old hat: he re-imposed martial law on 17 October 1972. This signalled the end of the Third Republic. A broadcast heralded a new era of authoritarian control, denouncing "factional strife and discord" amongst political parties and championing the need to combat disorder.

Ten days later, a new constitution was unveiled, which talked about the "historic mission for the peaceful unification of the fatherland". Known as the *Yushin* constitution (the characters, 'revitalising', duplicate those of Japan's *Meiji* restoration a century earlier), power was moved from the legislature back to the president: he could serve for as long as he wanted, providing he stood for re-election every six years; he could dissolve the now emasculated National Assembly; and he was able to suspend all freedoms at "times of crisis". A claimed 95% of voters approved the new powers in a November referendum, and martial law was subsequently lifted. The Fourth Republic had begun.

The third five-year plan (1972-1976) completed the foundations for industrial growth. The focus shifted from textiles to heavy industry. P'ohang steel mill began operating in 1973, reducing the need to import rolled steel; by 1975, steel output reached 2.6 million tons. Hyundai's Ulsan shipyard was expanded, and produced its first tankers in 1974: from a background where South Korea produced little more than fishing vessels in the 1960s, 313,000 tons were completed in 1974 alone. The domestic car industry, begun in 1962 with a basic taxi-cum-jeep known as the jeepney, advanced. In 1974, Kia produced a car, based on a Japanese design but using many local parts. Hyundai had built Cortinas from kits imported from Ford UK, but began to produce its own car, the Pony, in 1976. Cars were now to be built mainly for export (by contrast, the whole domestic quota for 1975 stood at 18,000). Exports, too, began to include labour, after the government sought construction projects overseas in 1973. The plan was to increase foreign exchange earnings, since it exempted companies and employees from tax providing 80% of earnings were repatriated. During the third plan, an 8.6% annual growth rate was predicted, but an average 10.9% was achieved, with an annual 46.2% increase in exports (the plan anticipated a 24.3% increase). Unemployment declined, from 4.5% in 1972 to 3.9% in 1976.

Industry grew in urban conurbations, but industrialisation led to an increasing disparity between urban and rural people. As the young flocked to the cities, the old remained in the countryside, hence villages were more and more associated with outmoded lifestyles and backward thinking. Virtually all farmers worked hardly-viable smallholdings of less than 3 hectares. By 1971, the annual farming income was $735 per family compared to an urban $991 per person. Cushioned by the buoyant level of the economy, the government responded with *Saemaŭl undong*, the 'new village' or 'new community' movement, a comprehensive rural development programme inaugurated in 1971 with the twin objectives of improving the rural environment and boosting farm income. To end village isolation, concrete was distributed for village teams to build roads. Mains electricity was brought to remote communities. Agricultural leaders were trained, who represented central control over local politics and eased the introduction and distribution of resistant or more productive crop strains and fertilisers. Loans were made available for the purchase of tractors, and thatch virtually disappeared when the government offered colourful tin roofs at subsidised cost. Within five years, $1780 million had been spent. By the late 1970s, farm household income was 6.2 times the figure it had been prior to the inception of the movement in 1971. By 1983, there were already over 14 million *Saemaŭl* projects in thousands of communities, with a total investment of almost 3.7 trillion *wŏn*. (The movement had, however, lost its momentum by the late 1980s.)

Domestic politics marred these impressive developments. At the time of the November 1972 referendum on the *Yushin* constitution, Kim Dae Jung, the chief opposition figure, was in Tokyo. From there, he denounced Park's actions as those of a 'dictator'. Some months later, in August 1973, he was kidnapped by the Korean CIA and forcibly repatriated; back in Seoul, he began a long period under house arrest, saying that in return for an undertaking by Park not to charge him further, he would renounce politics. A cycle of demonstrations was by now established, spreading beyond students and beyond Seoul.

In the first half of 1974, Park tried to strengthen his grip further, with first a decree punishing criticism of the new constitution with 15 years in jail, then a ban on demonstrations and strikes on pain of death. Kim Chiha, a poet and dissident, was sentenced to death, though the sentence was later commuted to life imprisonment. Kim Dae Jung, despite earlier clemency, was arrested on charges of breaking the law during the 1967 National Assembly elections and the 1971 presidential election. Some of the pressure on Park for reform abated in August when North Korean agents attempted to assassinate him. They succeeded in killing his wife. The agents had entered the country on Japanese passports, and the focus of ongoing protests shifted against Japan. In November, political and religious figures signed a declaration to found the National Council for the Restoration of Democracy. Kim Young Sam (who many years later, in 1993, would become president) and Yun Posŏn signed; Kim Dae Jung was present at the initial meeting.

In January 1975, Park announced a referendum on constitutional reform. But, since he refused to lift the decree that banned criticism of the constitution itself, the NDP announced a boycott. On 12 February, 80% of voters were claimed to have taken part in the referendum, 73% approving the *Yushin* constitution as it stood. Park took a few measures to appease his critics, releasing most people arrested under his two 1974 decrees, but some of these told of being tortured while in custody. This led to international criticism, which Park sought to stem by re-arresting those he had ordered released and enacting a new draconian law: a seven-year sentence for anybody who criticised his regime to foreigners. Heightened security measures introduced in May, following the collapse of the US-backed Vietnamese regime, further stamped on any opposition. The government security apparatus was empowered to close universities (since many of those released earlier had been students), to arrest, detain and search without warrants. Circulating 'false rumours' and 'misrepresenting facts' became criminal offences. Kim Dae Jung, Yun Posŏn and 16 other opposition figures were prosecuted and sentenced to between two and eight years in jail for signing a declaration on 3 March 1976 that called for Park to resign.

Against political vacillations, Park's fourth five-year plan began in 1977. This was designed to end the balance of payments deficit exacerbated by the oil crisis and the loss of international aid. It relied on a tight fiscal policy, charging higher prices for transport and utilities, and shifted investment from export-led heavy industry to light manufacturing that would stimulate domestic consumption. The plan was destined never to be completed.

Park was elected by a government-biased National Conference in July 1978 to a new six-year term. He was now deeply unpopular, and in National Assembly elections on 12 December his DRP gained just 32% of the vote, against 34% for the NDP. In May 1979, Kim Young Sam became the NDP leader, Kim Dae Young having been returned to house arrest after a brief amnesty. The new five-year plan required considerable adjustment. Consumer costs rose, as did inflation. As the fiscal policy bit, so some large employers went bankrupt. Public disquiet increased. After Kim Young Sam was expelled from the Assembly on 4 October, his hometown of Pusan erupted. Students and workers battled police, and demonstrations spread to Masan and other cities in Korea's southeast. (It was in Masan that the final wave of demonstrations against Syngman Rhee had started: could history repeat itself?) The clock stopped at 7.35 pm on 26 October 1979. Before Park could order what was expected to be a massive suppression of the demonstrations, he was shot dead by Kim Jae Kyu, Park's appointed head of the Korean CIA.

Park's rule was characterised by repression, yet he remained firmly in control for almost two decades. Five factors allowed him to do so:

— *fear* of North Korea and of a possible Communist invasion, sharpened by North Korean actions. During Park's presidency, they seized a US intelligence ship, shot down a reconnaissance plane, assassinated Park's wife, regularly dropped propaganda leaflets over Seoul and were discovered to have dug invasion tunnels.

— *support* from the conglomerates, who relied on the government to grant preferential loans.

— *acceptance* by the US, who were unwilling to pressurise Park on human rights issues, particularly during the Vietnamese involvement.

— *success* of economic developments, which brought tangible benefits to the populace.

— *sympathy*, but only for a short time, for a president whose popular wife had been assassinated.

The Fifth Republic

Martial law was declared, Kim Jae Kyu was arrested, and Choi Kyuha stepped in as acting president. On 7 December, Choi was elected as president. The army agitated in the background, though, even as Choi released 68 dissidents from jail and Kim Dae Jung from house arrest. On 12 December, Major General Chun Doo Hwan, head of Army Security Command, arrested the martial law commander, Chung Sung-hwa, for 'improperly' handling the assassination investigation. Choi refused to sign the arrest warrant, and only at 1.00 am the following morning did the defence minister agree to sign. By then, Chun had called on the Ninth Army, under General Roh Tae Woo, a colleague in the secretive *Hanohoe* (Society of One), to enter Seoul and suppress opposition. By the time of Choi's inauguration on 21 December, Chung had been sentenced to 10 years imprisonment, Kim Jae Kyu and four accomplices faced death sentences, and 30 officers had been removed from their posts. Not until the end of 1995 was the government prepared to consider this might have constituted a 'coup'. Despite a constitutional ban on military officers holding civilian positions, Chun took over the Korean CIA in April 1980. Students were busy demonstrating, and workers, seeking wage increases to counter rampant inflation, had joined them in Seoul and Kwangju.

The crunch came on 17 May 1980. Chun declared nationwide martial law, banned all political activity, barred the National Assembly from meeting and closed universities. Hundreds of politicians were arrested, amongst them Kim Dae Jung, Kim Young Sam, and Park's former ally Kim Jong Pil. The following day, a demonstration in Kwangju, the capital of South Chŏlla Province in the southwest, was suppressed with the loss of two dozen lives. Over the next few days, some 200,000 demonstrators took over Kwangju, ransacking the police station and taking control of the local media. By 23 May, Chun had 10,000 troops surrounding the city, blocking access and escape. The US announced it had released four South Korean battalions normally under its control "to suppress rebellion".

The US State Department said it supported the restoration of authority. In Kwangju, a citizen's council had collected many of the weapons seized earlier by demonstrators. On 27 May, after the US declined to intervene, Chun's troops entered the city, carrying out a door-to-door search for students. Official statistics declared some 200 people died; citizens' groups in Kwangju document over 2,000 deaths.

In the aftermath, troops were decorated for 'gallantry'. Kim Dae Jung, at the time already in prison, was tried for sedition in inciting the demonstration and on 17 September was sentenced to death (American pressure led to the sentence being commuted, and Kim later went to America for 'medical' treatment). On 16 August, Choi resigned the presidency. On 22 August, Chun resigned from the army, and on 27 August, an electoral college elected him president. Chun had made a claim to hold power on the basis of ruthlessness. The Kwangju 'incident' established that demonstrations would continue to be suppressed and that unrest would increasingly be concerned with human rights abuses. It maintained a rivalry between the southeast—where industry had been developed, where Park, Chun and Chun's successor, Roh, were born, and which maintained its axis with Seoul—and the poorer, agricultural southwestern provinces. It also proved that the US no longer controlled South Korea and was not prepared publicly to denounce domestic politicians. And it revealed Chun's personality, as cold and arrogant.

Chun recycled Park's style of government. He revised the constitution, once more reducing the power of the National Assembly and granting himself a single seven-year term of office. Established opposition figures were deprived of political rights, hence when the Assembly was reconvened, it was controlled by Chun's party, the Democratic Justice Party (DJP). Like Park, Chun embarked on a 'social purification' programme, dismissing bureaucrats and journalists and, between August 1980 and January 1982, rounding up many teachers, prostitutes, gamblers and beggars for militaristic 're-education' in the *Samch'ong* programme (according to the *Far Eastern Economic Review*, around 40,000 were sent to camps in August 1980 alone). A new labour law, introduced in December, tried to force workers' compliance. Unions would be allowed only if 20% of the total workforce approved, but there would be no compulsory membership, nor national negotiations for regional companies, and strikes could only take place after a 40-day cooling-off period. This was coupled to a fifth five-year plan, to cover 1982-1986, that sought to restore economic development. To counter domestic inflation, Chun cut interest rates and encouraged greater international investment by reducing restrictions on joint ventures. To generate growth, he forced the conglomerates to shift or swap interests in key areas. For example, Kia was forced to concentrate on trucks and abandon cars, Hyundai to build up its car production. To do this, and to guarantee compliance in terms of contributions to party funds, the government showed it still controlled the banks.

Kukje, at the time the seventh largest conglomerate, refused to co-operate, and found its lines of credit frozen: it was soon forced into bankruptcy. Small-scale industry was to be encouraged as domestic consumption rose, with a shift away from the heavy industries of Park's era.

Chun's Korea was still reliant on international credit. Despite improvements in alliances with the US and Japan, by the mid-1980s trade imbalances were noticeable. The state debt reached $40 billion by 1985; a year later, exports to the US created a trade surplus of $7 billion, compared to a deficit with Japan of $5.5 billion in 1987. America, the source of local criticism after it failed to act in Kwangju, began to act against Korean 'dumping' in 1985, which in turn generated more ill feeling amongst the Korean populace. Chun's government still controlled all imports, in what remained a protected domestic economy. Hence, the deficit with Japan grew as Korea sought what it needed for its own development of exports, the import of innovative technology. The relationship with Japan, still bitter after the colonial experience, improved markedly after Nakasone visited Korea in 1983 and Chun visited Japan in 1984. Contacts with China had begun in 1983, with negotiations over the return of a Chinese aircraft fortuitously hijacked to Seoul. Any relationship with North Korea remained more problematic. In October 1983, a bomb planted by Northern agents killed 17 South Korean officials accompanying Chun on a state visit to Burma (it exploded before Chun reached the scene). In 1984, the North sent rice, cement and some medical supplies to assist flood victims in the South. In 1985, 50 families divided since the Korean war were reunited before TV cameras. In November 1987, a Korean Air flight was blown up over Thailand by a bomb planted on board by North Korean agents.

As Chun sought to control a restless public, demographics and international events acted against him. At the local level, a 'youth bulge' led to ever more demonstrations. In 1975, some 1,123,000 students were enrolled in high schools and 296,000 in college; by 1985, the numbers had reached 2,152,000 and 1,260,000. Radicalism led some to look to Kim Il Sung for inspiration, and they joined churchmen arguing for freedom within the liberation-theology inspired *minjung* mass movement. Others saw in the downfall of Marcos in the Philippines a prophetic view of what could be achieved in Korea. Opposition politicians courted the middle classes, and began to agitate in 1984 after Kim Young Sam—still officially banned from politics—formed the Committee for the Promotion of Democracy together with Kim Dae Jung. The latter Kim, returning to Korea from America on 8 February 1984, was arrested at Seoul's Kimp'o Airport and put under immediate house arrest. This encouraged more demonstrations. In legislature elections in February 1985, Chun's DJP gained only 35.3% of the vote. On 6 March, Chun removed the bans on politicians, including the two Kims. Kim Dae Jung, however, was repeatedly put back under house arrest.

In January 1987, Pak Chongch'ŏl, a student at Seoul National University, was tortured to death by police. An investigation revealed on 19 January that he had suffocated when his throat had been crushed against the edge of a bath. The Minister of Home Affairs resigned, but Chun high-handedly replaced him with a general, General Chung Ho Yong, who had been instrumental in the events of December 1979 that brought Chun to power. A coalition of opposition politicians began to emerge, which in February Assembly elections gained control of the five largest cities. Unrest increased. Christian clergy went on hunger strikes, demanding reform, and workers joined students on the streets of Seoul. Chun tried to avoid direct confrontation, perhaps remembering what had happened to Syngman Rhee in 1960 and Park Chung Hee in 1979. He merely repeated the rhetoric favoured by his predecessor, promising on 13 April to restore civil order and to deal harshly with those seeking to create 'social chaos'. May saw the two Kims establish a new party, the Reunification Democratic Party, against the official opposition. Revelations about the murdered student returned to haunt Chun and, after Roh Tae Woo was nominated as Chun's successor on 10 June, unrest escalated. Roh represented more of the same. He was the commander Chun had called on to send troops to Seoul in 1979, and had been head of the Military Security Council until 1985. Finally, on 29 June, Roh gave a TV address in which he announced a liberalisation of politics, the release of political prisoners and, most importantly, that he would stand in a direct presidential election.

The constitution was duly revised, and elections prepared. Korean politics are a matter of individuals, and the two main opposition figures who stood against Roh were Kim Young Sam and Kim Dae Jung. The two Kims were poor bed-fellows. Kim Young Sam, from the southeast, was a moderate; Kim Dae Jung, from the southwest, was a folk hero and radical. Neither would stand aside for the other, and the inevitable split gave Roh a narrow victory. He got 35.9% of the vote, Kim Young Sam 27.5% and Kim Dae Jung 26.5%. The fourth candidate, Kim Jong Pil, returned to politics with 8% of the vote.

The Sixth Republic

This was a time of change, a feature confirmed in National Assembly elections on 26 April 1988, which left Roh's DJP in need of opposition support to achieve anything, since it gained only 125 seats against a combined opposition total of 164. Under Roh, the economy was to prove inconsistent. GNP growth was still maintained, but surpluses in 1989 were followed by deficits in 1990 and 1991. This, however, was an expected consequence of liberalisation and the decision to lay the foundations for more democratic rule.

Indeed, the erratic nature of the economy was caused by the people. Rapid unionisation, labour demands and strikes doubled wages within four years, but led to inflation of 8.6% in 1990 that touched double digits in 1991. Amongst students, affluence allowed nostalgia and led to a nationalist movement that championed the past to revive dying but indigenous cultural forms. This was a time for self-examination, with an explosion of literary critiques and films exploring social issues, revisions in the civil code and the family law to enshrine women's rights, and a relaxation in censorship which occasionally allowed the publication of works such as *Das Kapital* and North Korean texts. Underlying all this was great social upheaval accelerated by the rapid economic development. By 1988, 41% of South Koreans lived in cities with populations above 1 million; Seoul was home to 25% of the population, while 48.1% of the total population lived in Seoul or Kyŏnggi, the province which surrounds it. People were mobile: in 1986, 21% of the population moved their residence. People were affluent: in 1989, there were more than 13 million telephones and 16 million radios in the country, and around 90% of the 42 million population had access to colour televisions; by 1990, 600 new cars daily ventured on to the congested streets of Seoul.

As wages increased, so the competitive edge Korea had enjoyed in international trade was eroded. Roh played the patriot, pleading for morality to counter the import of unnecessary luxuries, and as the world moved into recession, encouraged the domestic economy to absorb local production. For this reason, the rapid increase in, for example, car ownership was not checked. The government's new diplomatic initiative of *Nordpolitik*, which sought to establish diplomatic and economic ties with North Korea's former socialist allies, also meant that new markets were opening up abroad. Trade with China—indirect—had amounted to $19 million in 1979, but reached some $3.2 billion by 1989; in the early 1990s, China became South Korea's third largest trading partner. Once relationships were formalised in 1992, mutual interests could be realised, Korea supplying electronics and setting up joint ventures in, for example, cars (Kia), machinery (Daewoo) and electronics (Goldstar, now LG), and China trading textiles, minerals, agricultural and marine products. Indirect trade with the Soviet Union likewise grew from $36 million in 1980 to $600 million in 1989, but the end of the 1980s saw rapid expansion and an annual doubling of trade. Both Daewoo and Hyundai are rumoured to have lost considerable investments in the Soviet Union, but this was forgotten after the establishment of full diplomatic relations in September 1990.

Government policy further encouraged industry to develop high-tech products, using cheap finance to encourage research and development. This was only partially successful, since the management structure of many conglomerates, still controlled by founding families, was not always willing to accept change, and often moved liquid assets into land speculation and offshore production facilities. Government consistency was not a strong point; the need to mollify opposition politicians led Roh to walk a tightrope between conservative hardliners and liberal reformers. In November 1988, Chun had apologised on TV for the Kwangju 'incident' and other aspects of his period in power; he had then retired to a Buddhist temple to contemplate retirement. A year later, he testified before the National Assembly, as an embattled Roh sought to limit infighting in his party and in the Assembly at large.

In early 1990, Roh found a way around the political morass, when he joined in a tripartite coalition with Kim Young Sam and Kim Jong Pil, merging their three parties into the Democratic Liberal Party (DLP). The coalition gave the two Kims a fast track to power and isolated their rival, Kim Dae Jung. It gave Roh an overwhelming majority in the Assembly, and enabled him to get on with governing. Cohabitation meant establishing a centrist party much like Japan's Liberal Party, and eventually allowed Kim Young Sam to run as the DLP candidate in the December 1992 presidential elections. He did so and won, the inheritor of the reform package introduced by Roh but, and more significantly, the first civilian president for 30 years.

Readings

Robert E. Bedeski, 1994. *The Transformation of South Korea: Reform and Reconstitution in the Sixth Republic under Roh Tae Woo, 1987-1992.* London: Routledge

James Cotton (ed.), 1993. *Korea under Roh Tae-woo.* St Leonards, NSW: Allen and Unwin

Hagen Koo (ed.), 1993. *State and Society in Contemporary Korea.* Ithaca: Cornell University Press

Robert A. Scalapino and Jun-yop Kim (eds), 1983. *North Korea Today: Strategic and Domestic Issues.* Berkeley: Center for Korean Studies

Dae-Sook Suh, 1988. *Kim Il Sung: The North Korean Leader.* New York: Columbia University Press

4

DIVISION AND WAR

Prelude

War came to Korea early in the morning of 25 June 1950. Before dawn, artillery opened fire from the North Korean side of the 38th parallel, along which Korea had been divided in the closing stages of the Pacific War. Under cover of a heavy barrage, infantry and armoured troops crossed the parallel along the traditional invasion routes near Kaesŏng and Ch'unch'ŏn. Simultaneously, amphibious landings began on the east coast. Within three days, Seoul, capital of a unified Korea since 1392, was in North Korean hands. When the conflict ended some three years later roughly where it had began, many other countries had become involved, some three to four million people were dead, wounded or missing, millions more had become refugees, the families of some ten million Koreans had been broken up and much of the Korean peninsula was in ruins. Korea, little known before, was, for a brief period, a household word throughout most of the world.

4.1 The division of Korea

The rapid end of the Pacific War in 1945, brought about by the dropping of two atomic bombs on the Japanese cities of Hiroshima and Nagasaki, came as a surprise to those planning for the post-war world. Decisions which it had seemed could be postponed for years now had to made with great speed. One such was how to handle the surrender of Japanese forces. In some places it was straightforward, since there were already Allied forces on the ground in contact with the enemy. Korea was different. US forces were at a distance and unlikely to arrive before mid-September 1945. Soviet forces, however, were just across the frontier and the Soviet Union had entered the war against Japan in its final days. But even in August 1945, the Cold War was casting its shadow, and the United States was anxious to prevent Soviet forces from occupying the whole peninsula to take the Japanese surrender. The American officials charged with this task looked at the map of Korea and selected the 38th parallel as a possible division line, though there was no obvious geographical feature to mark the parallel. But it placed Seoul, the port of Inch'ŏn and most of the population in the American half. While nobody was yet thinking of a permanent division of Korea, there seemed no harm in getting the best possible deal. For so far unexplained reasons, the Soviet Union accepted the proposal, and Soviet troops moved into Korea, stopping at the 38th parallel. In the southern half of the peninsula, the Japanese continued in charge until the arrival of the first US forces in September. In this haphazard and unplanned manner, the division of Korea began.

Most Koreans who knew about it had probably thought that the declaration at the 1943 Cairo conference that Korea should "in due course" be independent, meant that independence would follow the end of the war. Once the defeat of Japan was known, the Korean people behaved as though this was the case. Political organisations emerged north and south of the 38th parallel, and the beginnings of a state structure were put in place in each half of the peninsula. The Soviet forces did not stop this but took steps to make sure that only left-wing groups were able to function in the north. To help them organise administration, Soviet forces brought with them a number of Soviet-Koreans and former anti-Japanese guerrillas, including one Kim Il Sung.

The US forces which landed in the south in September were less well prepared. There was much American suspicion of the widespread political activity and the spread of parties, and steps were taken to suppress both. At first, the US commander, General Hodge, used Japanese forces to maintain order, but this was quickly abandoned in the face of Korean opposition. With few Korean-speaking American officers, the US forces had to rely on such English-speaking Koreans as were available. Many of these had lived abroad for long and were out of touch with popular feeling at home.

In order to implement the arrangements, the UN established a Temporary Commission on Korea (UNTCOK), which began work in January 1948. The Soviet Union refused to allow the commission to operate in the north, and so it was only south of the parallel that elections could be held in May 1948. A hundred seats were allocated to the north and were left unfilled. Even in the south, many who wished to see a united Korea boycotted the elections as divisive. The elections over, a new assembly met on 31 May 1948, adopted the name Republic of Korea for the country and began work on a constitution. On 15th August 1948, the Republic of Korea (ROK) became independent. Meanwhile, a similar process was under way in the north, and the Democratic People's Republic of Korea (DPRK) was proclaimed in September 1948. The temporary division of 1945 had become fixed.

Both Korean states claimed to be the only lawful government and each claimed jurisdiction over the whole peninsula. In December 1948, the United Nations partially endorsed the ROK position, declaring it the only legitimate government on the peninsula, and at the time establishing a Commission for the Unification of the Peninsula. The

United States and its friends established diplomatic relations with the ROK, while the Soviet Union and its friends did so with the DPRK.

4.2 War comes to Korea

By mid-1949, both occupying powers had withdrawn their troops, and the two Koreas were left to fend for themselves. The Soviet Union left behind a considerable amount of military equipment and had gone a long way towards establishing a modern army. From late 1949, the DPRK also began to absorb Koreans who had fought in the Chinese civil war. By contrast, the United States had left little more than an advisory group and an armed police in the ROK with no reinforcements. Both sides loudly proclaimed their intention of unifying the peninsula, and there were frequent armed clashes and raids along the 38th parallel. In January 1950, the United States declared that while it was concerned about the future of the Korean peninsula, the area lay outside direct US security interests. Many have seen this as the signal that the DPRK was waiting for to begin planning for unification by force. Evidence now clearly indicates that both the Soviet Union and China—by then under a Communist government—were informed of the DPRK's plans but that the decision to go to war was taken by the DPRK leadership.

Once the attack began in June 1950—without any declaration of war—the DPRK forces swept all before them. They were much better armed than their opponents, with tanks and other heavy equipment. The ROK government fled south, first to Taejŏn, then to Taegu and finally to Pusan in the southeast corner of the peninsula. Behind them, the DPRK sent officials who carried out land reform and established a new government structure. They also killed or imprisoned government representatives, religious leaders and other 'suspect' groups left behind. By mid-July, ROK-held territory was reduced to a small pocket around Pusan. What saved the ROK was the United States decision that, after all, it did matter. In the absence of the Soviet Union from the United Nations in protest over UN failure to seat the new People's Republic of China, the US got UN backing for intervention in Korea to combat North Korean 'aggression'. The first US troops went into action on 5 July 1950, and other forces, including British, followed. Overall military command of the various 'UN' forces was given to the US president, who appointed the Commander in Chief in Japan, General Douglas MacArthur, as Supreme Commander.

Trapped in the 'Pusan perimeter', the UN and regrouped ROK forces prepared to break out to the north. At the same time, MacArthur planned an ambitious amphibious landing behind enemy lines. This took place at Inch'ŏn on the west coast on 15 September 1950 and was a great success, partly because it met little opposition. The next day, UN forces began to break out of the Pusan perimeter and fight their way north.

DPRK resistance crumbled as the weeks of intensive fighting and long supply lines took their toll. ROK forces played a major role in this campaign but there were also reports of reprisals against those who were believed to have collaborated with the enemy. By the end of September, the combined UN/ROK forces had retaken Seoul and driven the invaders back across the 38th parallel.

No precise plans had been worked out about what to do in these circumstances. It proved easy therefore for General MacArthur and others to argue that UN forces should cross the parallel and, perhaps, reunify the peninsula. A UN resolution on 7 October endorsed this move and, assuming victory was imminent, set up a Commission for the Unification and Rehabilitation of Korea. The UN forces swept north, capturing the DPRK capital, P'yŏngyang, on 19 October 1950. On 26 October, ROK forces reached the Yalu river and the North Korean army virtually ceased to exist. Other UN forces followed in the wake of the ROK. A unified Korea now seemed a distinct possibility, and it was confidently believed that the UN forces would be "home by Christmas".

The Yalu marked the border with China, and at first there was some caution on the UN side about getting too close to it. The enthusiasm of victory overrode such considerations. It also led MacArthur to discount reports of Chinese concern, especially as these were relayed through third parties, such as the Indians, who were seen as being soft on Communism. When these warnings were ignored, the Chinese moved.

UN forces reported what seemed to be 'chance' encounters with Chinese patrols before the end of October. But the warning was not heeded, and before long the Chinese intervened in force. It may be that the Chinese were planning such an intervention from the beginning of hostilities. New evidence suggests that the Chinese leaders expected a conflict with the United States sooner rather than later. When non-Korean troops began to arrive close to China's border, the Chinese decided that it was time to act.

The first hammer blow came on the eastern side of the peninsula towards the end of November. Chinese troops in huge numbers smashed the South Korean 2nd Corps. Within days, Chinese forces had clashed with other, non-Korean forces, and the whole UN front crumbled. UN troops fell back southwards, some in orderly fashion, others retreating as fast as they could go, in what became known as 'bug-outs'. The arrival of a particularly cold winter made life miserable both for the retreating forces and for the large numbers of refugees who moved south to escape the renewed fighting. Seoul fell to the Chinese on 4 January 1951. Only as the Chinese ran out of supplies did the drive south stop, with UN forces holding a line across the country some thirty miles south of Seoul.

At times during the headlong UN retreated there were calls in the United States for the use of the atomic bomb against the Chinese, and for an extension of the air war into China. Occasional very restricted air raids did take place across the Yalu into China.

While the Chinese protested, they were not in a position to retaliate. For a number of reasons, including concern among other members of the UN forces and the likely consequences for troops on the ground, the atomic bomb was not used. Instead, other tactics prevailed. The UN passed a resolution on 1 February 1951 condemning China as an aggressor. In Korea, UN forces regrouped and re-attacked. Seoul was recaptured on 15 March and the Chinese pushed back across the 38th parallel. This time, however, the UN forces stopped, despite pleas from ROK president Syngman Rhee that they drive the Chinese out of Korea. There was a brief Chinese counter-attack in April, which saw one of the main British engagements of the war, when the 1st Battalion of the Gloucestershire Regiment and other forces held up an advancing Chinese force. But the Chinese, like the North Koreans before them, were tired and their supply lines were very extended. After ten months of movement, the war settled down to a stalemate reminiscent of World War I in Europe. Trenches stretched across Korea, and only occasional raids and short but often savage attacks broke the monotony.

4.3 Armistice talks

In a showdown with President Truman in April 1951, General MacArthur had been removed from his posts, including that of UN Commander in Korea. His dismissal cleared away an obstacle to armistice talks. Tentative soundings were made by the UN side, to which the Chinese and the North Koreans responded. Talks began at Kaesŏng on 10 July 1951. They were to last two years.

The talks were soon bogged down in disputes. Each side was highly suspicious of the other and it was some time before they could even agree on an agenda. Then other problems arose and the Communist side withdrew from the talks between 23 July 1951 and October of that year when they were resumed. Much of the tension was over the issue of the repatriation of prisoners of war—POWS. The UN side was reluctant to repatriate POWS who claimed that they did not wish to go back to North Korea or China, but tended to turn a blind eye to the methods used in some of the POW camps to persuade those captured that they did not wish to return. POW riots on Koje island in the far south in 1952 were firmly suppressed, which caused some disquiet among America's allies in Korea. Such disputes led to the US side withdrawing from the talks in October 1952.

By the time they resumed in April 1953, the death of the Soviet leader, Joseph Stalin (in March 1953), had led to a more favourable attitude among North Korea's allies towards a settlement. There was an exchange of sick and wounded prisoners, and foreign civilian detainees held since Seoul's capture in June 1950 were released. There were also moves to solve the POW issue. The POWS who did not wish to return would be handed to a neutral country who would hold them for four months. During that time, representatives of their home countries would be given access to them, to persuade them to return. Just when the atmosphere seemed better, however, Syngman Rhee's opposition to any settlement seemed likely to threaten the whole armistice process. In an effort to disrupt the negotiations, he ordered his troops guarding the North Korean POWS to release those who did not wish to be repatriated.

The possibility of an armistice was in jeopardy, especially since ROK forces held most of the front line and could not be relied upon to abide by a truce if one was agreed. The North Koreans and the Chinese demanded assurances that Rhee and his forces were in fact subordinate to the UN Command. Eventually the UN Command was able to confirm they were, Rhee having been persuaded not to oppose the armistice even if he would not agree to it. With that assurance, the Communist side agreed to sign the armistice.

Signing took place at the small village of P'anmunjŏm on 27 July 1953. There was little rejoicing and no fraternisation between the two sides. The war ended more or less where it began, with a military demarcation line following the line of actual control on the morning of the armistice. The armistice provided for a Military Armistice Commission to supervise its implementation and a Neutral Nations Supervisory Commission to monitor movements of equipment and personnel into the two Koreas. Poland and Czechoslovakia were nominated by the Communist side to serve on this commission, Sweden and Switzerland by the UN side. It also provided for a Neutral Nations Reparations Committee to handle the POW issue. The signatories recommended to their respective governments that a political conference should be held within three months of the armistice, to settle the issue of Korean re-unification.

Readings

Bruce Cumings, 1981 and 1990. *The Origins of the Korean War*, 2 vols. Princeton: Princeton University Press

Anthony Farrar-Hockley, 1954. *The Edge of the Sword*. London: Frederick Muller Ltd. New edition, 1985. London: Buchan and Enright

— 1990 and 1995. *The British Part in the Korean War*, 2 vols. London: HMSO

Jon Halliday and Bruce Cumings, 1988. *Korea: The Unknown War*. London: Viking

Max Hastings, 1987. *The Korean War*. London: Michael Joseph

Peter Lowe, 1986. *The Origins of the Korean War*. London: Longman

Callum A. MacDonald, 1986. *Korea: The War before Vietnam*. London: Macmillan Press

David Rees, 1964. *The Limited War*. London: Hamish Hamilton

5

LANGUAGE AND LITERATURE

5.1 The Korean language

Koreans are devoted to their language in both its spoken and its written form. They admire its expressiveness and the accuracy of its alphabet, *han'gŭl*. While acknowledging the strong influence of Chinese on its development and admitting to some grammatical affinities between it and Japanese, they point with pride to the separate origins of Korean.

Those origins are thought to lie in the Altaic family of languages, spoken in a vast region covering much of central and northeast Asia. Korean may have descended from a branch of this family, Tungus, based in the area to the north of modern Korea. This 'northern' theory is in general accepted, although some scholars point to the possible contribution to the formation of Korean of a 'southern' linguistic strand deriving from the Malayo-Polynesian languages. Other scholars consider Korean has grown out of the grafting of these two different linguistic types. It seems certain that within the Korean peninsula two groups of Korean were known: the Puyŏ languages, spoken in the north in the area controlled by Koguryŏ (see chapter 1.1); and the Han languages, current in the south, out of which the Shilla language developed. Modern Korean has evolved from the language of Unified Shilla, imposed on the whole of the peninsula in the wake of political unification (see chapter 1.2).

Characteristics of Korean

In its structure Korean differs greatly from its important neighbour, Chinese. Kim Chinu, a Korean scholar, in his contribution to *The Korean Language* (pp. 13-42), describes some of its features. In its sound pattern it displays a tendency to close articulation, that is, sounds are produced through as narrow an aperture as possible in the mouth. Consonants such as -n and -t tend to be pronounced as -m and -p when they appear in the middle of a compound word. Certain consonants—k, t and p—may appear in one of three forms: unaspirated, aspirated and emphasised (doubled). S also has an emphatic form. Grammatically, Korean is characterised by an "extremely richly developed set of derivative and conjugational affixes" that "agglutinate one after the other", that is, are added in succession to the end of the root of a verb or a noun to denote "different styles of speech, express every conceivable mood and aspect" and serve as markers for a wide range of syntactical constructions. Verbs terminate in one of three honorific endings, depending on the relative status of the speaker and the person being addressed. Thus the greeting *annyŏng* ("how are you?"), used familiarly between those of equal standing, probably friends, becomes *annyŏng haseyo* when used as a more formal greeting, perhaps between strangers, and *annyŏng hashimnikka* when the person being addressed is acknowledged to outrank the speaker on grounds of social status or age.

The frequent use of affixes makes it possible to build up sentences of considerable length, where the subjects and even objects of verbs may not be stated, but can be inferred from the surrounding words. Sentence formation follows the pattern subject-object-verb. The language is richly nuanced and onomatopoeic. Kim Chinu lists 29 different words (each word repeated twice) to express movements in the flow of water. An outstanding feature of Korean vocabulary is the number of words—around 54%—taken from Chinese. A dual system of Chinese and Korean forms exists for expressing a number of concepts, such as numerals, and for certain common words. In some cases the two forms are interchangeable; in others one of them, usually the Chinese, is regarded as the more elevated form. Sometimes there is no great difference between Korean and Chinese; thus Namsan, the South Mountain that once formed the southern boundary of Seoul, is not so far removed from the standard Chinese *nanshan*, which has exactly the same meaning.

The influence of Chinese

Chinese exerted an even greater hold over the way Korean was written for many centuries. A knowledge of Chinese characters spread through the peninsula, probably at an early date. It is likely that they were introduced through the Chinese commandery at Nangnang (108BC-AD313; Lelang in Chinese; see chapter 1.1). The oldest surviving example of a text in Chinese characters, but with a Korean context, is the stele erected by King Kwanggaet'o of Koguryŏ in AD414, on the north side of the Yalu river, to commemorate his territorial conquests. The traditions of administration and scholarship that developed in the later Three Kingdoms (see chapter 1.1) on Chinese models assumed the ability to read and write in Chinese. No written form for Korean existed. It was, however, accepted that Chinese and Korean were very different languages in their spoken form and that the Chinese system of characters, each of which represents a concept and is pronounced as a single syllable, could not adequately convey the full range of Korean sounds.

Three ways evolved of adapting characters to make them more responsive to the needs of Korean. The first of these, *idu,* appears to have been developed by the mid-5th century, and two centuries later was used to transcribe *hyangga* verses (see chapter 5.2). As an American scholar, Marshall R. Pihl, described it in *The Korean Language* (p. 113), *idu* "was a complex system of writing that employed some Chinese characters for their sound...and others for their meanings...It was both written and read in Korean grammatical order and would have made little sense to a Chinese reader." Another contributor to the same volume (p. 122), Kim Hyŏnggyu, points out that *idu* put substantive words such as nouns, adjectives and verbs into Chinese characters, retaining their proper meaning, but employed other characters with a Korean phonetic value to render relative pronouns and adverbs. By the mid-8th century, certain phonograms (that is, characters identified with a particular sound) in common use had been put into a conventionally accepted form and even codified.

A later system, *kugyŏl,* took characters commonly used to signify purely grammatical elements, abbreviated them and then formed them into a single (new) character. *Hyangch'al,* yet another system, put all Korean words into Chinese characters. The three arrangements co-existed for quite a long time, each one being used for a different purpose. *Hyangch'al* died out in the 15th century, but *idu* and *kugyŏl* appear to have remained in service long after the introduction of *han'gŭl* in the mid-15th century. The intention behind each system of transcription was to convey the sounds of Korean more accurately, not to replace the use of Chinese characters. These kept their value as a mark of literacy and scholarship until almost the end of the 19th century, when the administrative and educational traditions that had sustained them themselves disappeared.

Invention of *han'gŭl*

The invention of *han'gŭl* is a remarkable achievement, even if its aim was somewhat limited in the early stages. King Sejong (r. 1418-1450) was anxious to devise a more accessible form of transcription for Korean for the benefit of the 'ignorant', that is, those who had not mastered Chinese characters. He instructed a group of scholars drawn from the *Chip'yŏnjŏn* ('Hall of worthies'), which he had himself founded to promote learning, to create a new alphabet. It is not known exactly how this committee set about its work, but it is clear that it focused on two essential aspects: the sounds of the Korean language, and an appropriate written way of conveying these sounds.

The chief source of incompatibility between Chinese and Korean lies in the fact that standard Chinese syllables, each represented by a character, end either in a vowel or in -n or -ng. Korean words do not have this simple formation. King Sejong's scholars analysed the phonetic structure of Korean syllables (in the state of development this had reached in the first half of the 15th century) and distinguished three separate elements: the initial, medial and final sounds. Of these the medial element was a vowel. Each sound was to be represented by a separate letter in the new alphabet. The new writing system, based on phonemes or sounds, thus differed radically from the Chinese system of ideograms, whereby a concept was conveyed in each syllable-bound character. King Sejong presented his 'Correct sounds for the instruction of the people' (*Hunmin chŏngŭm*) in 1443 and three years later promulgated them for popular use.

The new alphabet, commonly known as *han'gŭl*, consisted of 29 letters, comprising 22 consonants and seven vowels. (Modern Korean has 19 consonants and 10 vowels.) Five basic consonants were isolated and identified by letters held to represent, in simplified form, the position taken by the speech organs in producing that consonant. Further consonants were formed by adding a stroke to the basic letter or by doubling the letter (see paragraph 2 above). Quite different principles determined the creation of letters representing vowels. For these, three symbols were used, a dot, a horizontal line and a vertical line, representing respectively heaven, earth and man. All vowels were formed through combinations of these three basic symbols. Consonants and vowels are grouped into syllabic blocks to form a word, and letters are not written in linear fashion, as are the letters of the Roman alphabet. (For examples of the formation and use of *han'gŭl* letters see Factsheet 2.2.) Korean was formerly a tonal language, but tones had disappeared by the 16th century.

It is assumed that in creating the new letter forms of *han'gŭl* the members of King Sejong's working party considered other scripts known in East Asia at the time. These might have included Turkic runic script, Uighur script (which had been used by the Mongolians since the 13th century), Tibetan script (promulgated as a script of the Chinese Yuan empire) and Sanskrit, introduced through Buddhism. Ancient Chinese seal script would certainly have been familiar. However, no clear model can be pointed to. The dimensions of Chinese characters undoubtedly influenced the style and shape of words written in *han'gŭl*. For a while the two scripts appeared intermingled in printed books. At first *han'gŭl* had a geometric appearance, enhanced no doubt by the use of woodblock or movable metal type (the latter already well known in Korea by the time of the invention of the new alphabet). Eventually, as *han'gŭl* came to be written more frequently with a brush and a tradition of calligraphy developed, the proportions and appearance of the new script changed to reflect the influence both of brush strokes and of the strokes of Chinese characters. Calligraphic forms had an impact on printed type.

Language reform

Despite royal sponsorship, *han'gŭl* did not win easy acceptance and was long disdained by officials and scholars as a script suitable for use by women, Buddhists and commoners. It did, however, become the medium of novels and poetry. *Shijo*, the subtle, elliptical verses in which Korean poets expressed their emotions (see section 2 below and Factsheet 6.1), were written in *han'gŭl*. King Sejong's alphabet did not pass into popular use until the last years of the 19th century, when the old political structure of Korea was collapsing. External pressure and internal disorder were inciting reform and an examination of the Korean identity. Use of native forms of speech and writing was seen by some as a means of strengthening that identity, escaping from Chinese—that is, foreign—cultural norms and communicating directly with the mass of people. The continued employment of Chinese characters in the publication of government documents was questioned (after the *Kabo* reforms of 1895 a mixed script was introduced in official publications, combining characters and Korean letters in Korean syntactical constructions). The reform-minded Independence Club (see chapter 7.5), formed in 1896, in a spirit of patriotism published its newspaper *The Independent* in *han'gŭl*. The *Tonghak* movement (see chapter 2.2), which erupted in 1894, also supported the use of the vernacular *han'gŭl* .

With enthusiasm for the use of *han'gŭl* came a desire to re-examine the structure of the language itself. Modern linguistic studies of Korean date from the turn of the 20th century. The Han'gŭl Research Centre was established in 1907. In 1910 the linguistician Chu Shigyŏng published a Korean grammar and in 1914 a work on the sounds of speech. Chu's aim was to analyse and standardise the Korean language and give it solid theoretical foundations. His teachings were influential in subsequent reforms of spelling and usage. In 1921 the Korean Language Research Society (Chosŏnŏ yŏn'guhoe) was established by linguists and educators to promote standard use of the vernacular. Through the next twenty years (and a change of name in 1931 to the Korean Language Study Society, Chosŏnŏ hakhoe), the group worked on questions of orthography and transliteration of foreign loan-words and on preparation of a comprehensive dictionary (*K'ŭn sajŏn*) of Korean. In 1933 it published its Unified Orthography (*Han'gŭl match'umbŏp t'ongiran*). Its activities went on against the background of Japanese colonial policies. Inevitably, the society's work and the wider movement of language use and reform came to have nationalist overtones (see chapter 2.4). By the late 1930s the Japanese administration in Korea was taking a hard line on use of the native language. Korean as a means of communication was progressively forbidden in the bureaucracy in 1937, in schools in 1938 and in the press in 1939. The end of hostilities in 1945 brought release from such linguistic repression.

Post-war Korean

Discussion and research in both South and North Korea has since centred around the continued use of Chinese characters in written Korean and around suitable forms of romanisation. In South Korea, characters still appear in newspaper articles and other publications, in the post-1895 style, and name cards generally bear a person's name in characters. The flexibility of *han'gŭl* permits the assimilation of almost any foreign word, and modern Korean (in the South, at least) has taken in a number of new loan-words. In the North, however, Chinese characters have been dropped as a matter of policy. As early as 1949, school textbooks had replaced Chinese words and expressions with Korean ones, and ten years later the study of Chinese literature and of classical Chinese was removed from the curriculum. Words of other foreign origin, for example, Japanese, have likewise been expelled from the language and substitutes devised. The constitution of the DPRK undertakes to protect the language from attempts to 'destroy' it (see chapter 15.1).

Romanisation of Korean is made difficult by the variety of consonant and vowel sounds and the shifting relationships between them. In 1939 two American scholars, G. M. McCune and Edwin Reischauer, produced a system of romanisation that gained acceptance among Western users. The South Korean Ministry of Education put forward its own system in 1959, but in 1984 revised this along the lines of the McCune-Reischauer model. The resulting compromise has been in use ever since. However, individual Koreans remain free to devise their own romanisation for transcribing their names. North Korean romanisation is similar to the McCune-Reischauer system.

Readings

Baek Eung-jin, 1984. *Modern Korean Syntax*. Seoul: Jung Min Publishing Co.

Bruce K. Grant, 1986. *A Guide to Korean Characters*. Seoul: Hollym International Corp.

Handbook of Korea, 1993. Seoul: Korea Overseas Information Service

Korean National Commission for UNESCO (ed.), 1983. *The Korean Language*. Seoul: Si-sa-yong-o-sa Publishers

Lee Hong-bae, 1970. *A Study of Korean Syntax*. Seoul: Pan Korea Book Corp.

Gene S. Rhie and B. J. Jones, 1986. *Standard Korean-English Dictionary for Foreigners*. Seoul: Hollym.

Michael E. Robinson, 1988. *Cultural Nationalism in Colonial Korea, 1920-1925*. Seattle: University of Washington Press

Rinn-Sup Shinn *et al.*, 1969. *Area Handbook for North Korea*. Washington, D. C. : American University for Foreign Area Studies

Sohn Ho-min (ed.), 1975. *The Korean Language: Its Structure and Social Projection*. Honolulu: Center for Korean Studies

5.2 Literature

Poetry

In old Korea, skill in poetic composition was a very practical business: it was one of the major indicators of a man's ability to serve his country well as a public servant, and at the same time it was the yardstick of a man's personal cultivation. This approach to poetry had some interesting consequences. Firstly, poetry tended to be 'I'-centred, confessional. In the hands of any other than a consummate artist this sort of subjective tradition labours within severe limitations, but in the hands of great masters, the reader discovers his own experience, and perhaps the experience of all men, in the experience of the poet. Secondly, poetry was characterised by a pervasive movement toward transcendence, reflecting the Buddhist tradition of freedom and liberation, but also reflecting the Confucian tradition which though directed toward order and control still seeks the ultimate in wisdom. Buddhism and Confucianism have had an enormous influence on all facets of Korean literature: Buddhism was dominant during the Koryŏ period (918-1392) when *hanshi* (poems in Chinese characters by Korean poets) developed to maturity, and Confucianism was dominant throughout the Chosŏn period (1392-1910) when the *shijo* and the *kasa,* the two literary genres deemed to best express the Korean sensibility, reached their fullest development. Thirdly, Taoist influence is apparent. Composition tended to be spontaneous: a visit to a temple, meeting a friend, celebrating the arrival of spring, a gift of wine, etc. A concrete emotion prompted the writing of a poem. Fourthly, poets generally approached nature conceptually: that is to say, when they looked at a flower, they did not see this particular flower or this individual petal; they saw the universal essence of all flowers. This approach is symbolic rather than realistic: the poets concerned themselves with moral rather than physical beauty; they cultivated the heart more than the eye. This remains the core of the Korean poetic tradition to this day.

The earliest Korean poetry consisted of songs of ritual worship and songs designed to accompany work: these songs were invariably linked with music and dance. Unfortunately, there was no writing system in Korea until Chinese characters were introduced, probably in the second century. Chinese characters quickly became very popular with the elite, leading to the development of a tradition of *hanshi* poetry, that is, poems in Chinese, following the rules of Chinese prosody, but written by Korean poets (see Factsheet 6.1, poem 1, for an example).

During the Shilla period (about 300-668), a system of recording Korean sounds in Chinese characters, called *idu,* was developed, thus making it possible to record the vernacular *hyangga* or 'native songs' which flourished during Unified Shilla (668-918) and the early part of Koryŏ. Twenty-five *hyangga* are extant.

The pattern of Korean *hanshi* poetry had been solidly established by the time Yi Kyubo (1168-1241) began to write his *hanshi* in the middle of the Koryŏ period. Yi's poems are intensely personal, very often dramatic vignettes from the poet's own life. He describes an external landscape—a temple, a posthouse, an inn—and then he moves to an inner landscape of the heart. The poems are brief, songlike and revelatory; they describe moments of personal illumination. The reader meets the poet in the more intense moments of the daily grind: it may be a problem on the job, with one of his children or with his wife; it may be a visit to a temple or to a friend; it may be an occasion of sorrow or joy. Always, however, the occasion is intimately connected with the poet himself. The poem is his reaction to the situation, his personal experience:

> Desolate the monk's room beside the ancient tree;
> one lamp burns in the shrine, one incense burner smokes.
> I ask the old monk how on earth he spends his days:
> a chat when a guest comes; when the guest goes, a nap.

With a few deft strokes—tree, lamp, incense burner—the speaker paints the hermitage, before moving on, almost casually, to an intense Zen landscape of the heart. The monk represents that ideal of transcendence which cultivated men strove to attain. However, this poem is not about the monk; the focus is on the speaker, specifically on how the speaker's heart is touched by the monk's experience and the light generated thereby.

Hanshi poems are quite different from *shijo* in the feeling they engender. This difference in sensibility may derive from the fact that *hanshi* were written in Chinese, the language of literature and official business, whereas *shijo* were written in *han'gŭl*, the native Korean alphabet (see section 1 above). At any rate, *shijo* are freer, even more private and more personal than *hanshi*. (Two examples appear at poems 2 and 3 of Factsheet 6.1.) An image is introduced, developed, and the poet presents a statement of his own experience, all within the narrow confines of three lines and forty-five syllables. Nothing is allowed to get between the poet and his subject:

> The tree is diseased;
>   no one rests in its pavilion.
> When it stood tall and verdant,
>   no one passed it by.
> But the leaves have fallen,
>   the boughs are broken;
>   not even birds perch there now.

Notice the intensity of focus in this *shijo* by Chŏng Ch'ŏl (1536-1593). We see the tree as it is now, ragged and broken, and we see it as it was when it was tall and verdant. The final line "not even birds perch there now" penetrates right to the bone in its depiction of the fate of those who fall from political favour.

Towards the middle of the 15th century a new genre of vernacular verse, called *kasa*, more descriptive and expository than earlier Koryŏ songs, made its appearance. Chŏng Ch'ŏl is the finest master of the *kasa* form and his *Kwandong pyŏlgok* (1580), describing eight famous scenes in the Diamond Mountains and East Sea, represents the tradition at its best.

Chinese remained the written language of government and of literature until the end of the 19th century. From 1876 Japan and the Western powers forced the opening of the ports; an event which marked the beginning of a flood of Western influence. Following annexation by Japan in 1910, an increasing number of young Korean intellectuals went to Japan for university education, where they came into contact with current trends in Japanese literary circles. Within Korea the period was marked by a surge of nationalist sentiment which culminated in the 1 March Independence Movement of 1919.

The rise in nationalist sentiment was accompanied by a rejection in literature of Chinese and the Chinese tradition in favour of *han'gŭl* and the Western tradition. Working with Western models—Baudelaire, Verlaine, Yeats and Symons—young writers began to create a new literature. Symons's *The Symbolist Movement in Literature* was translated into Japanese quite early in the 20th century; in Japan it became a sort of critical bible. The young Korean poets had some English and less French. Most of their translations seem to have been made from Japanese texts—with an eye sometimes on the English; most of the theory came from Japanese translations of English sources. The result of this complex skein of influence was a poetry full of Pre-Raphaelite colours, characterised by a fin-de-siècle atmosphere of world weariness, decadence and pessimism, with Symons perhaps as the dominant influence.

Imitation was inevitable in the new poetry: the poets, all young men in their twenties, set out consciously to write a new Korean poetry based on their apprehension of Western models. The approach was one of trial and error.

Kim Sowŏl (1902-1934) was the first of these young poets to move away from imitation and create something new on the basis of influences assimilated. Sowŏl was much more than a writer of pretty lyrics; his essay *The Spirit of Poetry* (1925) is the first manifesto of mysticism in modern Korean poetry. Perhaps his most significant achievement was the flexibility and versatility he achieved in the use of the Korean language. He incorporated the saltiness and bite of the vernacular into a modern idiom which contrasts sharply with the more formal Chinese tradition.

Chŏng Chiyong (1902-?) and Kim Kirim (1908-?) ushered in the second stage of modern poetry. Steeped in the imagist mode, they show a literary world coming to grips with modernism. In them we see the discarding of the Pre-Raphaelite tints in favour of a more modern idiom. (An example of Chŏng Chiyong's work is at poem 5 of Factsheet 6.1.)

The Korean Artists Proletarian Federation (KAPF) was founded in 1925. Its forced dissolution in the mid-1930s introduced a period of intense Japanese repression. However, following the tradition of Han Yongun (1879-1944), monk, poet, patriot (see poem 4 on Factsheet 6.1 for an example of his work), the defiant note continued to ring out in the work of poets like Yi Yuksa (1904-1944) and Yun Tongju (1917-1945), who remain symbols of undying resistance to foreign domination. The Blue Deer Group, Pak Tujin (1916-), Pak Mokwŏl (1919-1978) and Cho Chihun (1920-1968), sought to sublimate the harsh reality of Japanese oppression in nature poetry. All three are recognised as masters of lyrical language.

The Korean War made the idiom of the pre-war period seem dated and unrelated to contemporary problems. The post-war era was characterised by a poetry that was experimental in form and highly critical of the contemporary scene. Beginning in the 1960s, the process of industrialisation bred a profound sense of alienation, isolation and dehumanisation, which was increasingly reflected in poetry. A new radical, political-social consciousness was awakened, and the more outspoken of the committed poets, the celebrated Kim Chiha (1941-), for example, or the man who has assumed his mantle in the 1980s, Kim Namju, paid for their dissent by spending long periods in jail. The old battle of accusation and counter-accusation between adherents of pure literature and those of a more committed revolutionary approach has erupted once again. The violence of the Kwangju revolution which ushered in the 1980s led younger intellectuals to lash out in anger against the poetry establishment, attacking it for its failure to find a poetic voice to prevent or even deal with such tragedy. The young intellectuals reacted forcefully, both in form and content, asserting the failure of the humanist stance to find adequate solutions.

The 1980s have also been characterised by the vigorous re-emergence of the genre of workers' poetry, a genre that traces its roots back to the KAPF literature of the 1920s and early 1930s. Pak Nohae's *The Dawn of Labor* took the literary world by storm.

Sŏ Chŏngju (1915-) is generally recognised as the best Korean poet of this century. The appeal of his work rests firstly in his use of language, so distinctively of his native Chŏlla Province, secondly in the sensuality apparent particularly in his earlier work, which has evoked comparisons with Baudelaire and Yeats, and thirdly in his return to the spirit of Shilla, mainly in Buddhist aspects, to find the values that should inform the new Korea that is to replace the tragic Korea of the recent past. His approach is that of a poetry of revelation: his lyrics are short, with an intense zen-style illumination. *Untitled* is typical:

```
        So hushed
          the sky
        an orchid
        wondering
              why
          opened
              its petals
          wide
```

There is a profusion of poetic talent in Korea, but how the moderns will measure up to the great poets of the past in the acid test of time remains problematical. In particular, the literary quality of much of the committed poetry still remains unestablished. There are literally hundreds of poets publishing work in authoritative literary magazines and academic journals, all introduced with suitable encomiums by well-known writers, all vying annually for a large number of lucrative literary prizes, The outstanding success in the 1980s of To Chŏnghwan's *My Hollyhock Love*—a linked series of love poems dedicated to his recently deceased wife, which sold over a million copies—has introduced a new note to poetry creation, the possibility of enormous commercial reward. These various factors contribute to creating a rather special environment for the writing of poetry in Korea. Poets and readers alike look to the future with optimism and a certain trepidation.

Narrative tradition

The sources of Korea's narrative tradition can be traced back to a rich storehouse of myths, legends and folk tales, the oldest surviving examples of which are recorded in *Samguk sagi* (History of the Three Kingdoms; compiled 1145) and *Samguk yusa* (Romance of the Three Kingdoms; compiled in the late 13th century). *New Stories of the Golden Turtle*, written in Chinese by Kim Si-sŭp (1435-1493), is usually taken as the beginning of fiction, the mastery of composition and form, in Korea: only the first book, containing five stories, survives today. The stories are marked by Korean settings and tragic endings in contrast with the Chinese settings and romantic happy endings that characterised earlier work.

Korean fiction in the vernacular begins with Hŏ Kyun's (1569-1618) celebrated *The Story of Hong Kildong*, an account of how the hero becomes the leader of a band of thieves and ends up establishing a classless utopia on Yul island. The novel advocates the abolition of the class system, the cleaning up of corruption and the elimination of the abuse of power by greedy bureaucrats.

The Nine Cloud Dream (1689) by Kim Manjung (1637-1692) marked the coming of age of the Korean novel. The story concerns a Buddhist monk who dreams that he is reincarnated as a successful Confucian bureaucrat. The *Nine Cloud Dream* employs a sophisticated symbolism to explore the tensions between the Buddhist and the Confucian approaches to life. The theme of the novel is in the title: 'nine cloud dream' - *ku un mong*. In the cloud-dream state the true face of reality is hidden. This implies a state of human imperfection. *The Story of Lady Sa* (1690), also by Kim Manjung, is a satire on the institution of concubinage, directed at King Sukchong's treatment of Queen Inhyŏn.

During the 17th century, *shirhak* (practical learning), emphasising empirical knowledge and practical living, came into prominence. With it came a movement away from poetry to prose as the mode of literary expression and a new more realistic kind of fiction satirising the social prejudices of the day made its appearance. Pak Chiwŏn (1737-1805), with his incisive satire on the hypocrisy of *yangban* (aristocratic) life, is representative of the new realism.

The Story of Ch'unhyang is by far the most popular of the Chosŏn-dynasty novels. Originally a popular tale, it was developed by travelling entertainers into *p'ansori* (a folk opera genre). The novel describes a love affair between the son of a nobleman, Yi Toryong, and the daughter of a *kisaeng*, Ch'unhyang. After the young couple's secret marriage, Yi Toryong is ordered to accompany his father to the capital. The provincial governor tries to make Ch'unhyang his concubine. She refuses on the grounds that she is a married woman. Enraged, the governor throws her in jail and inflicts the most severe torture on her. Ch'unhyang remains faithful. In the meantime Yi Toryong returns disguised as a beggar. He is, in fact, a royal inspector, and he duly punishes the cruel governor and restores Ch'unhyang to happiness. The novel presents a satirical treatment of corrupt officials, a sensitive delineation of social problems, a finely modulated humour centred in the minor characters, an extraordinary depiction of the ideal of faithfulness, and a lovely, playful picture of young love.

The historical novel is a distinct type of Chosŏn-dynasty literature. *Imjin nok*, by an unknown author, records the exploits of famous generals who fought against Hideyoshi. *Kyech'uk Diary*, by an anonymous court lady, records the sufferings endured by Queen Mother Inmok (1584-1632) under the tyrant Kwanghaegun (1556-1622). *Hanjung nok*, by Princess Hyegyŏng (1735-1815), is an elegant account of court life in diary form. The princess relates the untimely death of her consort Prince Sado (1735-1762), her own subsequent sad life in seclusion and her personal suffering at the hands of slanderers. *The Tale of Queen Inhyŏn* recounts court intrigue during the reign of Sukchong. The childless Queen Inhyŏn (1667-1701) brought in Lady Chang to bear Sukchong an heir. After bearing a son, Lady Chang indulged in intrigue until finally she succeeded in having Inhyŏn removed from the court. Afterwards Lady Chang had many of Inhyŏn's followers killed. Eventually Sukchong felt remorse, killed Lady Chang and restored Queen Inhyŏn to her rightful place.

The late 19th century was marked by a decline in the classical novel. Towards the end of the century Korea entered a period of profound political and social change. Before 1876, when the first treaty opening up the ports was signed, Western influence had been restricted to contacts with Western art and science provided through the Catholic missionaries in Beijing, whom Koreans met on the annual visits to bear tribute, and to contacts with priests who actually began to work in Korea. After 1876 the wave of Western influence grew to tidal proportions, with Protestant missionaries, working particularly in education, forming the vanguard.

At this time a new national consciousness began to emerge, its first dawning being signalled by the *Tonghak* (meaning 'Eastern learning' as opposed to 'Western') Movement towards the end of the century. This was an unprecedented popular revolt against corruption and injustice. In the years immediately before and after annexation in 1910, the new national consciousness began to be expressed through the medium of a literature written in *han'gŭl*, called *shinmunhak* or 'new literature'. These were crisis years of alternating hope and despair. Modernisation had begun: with it came new ideas, new fears. President Wilson's declaration of the rights of small nations became a rallying cry for young Korean intellectuals, educated in Japan, who had recently returned.

As in poetry, the new literature was a reaction against Chinese characters and the Chinese literary tradition in favour of *han'gŭl* and a literature on European lines. The modern novel was a new concept in Korea. The work that appeared under this new heading was something between the old Chinese romances and the modern Western novel. *Tears of Blood* (1906) by Yi Injik (1862-1916) was the first new offering. It is a romance with the old formula of rewarding good and punishing evil and it still assigns a significant role to dreams. Although it had not fully developed an acceptable realistic idiom, nevertheless it expressed the ideas that were the rallying cries of the age—freedom to pick one's partner in marriage, the need for education, the call to enlightenment and the urgency of the task of modernisation.

In 1908 Ch'oe Namsŏn (1890-1957) produced *Youth* (*Sonyŏn*), a kind of quasi-literary magazine. It and a series of others produced between 1908 and 1928 provided a forum for young writers to express their ideas. Ch'oe Namsŏn worked closely with another fervent young nationalist and writer, Yi Kwangsu (1892-?). Yi's *The Heartless* (1917), was the first modern novel. It is a romantic story with a complicated pattern of love versus arranged marriages, great emphasis on the value of overseas education, the need for sacrifice for one's country, and the opposition between the values of the old world and the new. The interests of both Ch'oe Namsŏn and Yi Kwangsu were not primarily literary: their concern lay in the promotion of nationalism and enlightenment. Young men rallied to the cause, bright-eyed with visionary hope. The dark days that had followed annexation were over; hope was viable again.

However, the failure of the Independence Movement in March 1919 shattered all the expectations that had been built up in the preceding decade. In particular it bred a climate of intellectual pessimism and disillusion that limited the roads an intellectual might take: he could be completely escapist and ignore the situation altogether; he could adopt the nationalist platform of 'strengthen the nation'; or he could take the Marxist option which developed in literature from the New Direction Group and reached its culmination in the organisation in 1925 of KAPF.

One of the lessons learned from the March 1919 Movement was that independence was not going to be won by emotional appeals alone. This realisation gave considerable impetus to the 'strengthen the nation' approach. Yi Kwangsu threw his weight behind this programme. Up to 1919 Yi had been a radical idealist preaching independence through education, modernisation and popular demonstrations. Now he became a realist thinking in terms of what was feasible here and now, with independence as a long-range goal.

A reaction against this kind of doctrinaire literature came in the form of Korea's first purely literary magazine, *Creation* (1919). Written by a group of young men studying in Japan under the leadership of the brilliant if rather eccentric Kim Tongin (1900-1951), it stated that the purpose of literature lay not in political propaganda but in depicting life as it is. Art for art's sake was the imported catchword.

Young Korean students in Japan had been introduced, in Japanese translation for the most part, to Zola, Maupassant, Tolstoy, Turgenev, Dostoevsky and Wilde, an exposure which opened up new worlds to them. The negative, pessimistic side of what they read seemed to influence them most; they felt trapped by a whole range of historical, social, economic and biological forces which they regarded as fate, the result emerging in their fiction as a kind of hyperrealism close in end-product if not in theory to the determinism of French naturalism.

Kim Tongin, Hyŏn Chin'gŏn (1900-1943), Yŏm Sangsŏp (1897-1963) and others, aiming to depict life as it was, began to write about Korea as they saw it, a dark, gloomy, sordid world. Kim Tongin was the foremost fiction writer of the new generation, an Oscar Wilde-type figure complete with morning coat, carnation and cane. His stories run the gamut of all the -isms current at the time, from naturalism to aestheticism. Hyŏn Chin'gŏn was arguably the best short story writer of the generation. In style and technique his work was reminiscent of Maupassant and Chekhov. *A Lucky Day* (1922), a particularly fine depiction of the tragic fate of a poor rickshawman in Japanese times, is typical of his approach. Many commentators feel that the Korean novel came of age with

Yŏm Sangsŏp's *Before the Cheers* (1923) and *Three Generations* (1931). These novels are remarkable for the realistic picture they give of life in colonial Korea: the cruelty of the oppression, the backwardness of the people.

From 1923 onwards, the New Direction Group began to herald a change from pure literature to a propaganda literature dedicated to spreading socialist principles. In 1925 KAPF was formed and it absorbed the New Direction Group. Pure literature was forgotten. The literary world became a battlefield between Marxists and nationalists, an arena of theoretical disputes without any real literary creativity. The proletarian groups remained in the ascendancy until the mid-1930s when they were rooted out by the Japanese police.

For the rest of the decade there was no real dominating influence in literature. There was, however, a good deal of experimentation, notably in the work of Yi Sang (1910-1938), who tried to plumb the depths of the subconscious mind in a series of stories set in red light areas. The mind being analysed is his own, helpless as he gradually sinks into inevitable degradation.

During this period, Ch'ae Manshik (1902-1950) wrote his inimitable *Peace under Heaven* (1937). There is nothing quite like it in Korean fiction; in fact, there is nothing quite like it in fiction anywhere. It seems to be almost a new genre, reminiscent of Dickens in the vividness of the hero's character, of Fielding in the intrusive narrator, and of *p'ansori* folk opera in narrative technique. It represents the marriage of realism to the classical romance. This is a funny, funny novel, and the hero, Master Yun, is the most fully realised character in all of Korean fiction. Greedy, vain, unscrupulous, philandering, stingy, Master Yun, in manipulating and being manipulated by the family of wastrels, ne'er-do-wells and incompetents with which he has surrounded himself, manages to preserve an almost childish innocence so that it is impossible to stay angry with him. Ch'ae Mansik through this genial monster is satirising the foibles of the Korean people under the Japanese.

During the 1930s another group of writers—notably Kim Tongni (1913-), Hwang Sunwŏn (1915-) and Yi Hyosŏk (1907-1942)—had begun writing a completely new type of story. Before them the whole trend of literature had been away from the past because the past represented all that was opposed to enlightenment, modernisation and nationalism. These writers began to examine what was uniquely Korean, writing in lyrical prose of the real spirit of Korea, which they looked for in the past.

Hwang Sunwŏn is Korea's premier short story writer. His approach is classical in that his stories usually focus on an emotion. *Cranes* (1953) is representative. Two childhood friends find themselves in the role of captor and captive during the Korean war (1950-1953). The story delineates the subtle changes of emotion experienced by the captor—

rage, anger, shame, responsibility, compassion—until finally the roles of the two men become reversed: psychologically, captor becomes captive and captive becomes captor. The story ends with the captor letting the captive go. The theme is obvious: humane feelings triumph over the absurdity and cruelty of war. The beauty of the story lies in the subtlety of the exposition: the suggestion of mood changes through a glance or a gesture rather than through direct statement.

The 1950s saw the emergence of young writers who, having experienced the horrors of civil war, were now looking for meaning amidst the cruelty and corruption of post-war society. Existentialism became something of a vogue, exerting a marked influence on the literature of the period. Chang Yonghak (1921-) and Son Changsŏp (1922-) are typical of the new generation in their search for meaning in a society where all order had broken down.

The quest for freedom was central. Post-war intellectuals were concerned to discover or rediscover the self, the value of the individual self. *The Square* (1961) by Ch'oe Inhun (1936-) is a representative expression of this quest for freedom. The story deals directly with the consequences of the war and a dilemma which must have faced many POW intellectuals: whether to choose South, North or a neutral country after the armistice.

The Square reflected the existential mood that was dominant in European literature in the 1950s. It was a towering bestseller, which interestingly enough returned to the success charts during the democratisation crisis of recent years. As a depiction of a young Korean intellectual under stress, nothing better has been done. *The Square* combines the best qualities of Camus and Hemingway. Yet, it is a difficult book: the philosophical asides are distracting, and the theme is extremely dark and pessimistic. The characters seem quite unable to get outside themselves, to attain any sort of vision of a world that does not turn within the confines of their own private experience. Lee Myŏngjun is unabashedly self-centred. His quest for meaning is totally personal and selfish. When he is also revealed to be diabolically cruel, the reader unfamiliar with Korea finds it virtually impossible to empathise with him in his dilemma.

The new generation of writers of the mid-1960s and early 1970s had either been children during the Korean War or been so young that they had no vivid memories of its horrors. As a consequence the war and its aftermath began to lose their dominance as subject matter of literature. *Seoul: Winter 1964* (1965) by Kim Sŭngok (1941-) is a brilliant satire of a society where all order has broken down and human relationships have become meaningless. Highly experimental in form, it is a horrifying tragi-comic depiction of alienation and the absurdity of human existence.

During this period a new awareness of social and political issues came to the fore, bringing a consequent concern with corruption and the abuse of power. The characters of

Hwang Sŏkyŏng (1943-) are mostly from the lowest social levels of people who find themselves in conflict with an unjust society and who face inevitable defeat. *Chang Kilsan* (1975) provides a panoramic picture of the 18th century in the course of depicting the tragic life of a legendary rebel hero. *A Strange Place* (1971) shows management and corrupt overseers cruelly exploiting the workers on a reclamation project. *The Road to Sampo* (1975), one of Hwang's finest stories, is a delicate mood piece, told almost entirely through dialogue, without the overt social message of *A Strange Place*, though the inferences are there for the reader to make.

Pak Kyŏngni's *The Land* (1970), a massive historical chronicle portraying a traditional landowning family against a panorama of cultural conflict between old world values and the values of the emerging new world before, during and after Japanese colonisation, was greeted with critical acclaim. Pak displays a marvellous historical sense in creating a detailed, totally convincing world, peopled by a vast cast of finely realised characters moving around the central heroine, Ch'oe, who is a commanding presence throughout the novel.

The Kwangju revolution in 1980 brought the anomalies of contemporary society into even sharper focus. There was a surging sense of the urgent need to solve the problems that beset society, in particular, the gaping wound of a divided country. A literature of 'division' has emerged in recent years, which traces its roots back to Ch'oe Inhun's *The Square*, but with a rather different emphasis. *The Age of the Hero* (1984) by Yi Munyŏl (1948-) depicts a hero who has freely chosen the Communist way of life, emphasising personal responsibility in choices; *Taebaeksanmaek* (1986) by Cho Chŏngnae (1942-) asserts that division was part of an inevitable revolutionary process inherent in the class struggle between landowners and tenants.

In addition to *The Age of the Hero*, Yi Munyŏl has written other novels and novellas: *The Son of Man* (1979), *Our Twisted Hero* (1987) and *Even Fallen Things Have Wings* (1989). All have been bestsellers.

Our Twisted Hero, an allegory on the abuse of power, delineates the latent tendency in man towards dictatorship, examining its theme against the background of an elementary school. Ŏm Sŏktae, monitor of the sixth grade, rules his class with an iron fist. A sinister, shadowy figure, he terrorises the class into submission, reducing them to cringing, fawning pawns. He beats them, takes their money, uses them to cheat on exams, collects 'dues', sells preferment, and in general insists on being treated as a king. A transfer student from Seoul challenges Sŏktae's dictatorship, leading to a long, lonely struggle that ends in the capitulation of the Seoul boy. However, in capitulation he discovers a new side to Sŏktae's corrupt regime: he begins to taste the sweets of special favour and power. The Seoul boy becomes Sŏktae's reluctant lieutenant.

A new teacher takes over the class and immediately becomes suspicious of Sŏktae. An investigation reveals that Sôkdae has been cheating on his exams. The teacher gives him a severe beating in front of the class, humiliating him in the process. Seeing their king reduced to a snivelling weakling, the boys, once such loyal supporters, now turn on him like snakes. The only exception is the Seoul boy. After Sŏktae's departure the long process of restoring democratic procedures in the class begins. Boys are elected to positions of responsibility and just as quickly deposed; some groups act recklessly, some groups do not act at all. In the end, after much pain and toil dignity is restored to all.

The 1980s have also been marked by a wave of 'novels of the masses' (*minjung*) and 'novels of workers' (*nodongja*), which focus on the entire gamut of social problems associated with industrialisation. They see the working class as pivotal in social reform and the future development of the nation. The part played by workers in the events leading up to the establishment of the Sixth Republic in June 1987 has provided a strong incentive to the production of workers' literature.

The canvas of contemporary Korean fiction shows a wonderful variety. Much could be said about the intense alienation that characterises the work of Pak Wansŏ (1931-); the special atmosphere evoked by Yi Ch'ŏngjun (1939-) in many of his stories, in particular the celebrated novella *The Prophet* ; the gentle humour of Yun Hŏnggil (1942-); the range of technique employed by O Chŏnghŭi (1947-). Korea has an abundance of talented novelists and a great variety of outlets. All the daily newspapers feature serial novels. Add to this a plethora of valuable literary prizes to be won every year, and there is a ready-made formula for a vibrant market in fiction. Korean fiction has had to struggle to develop its own distinctive voice, and the full fruits of the struggle have perhaps yet to be reaped.

Readings

Ch'oe Inhun, 1961. *The Square*, trans. Kevin O'Rourke, 1985. Barnstaple: Spindlewood

Chung Chong-wha (ed.), 1995. *Modern Korean Literature: An Anthology 1908-1965*. London: Kegan Paul International

Kathleen J. Crane Foundation, 1992. *Tiger, Burning Bright*. Elizabeth, NJ, and Seoul: Hollym

Daniel A. Kister (trans.), 1994. *Distant Valleys: Poems of Chong Chi-yong*. Berkeley: Asian Humanities Press

Korea National Commission for UNESCO, 1994. *Reunion So Far Away: A Collection of Contemporary Korean Fiction*. Seoul: Seoul Computer Press

Ku Sang, 1990. *Wastelands of Fire: Selected Poems*. Trans. Anthony Teague. London and Boston: Forest Books

– 1991. *A Korean Century: River and Fields*. Trans. Brother Anthony of Taize. London and Boston: Forest Books

Midang So Chong-ju, 1993. *The Early Lyrics 1941-1960*. Trans. Brother Anthony of Taize. London and Boston: Forest Books/UNESCO

– 1995. *Poems of a Wanderer*. Trans. Kevin O'Rourke. Dublin: Dedalus

Peter H. Lee (ed. and trans.), 1974. *Poems from Korea: A Historical Anthology*. Honolulu: University of Hawaii Press

– (ed.), 1975. *The Traditional Culture and Society of Korea: Art and Literature*. Honolulu: University of Hawaii Press

– (ed. and trans.), 1981. *Anthology of Korean Literature: From Early Times to the Nineteenth Century*. Honolulu: University of Hawaii Press

– (trans.), 1991. *Pine River and Lone Peak: An Anthology of Three Chosôn Dynasty Poets*. Honolulu: University of Hawaii Press

David R. McCann, 1988. *Form and Freedom in Korean Poetry*. Leiden: E. J. Brill

– (trans.), 1989. *Selected Poems of Sŏ Chŏ ngju*. New York: Columbia University Press

Kevin O'Rourke (ed. and trans.), 1987. *The Sijo Tradition*. Seoul: Jung Eum Sa

– (ed. and trans.), 1988. *Tilting the Jar, Spilling the Moon: Poems from Koryŏ , Chosŏ n, and Contemporary Korea*. Seoul: Universal Publications Agency

– (trans.), 1995. *Singing Like a Cricket, Hooting Like an Owl: Selected Poems of Yi Kyu-bo*. Ithaca: Cornell East Asia Program

Marshall R. Pihl, 1973. *Listening to Korea: A Korean Anthology*. New York: Praeger Publishers 1993. 'Contemporary literature in a divided land', in *Korea Briefing, 1993*, D. N. Clark (ed.). Boulder, CO: Westview Press:79-97

Marshall R. Pihl, Bruce and Ju-Chan Fulton (eds), 1993. *Land of Exile: Contemporary Korean Fiction*. New York: M. E. Sharpe/UNESCO Publishing

Richard Rutt (ed. and trans.), 1971. *The Bamboo Grove: An Introduction to Sijo*. Berkeley: University of California Press

Richard Rutt and Kim Chong-un (trans.), 1974. *Virtuous Women: Three Classic Korean Novels*. Seoul: Royal Asiatic Society

Hyun-jae Yee Sallee (ed.), 1993. *The Snowy Road and Other Stories: An Anthology of Korean Fiction*. Trans. Hyun-jae Yee Sallee and Dr Teresa Margadonna Hyun. New York: White Pine Press

Yi Munyol, 1987. *Our Twisted Hero*. Trans. Kevin O'Rourke. Seoul: Minumsa Publishing Company

– 1992. *The Poet*. Trans. Chong-wha Chung and Brother Anthony of Taize. London: Harvill Press

6

FINE ARTS, MUSIC AND DANCE

6.1 Fine arts

Introduction

The cultural legacy enjoyed by Korea in the 20th century has unbroken links to an ancient past. The Korean peninsula has been home to craftsmen and artists producing distinctive work in various materials, ranging from elegant paintings for scholars to brightly embroidered accessories for women, and including splendid golden ornaments and holy relics unearthed in tombs and temple ruins. Koreans are particularly proud of types and styles of artistic decoration unique to their country. A first look at the fine arts of Korea, China and Japan draws our attention to common features shared by all three. But on longer acquaintance, it becomes clear that Korean ceramics, brush painting, textile arts and furniture have recognisable and distinctive qualities. Chinese styles and techniques were of great importance, but Korean artists and craftsmen brought local aesthetic values to their work and created art objects notable for their unforced enjoyment of colour and form.

Korea's artistic heritage is an interesting field of study, not least because the rapid industrial development of south Korea in the late 20th century has thrown up unimagined treasures as archaeologists and art historians race to rescue buried relics from the jaws of developers' bulldozers.

Three Kingdoms and United Shilla (to AD668)

Koguryŏ, Paekche and Shilla were the Three Kingdoms ruling the greater part of the Korean peninsula by about the 4th century AD, although Koguryŏ's authority dates from much earlier. The geographical differences between them are reflected in a great diversity of artistic production. Koguryŏ, the most northerly of the three, established capitals first in the far north, on the Yalu river, and later at P'yŏngyang, the modern capital of North Korea, on the Taedong river. Koguryŏ kings and nobles are remembered particularly for the wall paintings which decorate chambers in their tombs of the 5th to 7th centuries. The subjects include animated hunting scenes where galloping hunters take aim at deer and tiger, and a depiction of a feast with dancers dressed in loose trousers and long tunics entertaining two seated nobles, whose status is indicated by making their figures more massive than those of the dancers. These scenes are a unique source of information about the style of life of people in Koguryŏ, and they also provide evidence about the way painters handled scale and perspective and about their conventions for placing figures in a landscape.

The Buddhist religion reached Koguryŏ in the 4th century, and later spread southwards, first to Paekche and in the 6th century to Shilla. Numerous statues representing Buddhist deities were produced and precious holy relics were buried in the temples and monasteries that were founded across the length and breadth of the Korean peninsula.

Paekche occupied the territory south of modern Seoul and along the western coastal areas, facing towards China. During the 1970s, the tomb of King Munyŏng (also spelled Muryŏng by some writers; r. 501-523) was excavated, revealing golden regalia of high quality as well as carved tiles and silver and jade objects. These allowed historians to construct a more accurate picture than hitherto of the high quality and Chinese-influenced style of Paekche artefacts. Magnificent pictorial tiles depicting mountainous landscape scenes were produced in the Paekche region, probably reflecting the painting style of the time.

The third of the Three Kingdoms, Shilla, grew from origins as a group of walled cities in the far southeast of the country. Shilla flourished and became a strong and accomplished kingdom which attracted travellers from far and wide. By land, the Silk Road brought merchants and goods from Central Asia and India. Tomb goods discovered in the area of the Shilla capital, Kyŏngju, include glass vessels imported from the western Mediterranean. Sea trade also flourished, bringing contacts with Japan and with south China.

In 668, Shilla unified the entire Korean peninsula from the Taedong river southward, having defeated Paekche in AD660 and Koguryŏ in 668. By that time, the Buddhist faith had gained adherents at every level of society. For the common people, calling out the name of Amitabha, who ruled over the Western Paradise, brought reassurance amidst the hardships of daily life. At court and among the elite, Buddha's protective powers were invoked at times of crisis and war. The magnificent rock grotto of Sŏkkuram, which stands near Kyŏngju, is a case in point. Built in the 8th century AD, it is a monument to belief in the Buddha's protective powers, and to the devotion of the artists who commissioned it. Blocks of white granite were painstakingly carved out of the cliffside, to allow the huge figure of Buddha to look out to the eastern sea, towards the rising sun.

Still today, visitors to nearby Pulguk temple climb the hillside at dawn to view the unforgettable sight of the massive seated Buddha figure catching the sun's rising rays. Numerous temples and monasteries of the Kyŏngju area were imposing edifices that accumulated great wealth and extensive lands. In the service of the Buddha, sculpture in stone and metal was produced. Deities such as Maitreya, Buddha of the Future, and Avalokitsvara, god or goddess of mercy, were popular subjects.

Buddhism was thus an important impetus for artistic creativity in the Three Kingdoms period. When sculptors using granite or stone, and metal casters using bronze or iron, created images of holy figures, their aim was to praise or invoke a divine creature. In some cases the spirituality and joyful tranquillity that their works express can be sensed even by those who do not share the religious faith of the anonymous artist.

Buddhist temples were rich and powerful, commanding the service of numerous labourers as well as those of monks and novices. Temples would operate foundries and employ painters to produce the bells, drums, ritual vessels and banners and other holy images required for the ceremonies that occurred on prayer-chanting days, fasting days and other holy days of the Buddhist calendar. Many temples had special towers in their courtyards, known in Korean as *t'ap*, and in these were buried particularly valuable icons of faith. In the *t'ap* at Pulguk temple near Kyŏngju for example, a holy scripture with an image of the preaching Buddha was buried in the foundations. It was uncovered during excavations in the 1960s, and is now famous as the earliest printed document in the world.

Of the many achievements of the artists and craftsmen of Shilla, however, the most astonishing are the splendid golden crowns, belts, head ornaments, earrings and regalia which have been excavated from tombs in and around Kyŏngju.

Because Kyŏngju is far from the Han river delta (the area which has been the economic and political centre of Korea since the 14th century) and—more importantly—because Shilla royal tombs were covered after closing by massive mounds of granite boulders, making them safe against robbers, many important royal tombs remained undisturbed until the 20th century. Significant numbers of their contents have now been systematically excavated and described. Unlike the Koguryŏ chamber tombs, which long ago yielded their treasures to tomb robbers, Kyŏngju tombs held many surprises for archaeologists and art historians. As well as golden regalia, there have been glass beads and vessels, a painting of a flying horse done in mineral colours on birchbark, and many comma-shaped jade ornaments. The unusual construction style of Shilla crowns and head-dresses, using beaten gold and often incorporating tree and antler motifs, is thought to link Shilla artistic traditions to those of nomadic peoples of the steppe and mountain area of central and northeast Asia. Shilla royal tombs and the objects unearthed in them have features also found in buried funerary goods discovered in that region, that date to between the 5th and 1st centuries BC. Recognition that non-Chinese prototypes play an important role in the history of artistic transmission in East Asia is a major advance in art historical studies, and one which broadens our understanding of the origins and regional complexities of Korean art and culture.

Objects fashioned from other materials were also buried in Shilla tombs. Because most pieces surviving from these distant times are made of non-perishable materials, we know more about the ceramics than we do about textiles and clothing or about wooden objects or those made of base metal. Shilla ceramics were thrown on a potter's wheel, using a clay that was high in iron and yielded a greyish-black colour when fired. In the 5th and 6th centuries, sculptural ceramics like the horse rider and servant were made alongside monumental vessels standing on high pierced pedestals. Somewhat like steamers, these high-footed stonewares often consisted of base, vessel and cover. The base might have decorative bands of regularly shaped cut-outs, as well as raised, incised and stamped patterns to add interest to the surface. The most common types of ceramic throughout the entire Korean peninsula before the 10th century were varieties of high-fired stonewares, produced in shapes that reflect local preference, and using clay that fired to a range of tones from whitish-grey through warm ochres to deep charcoal. These Three Kingdoms-period vessels are admired for the austere simplicity of their forms.

Koryŏ (918-1392)

During the 10th century, political rule shifted away from Shilla. Koryŏ, a state that chose the central area for its capital, was founded in 918. At about this time, a major shift in ceramic production began. Korean potters had learned how to apply glaze to their unfired vessels, and green-coloured ware became increasingly popular. They also introduced new shapes and styles of ceramics to the range of vessels and architectural ceramics they produced. The taste for green vessels originated in China and appears to have reached Korea through seaborne trade. It seems to have been spread by travellers and diplomats who made regular official journeys throughout most of the 10th and 11th centuries. The Koryŏ court and aristocracy enjoyed the refined pleasures of wine, poetry and contemplative Buddhism. Ingenious potters made incense burners, jugs and vases that imitated plants, animals and figures. They became prized objects in the dwellings of the powerful elite. Green-glazed tiles adorned the roofs of pavilions; wine was served from delicately shaped cups with petal-like lobes. During the 12th century, the technique of inlaying black and white designs under the glaze was introduced: this type of decoration is known in Korean as *sanggam* and is recognised by art historians as one of the great achievements of Korean ceramic art. Using the inlay technique, patterns such as flying cranes, repeating chrysanthemum heads and meandering vines could be applied. The combination of green glaze with sparkling glassy black and white pictorial designs has enduring appeal to collectors, who even today compete fiercely at art sales to buy the finest examples.

In the devoutly Buddhist ambience of Koryŏ high culture, devotional art was predominant. Temples and museums in Korea and throughout the world have preserved a few precious examples of scroll paintings of Buddhist deities. Other, non-Buddhist, subjects were certainly depicted by the painters of the time, but little survives to tell us which were the favoured styles and subjects. The entire body of Buddhist scriptures was printed on woodblocks in the 11th century and again (following the loss of the first set of blocks in a fire) in the 13th century. Holy texts were also carefully copied by scribes: the most luxurious versions were done using gold or silver pigment on paper dyed to a deep inky blue using a plant dye, indigo. To hold these holy texts, large chests covered in lacquer inlaid with mother-of-pearl were made. The designs on these chests often include scrolling flower heads which resemble the inlaid floral motifs on green-glazed ceramics of the same period. Bronze vessels with decoration inlaid using silver wire were also produced: these included bottles and sprinklers for temple altars, as well as incense burners and on a larger scale bells, drums and statues.

Chosŏn (1392-1910)

After the Mongol invasions of the 13th century, the Koryŏ state never regained the heights of artistic and literary endeavour that had been reached in the 11th and early 12th centuries. In the latter part of the 14th century, a powerful general, Yi Sŏnggye, led Koryŏ forces resisting Chinese invaders along the Yalu river. Yi subsequently rebelled against the Koryŏ royal house and founded a new dynasty, which later took the title Chosŏn.

The new dynasty gradually turned away from the Buddhist fervour of earlier times, and introduced measures to bring the teachings of the Chinese philosopher-sage Confucius into all spheres of Korean life. In the arts, this led to a gradual decline in the output of Buddhist paintings and banners, although belief in Buddhism was by now so deeply ingrained that temple culture persisted despite the withdrawal of court and official patronage. Supporters of Confucian morality introduced the practice of honouring one's ancestors, and new, plain vessels of ceramic and bronze were fashioned to bear offerings and to stand on family shrines erected for this purpose.

In contrast to the predominantly Buddhist subject-matter of paintings that survive from Koryŏ times, Chosŏn dynasty painting spread to a greater variety of genres. There are landscape scenes such as *The Journey to Peach Blossom Land* by An Kyŏn, who was active in the mid-15th century, and portraits of high-ranking ministers and members of the royal family, commissioned to pay homage to a distinguished ancestor and to record his conformity to the qualities of a virtuous leader. In the later centuries of Chosŏn rule, there are landscapes and still-life paintings that record details of the world as it appeared to the painters of the time. Genre paintings by artists like Kim Hongdo (born 1745) and depictions of the soaring peaks of the scenic Diamond Mountain area by Chŏng Sŏn (1676-1759) have survived to give us insights into the daily life of the people, and into the unchanging beauties of Korea's landscape.

Ceramics and other decorative arts also developed rapidly and in distinctive ways during the long unbroken rule of the Chosŏn. White porcelain, fired to a higher temperature than the green-glazed stoneware of the Koryŏ period, was the preferred type of ceramic of the court and educated elite. Strongly adhering to Confucian ideals of austerity and avoiding any hint of ostentation, the Chosŏn aristocratic class, known in Korean as *yangban,* preferred the understated beauty of plain white ceramics. The only colours used in decorating these vessels, which are distinctive because of their thick walls and natural, unforced shapes, were pigments of red deriving from copper, brown and black deriving from iron, and blue, taken from the precious mineral cobalt, also known as 'Mohammadan blue' because before a native supply was identified it had to be imported from further west.

Ceramics were used for everyday living, for example, as eating utensils, as flower vases, as teapots and wine jugs. The scholar's study used desktop ornaments that were also functional: waterdroppers for mixing ink, brushrests on which to lay the calligrapher's brush when pausing between strokes, and brushholders shaped like cylinders or like hollow rectangles that held the numerous brushes used in composing texts or in painting. Other porcelain objects on the scholars' shelves might also have included purely decorative knick-knacks such as paperweights in the shape of a mountain or a fruit, all produced on a small scale for handling and enjoying individually. Larger-scale jars and bowls were also made, often in rather plain shapes: one very characteristic feature of later Korean ceramics is the prominence of form over decoration.

Furniture, decorated lacquer boxes and brightly coloured wrapping cloths are among the fine arts of the Chosŏn that have survived to our times. Boxes inlaid with mother of pearl were made to contain the precious belongings of ladies and gentlemen, and a few particularly high-ranking ladies could own a storage chest lacquered with red lacquer. People of lower rank might own a chest strengthened and ornamented with iron or ornate brass plates and hinge-pieces. In the plain and sparsely furnished rooms that Koreans, including those in more prosperous families, lived in, these pieces of furniture provided colour and pattern while serving a useful storage function. Korea in the Chosŏn period advocated a Confucian, hierarchical view of society. Women were systematically excluded from status in public life. Living in seclusion in the inner quarters of a family compound (see Factsheet 2.4), many well-born women cultivated needlecraft, embroidery and dress ornamentation, producing wrapping cloths, purses, perfume pouches, embroidered thimbles and other accessories which have a fresh and direct appeal. Even some of the clothes worn on special occasions, such as bridal gowns or court robes, were embellished by exquisitely embroidered designs of flowers, birds, clouds and rocks, which today are considered works of art (see Factsheet 2.6).

Arts in present-day Korea

In the 20th century, Korean artists have experienced changes and great suffering along with the rest of the population. Many of their works have reflected shifting moods: despair at the colonial occupation of the country by Japan, elation following independence in 1945, and anguish at the suffering of the Korean War and the division of the peninsula that followed it. The first half of the century was a time when Korean artists learned about Western techniques such as oil painting and the creation of three-dimensionality in landscapes and portraits. Often they assimilated such new concepts and practices through study in Japan, where painters were themselves experimenting. To a people whose experience of art had been restricted to Oriental brush painting, which uses ink and colours on paper and silk and follows well-established conventions about subject-matter and manner of depiction, the new Western concepts of art were exciting or even shocking. The earliest Korean oil paintings included portraits of nudes, considered indecent by Confucians, and departed from the conventions of Oriental portrait painting by emphasising the individuality of their subjects. (Portrait painting had hitherto been closely tied to the tradition of paying respects to ancestors, and had produced idealised versions of statesmen and rulers that excluded all hint of fallibility.) Landscape and figure brush painting in the traditional manner continued alongside the new experiments and indeed flourish to this day.

With the healthy economy in South Korea since the 1970s, interest in art has grown, and colleges and universities each year produce thousands of graduates specialising in the visual arts and in art history. Some painters have turned towards the meditative traditions of Buddhism to produce plain, undecorated canvases which recall the quiet austerity of early ceramics and textiles. Politically engaged artists of the People's Art (*Minjung misul*) school began in the 1980s to portray ordinary working people, as a conscious protest against inequality and injustice in Korean society.

In recent years, a new spirit of experimentation has informed the work of some distinguished artists, such as the abstract painter Kim Hwangi, the Japan-based artist and critic Lee U-fan and the conceptual artist Paek Namjun. Artists active in applied media such as ceramics, lacquerware and textiles have taken diverse paths, and have produced exciting and challenging work with links in some cases to Korean themes and attitudes and in others to international and technological developments in the art world. After the hardships of colonialism and war, artists in South Korea are able to work more freely. They are actively leading the educated public, which has increasing leisure time, into the study and enjoyment of the visual arts of all periods.

The situation in North Korea is very different. Although the arts are fostered, they are given first and foremost a didactic role and are not intended as a means of untrammelled free expression. The style of Socialist Realism, developed first in the 1930s in the former Soviet Union as an adjunct to state propaganda and promoted in the People's Republic of China, has dominated North Korean art for decades. The result has been innumerable paintings on the themes of resistance to foreign aggression and the socialist reconstruction of the country, often composed around the central figure of Kim Il Sung or his son Kim Jong Il. These are intended as realistic depictions, and often give a flat treatment of the subject as if they were little different from wall posters. Sculpture has likewise often been restricted to enormous statues of Kim Il Sung or other heroic figures. More successful is the vigorous bronze *Ch'ŏllima* monument near the Museum of the Korean Revolution in P'yŏngyang, which depicts the fabled winged horse that could cover 1000 *li* (300 miles) in a day. The horse with its riders commemorates the reconstruction campaign of the late 1950s.

Readings

Edward B. Adams, 1986 and 1989. *Korea's Pottery Heritage,* 2 vols. Seoul: Seoul International Publishing House

R. Goepper (intro.) and R. Whitfield (ed.), 1984. *Treasures from Korea: Art Through 5000 Years.* London: British Museum Publications Ltd

G. St G. M. Gompertz, 1963. *Korean Celadon.* London: Faber and Faber

– 1968. *Korean Pottery and Porcelein of the Yi Period.* London: Faber and Faber

Wanne J. Joe, 1972. *Traditional Korea: A Cultural History.* Seoul: Chung'ang University Press

Kim Won-Yong, 1986. *Art and Archaeology of Ancient Korea.* Seoul: Taekwang Publishing Co.

'Korean art today', *Koreana* 9, no. 2 (Summer 1995): 4-63 [nine articles]

Young Ick Lew (ed.), 1993. *Korean Art Tradition.* Seoul: Korea Foundation

Evelyn B. McCune, 1962. *The Arts of Korea: An Illustrated History.* Rutland, VT, and Tokyo: Tuttle

Beth McKillop, 1992. *Korean Art and Design: The Samsung Gallery of Korean Art.* London: Victoria and Albert Museum

Robert Moes, 1987. *Korean Art from the Brooklyn Museum Collection.* New York: Universe Books

Ken Vos, 1994. *Korean Painting: A Selection of Eighteenth to Early Twentieth Century Painting from the Collection of Cho Won-Kyung.* Leiden: Ukiyo-e Books

6.2 Music

Overview

Korean music is often overshadowed by better-known Japanese and Chinese sound worlds. This is hard, given its long independent tradition. While court music may seem slow and dreary—a combination of the upright correctness demanded by Confucian etiquette and an apparent slowing down in many melodies over centuries—it remains enigmatic and curious. And although folk music may use different modes to Western music, particularly several differently tempered pentatonic systems, the rhythms are immediately catching: they make you want to get up and dance, said one reviewer in the *New York Times*. Folk music is earthy and energetic, almost as spicy as Korea's pickled cabbage staple, *kimch'i*. Indeed, music is in the bones of every Korean, and no party is complete without singing, dancing and the beating of drums and gongs. The main characteristics of Korean music can be summarised thus:

style. There are two types: court music, which is upright and controlled, with little obvious emotion; and folk music, which is lively, earthy and full of emotion and enthusiasm. By contrast, Japanese music uses more 'delicate textures', which mean less outpouring of emotion is possible; Chinese is normally full of vitality and energy.

melody. Melodic contour is less important than the treatment of individual tones. As a consequence, melodies are full of ornamentation, particularly before or after the main pitch of a tone sounds. Japanese music is quite similar, but builds from small repeated melodic cells. Melody is the fundamental building block in Chinese music.

harmony. Korean music is homophonic; there is virtually no harmony. However, different instruments use different ornamentation, which when combined can sound harmonic or, more correctly, heterophonic

rhythm. The key to Korean music is rhythm. Rhythmic cycles underpin virtually all music, giving a collection of downbeats and accents that ensure no single musician can get lost. Compound time is preferred, such as 6/8 and 12/8. In contrast, Japanese music tends to have freer rhythm with less focus, while Chinese music is typically in simple time, usually 2/4 and 4/4.

scales. Pentatonic scales are favoured, with even more restricted three-tone scales in the southwest of the peninsula. The Chinese system on which Korean modes are based actually has all 12 semitones of Western music, but from this palette three or five tones are chosen. The exact tuning of notes varies from instrument to instrument. The scales are different in details to those of China and Japan.

instruments. Some 65 instruments are used in Korean music today. Many of those imported originally from China survive only in court rituals or in new compositions. Korean instrumental timbres tend to be soft, but always incorporate elements of noise (the plucking of a silk string, the sound of a plectrum hitting wood after a string is struck, the sound of air on a wind instrument). Chinese music sounds much 'cleaner' but brighter, while the Japanese say their instruments use 'natural' timbres.

Historical sketch

The Silk Roads reached Korea from China. Many centuries ago, music with roots in the Near East and India merged with Central Asian and native Chinese music before passing to an eastern outpost of the Chinese empire, Lelang (Kor.: Nangnang). Lelang, near modern P'yŏngyang, survived from 108BC to AD313. Some of the earliest references to Korean music thus occur in Chinese sources. For example, Chen Suo's 3rd-century *Sanguo zhi* (History of three kingdoms) describes how people in Mahan to the southwest of Korea sang and danced at times of planting and harvesting. Tomb murals also illustrate musical scenes. The Anak No. 3 tomb, completed around AD357, portrays Chinese instruments—panpipes (*xiao*), standing drums (*gu*), horn (*qiao*), handbell (*nao*), zither (*zheng*), lute (*yuanxian*) and flute. Across the border in today's Jilin Province of northwest China, murals in the 5th-century Changchuan No.1 Tomb depict nine instruments that by then were considered Korean: transverse flute (*hoengjŏk*), vertical flute (*changso*), two lutes (*ohyŏn pip'a* and *wanham*), zither (*kŏmun'go*), five-string zither (*ohyŏn'gŭm*), long horn (*taegak*), oboe (*p'iri*), and suspended drum (*tamgo*).

The literary tradition tells us more. The 1145 *Samguk sagi* (History of the three kingdoms), written by Kim Pushik (1075–1151), and the less rigorous *Samguk yusa* (Romance of the three kingdoms') by the monk Iryŏn (1206–1289), indicate that among the so-called Three Kingdoms (traditional dates 57BC—AD668), Koguryŏ (extending over the north and west) sent ensembles to the Chinese Sui court. Koguryŏ's favoured instruments were the Central Asian lute and cylindrical oboe. It was in Koguryŏ that the *kŏmun'go*, a six-string plucked long zither, was invented. Legend recounts how Wang Sanak devised the instrument on the orders of the king and, as he played it, black cranes flew into the room and danced (hence in some texts it is called *hyŏnhakkŭm*, 'black crane zither'). Paekche (in the southwest and centre) imported the South Asian harp and a Southern Chinese flute with a raised mouthpiece. Paekche developed relations with Japan, and in the 7th century one of its musicians, Mimashi, taught mask dances learnt in China at the Japanese court.

Shilla (based initially in the southeast) began with two important instruments. One, the *kayagŭm*, a 12-string plucked long zither that is now the most popular of traditional instruments, was actually developed on the orders of a king, Kashil, in the Kaya tribal federation. The legend tells how the king saw a Chinese zither being played and commented that, since Korea has a different language, the people should not use the same music as China. Hence, his musician U Rŭk created the *kayagŭm*. This was in the 6th century, and U Rŭk fled to Shilla by 551, shortly before Kaya was overrun. Four of these peculiar zithers, characterised by an endpiece shaped like ram's horns that holds the strings taut, survive in the 8th century Shosoin repository in Nara in Japan. The instrument design has hardly changed over 1400 years! The other Shilla instrument was the transverse flute, *taegŭm*. Again, there is a legend. In 683, King Shinmun was told of a mountain floating in the Eastern Sea. A bamboo plant grew on it that split in two during daylight but fused as a single trunk each night. Storms raged whenever the bamboo fused as a single trunk. Astrologers divined that the king's dead father had come back to earth as a dragon and wanted to give a treasure that would protect the kingdom. The bamboo was recovered and made into a flute. Whenever the flute was blown, the seas became calm and peace ruled the kingdom.

The legend in fact came after Shilla, ousting the rival kingdoms of Koguryŏ and Paekche, had unified the peninsula in 668. The new state created a mixed ensemble called *samhyŏn samjuk*, the 'three strings, three winds' ensemble, which boasted the Shilla *kayagŭm*, Koguryŏ *kŏmun'go*, Central Asian *pip'a*, three sizes of transverse flutes—big (*taegŭm*), medium (*chunggŭm*) and small (*sogŭm*)—and Tang Chinese clappers (Ch.: *paiban*; Kor.: *pak*).

Music at the royal court

The music of the next dynasty, Koryŏ (918–1392), is described in the *Koryŏsa* (History of the Koryŏ dynasty), officially dated 1451, written by Chŏng Inji (1396–1478). Court music was by now divided into three types: *aak* (Chinese ritual music played in what was considered an authentic style), *tangak* (other music of Song Chinese origin) and *hyangak* (indigenous music; other texts refer to this as *sogak*). The most significant dates for music were 1114 and 1116, when the court received two gifts from the eighth Song emperor, Huizong. Korea was fast becoming a Confucian state, and kings had begun to observe Confucian rites to heaven, to agriculture, land and grain, and to royal ancestors. They needed suitable music and appealed to Huizong. The first gift, in 1114, of *dasheng xinyue*, music for banquets, consisted of 167 instruments, scores and illustrated instructions for performance. The second gift, in 1116, was what the Koreans wanted. This was *dasheng yayue*, music for rituals. It comprised a massive 428 instruments together with costumes and ritual dance objects. Musicians were sent as gifts along with their instruments.

Virtually all the Chinese instruments were lost in a 1361 invasion; by then, the Chinese music was well mixed with local tunes. Confucianism was strengthened by the following dynasty, Chosŏn (1392-1910). The need to keep appropriate rituals, the loss of instruments and the infiltration of indigenous music led in 1430 to a thorough revision, which is documented in the *Aakpo* (Notations of ritual music), where 456 suggested melodies and transcriptions are prescribed for court rituals. Only six of these melodies are still played and they come in a single rite, the twice-yearly *Munmyo cheryeak* (Rite to

Confucius). A second extant court rite, the annual *Chongmyo cheryeak* (Rite to royal ancestors), uses two song suites composed during King Sejong's reign (1418–1450). All other Chinese music was soon Koreanised, and today only two pieces are still played, the orchestral *Nagyangch'un* (Spring in Lelang) and *Pohŏja* (Walking in the void). These are overshadowed by a long Korean suite, *Yŏmillak* (The king shares pleasure with his people). The 15th century ended with Sŏng Hyŏn's musical compendium, *Akhak kwebŏm* (Guide to the study of music; 1493), which quotes Chinese sources and gives notations and prescriptions for rituals and dance.

In Chosŏn society, beyond the confines of the court, a new musical culture developed. Normally associated with the emergence in Korean society from the late 17th century of a class of professionals, the *chungin*, this music came to be known as *chŏngak* ('correct music'). The *kŏmun'go* zither was central, providing the lead for ensembles known as *p'ungnyu* and *chul p'ungnyu*. The most sophisticated surviving *chŏngak* chamber piece is the suite *Yŏngsan hoesang* (the name derives from syllables matched to the opening notes in the oldest surviving score: 'Buddha preaching on Spirit Mountain'). New styles of vocal music also emerged, including *kagok* (lyric songs), *kasa* (narrative songs) and, latterly, *shijo* (sung short poems). The literati left many manuscripts, the majority of which provide notations for the *kŏmun'go*, and these tell us much about performance practice from the 15th century onwards.

Folk music

At the professional end of folk music, *p'ansori* (epic storytelling for solo singer accompanied by *puk* drum) and *sanjo* ('scattered melodies' for solo instrument and *changgo* drum accompaniment) remain particularly popular. *P'ansori* is a composite art form that combines song (*sori*), narration and dialogue (*aniri*), and simple dramatic action (*pallim*). Each *madang* (story) is long and can take five or more hours to perform in its entirety. Historical documentation is sketchy, and although *p'ansori* is considered to be an old musical form, we know nothing of it prior to a text dated 1751, documenting a performance. By the 19th century, *p'ansori* was popular amongst the middle and upper classes and had absorbed literary allusions and Confucian moralism. Five *madang* survive today—*Ch'unhyangga* (The song of "Spring Fragrance" or of Ch'unhyang), *Shimch'ŏngga* (The song of Shim Ch'ŏng), *Hŭngboga* (The two brothers), *Sugungga* (The underwater palace) and *Chŏkpyŏkka* (The red cliff). In South Korea a few new adaptations keep the old musical style, including Pak Tongjin's *Yesujŏn* (The story of Jesus) and Im Chint'aek's setting of the poet Kim Chiha's *Ojŏk* (Five enemies). In North Korea, *p'ansori* was disliked by Kim Il Sung. It was outlawed, and eventually a new operatic style evolved around the *P'i pada kagŭk tan* (The Sea of Blood Opera

Company). The first opera was called *P'i pada* (The sea of blood), setting the standards for works described as "immortal", since they relate the exploits of revolutionary heroes.

Sanjo is considered to have developed from *p'ansori*, folk songs, and the shaman music of Korea's southwestern Chŏlla provinces. Many claim Kim Ch'angjo (1865–1920) invented the genre. *Sanjo* was first played on the *kayagŭm* zither, but it was adapted for other instruments. Different master players developed their own schools, and six *kayagŭm sanjo* are today commonly taught in Seoul. *Sanjo* was once taught entirely by rote but, as training moved to university music departments in the 1960s, scores began to appear. *Sanjo* is now the most popular folk instrumental genre in the South, and a single performance can last around an hour. In the North, it is still taught but rarely performed. A performance consists of a sequence of movements, starting with a slow and emotional section following an 18/8 rhythmic pattern, and ending with a fast, jolly 4/4.

In rural Korea, egalitarianism and communal activities ensured an abundance of group genres. Folksongs (*minyo*) multiplied for work, entertainment and death. Folkbands (now known by the umbrella term *nongak*) were until recently used in village rites, for fund raising, farming and fishing, and entertainment. Some performers were amateur, and some were professional. Three folksong styles based on area are also distinguished: *namdo minyo*, from the southwestern Chŏlla provinces, are based on a sorrowful tritonic mode; *Kyŏnggi minyo*, from the central region around the South Korean capital, Seoul, are joyful and lyrical; *sŏdo minyo* once featured around P'yŏngan and Hwanghae provinces in the northwest of the peninsula, using wide vibrato and a lot of nasal resonance. Some scholars distinguish a fourth, Eastern area: *tongbu*, characterised by descending phrases. More popular songs took off with professional singers in the 1920s, a time when records began to be produced and sold. A similar amateur/professional division exists in folk bands. The three regional styles—*udo* around the rice plain of Chŏlla, *chwado* in the more hilly areas further east, *kyŏnggi* in the central Kyŏnggi and Ch'ungch'ŏng provinces—survive in festivals but are increasingly rare in the countryside. 1978, however, saw a new urban phenomenon. This was *samulnori*, a four-man band playing updated pieces from each region on the four basic percussion instruments, two gongs and two drums. *Samulnori* sit where local *nongak* bands stood, marched and danced. They play a repertory that develops sequences of rhythmic patterns in fixed time-frames, while local bands improvised around simple rhythmic models. *Samulnori* have proved remarkably popular. They have spawned several dozen professional rivals, and urban performances range from student groups to a massed band of 1100 that played at the opening ceremony for the 1993 Taejŏn Expo. The latter, in the words of one drummer, was indeed a "Big bang *samulnori*".

Music today

Approaches to music and musical instruments differ in North and South Korea. The South has, since the *Munhwajae pohobŏp* (Cultural Asset Preservation Act) of 1962, preserved and promoted traditional music. It has appointed 17 music genres, 7 dances, 14 dramas and 22 plays and rituals *Muhyŏng munhwajae* (Intangible Cultural Assets), all of which contain much old music. This sponsorship concentrates on what is dying, but it has certainly encouraged a revival: performances of traditional music are now very popular. The government has also maintained the high culture of the court, through direct sponsorship of the National Center for Korean Traditional Performing Arts, the direct successor to court music institutes going back to at least the 8th century.

The North began by adapting the principles of Socialist Realism. In Russia, Andrei Zhdanov had defined this in 1932 as both historic and dynamic: "Art must depict reality in its revolutionary development". Kim Il Sung promoted revolutionary songs and the marches of military bands, then programmatic music modelled on Russian composers. Chinese influence followed, first in the development of revolutionary opera, then as old instruments (*ko akki*) were 'improved' to increase their flexibility and allow them to compete with Western orchestral counterparts.

This, though, is not the whole story. The demands of socialist reconstruction and the headlong rush to modernise has meant that in both North and South Korea the dominant music culture is Western. Western music was first experienced 100 years ago as the hymns of missionaries and the bands of European and American armies. This new music soon sidelined traditional music in schools. The pervasive influence continues. In South Korea today, a Top-40 pop chart of *Han'guk kayo* (Korean songs) is published every week. Each song is modelled on Western equivalents, from ballads and 'unplugged' to reggae and rap. In 1990, there were 428 documented traditional music concerts, attracting less than 8% of the total nationwide audience, compared to 2719 Western music concerts. Korean music accounted for just 16% of recorded music sales. The import of Western individualism has led to a vibrant scene in composition, still largely modelled on the West. There are many active composers: 1539 composition BA majors were registered at 13 South Korean universities in 1989. Well-known composers include Byungki Hwang (b.1936), Lee Sung Chun (b.1936), Byung-dong Paik (b.1936), and Sukhi Kang (b.1934). Perhaps the best-known was Isang Yun (1917-1995). Resident in Berlin, Yun had a Europe-wide reputation. He was born in the South but was a regular visitor to the North, where an institute, the *Yun Isang ŭmak yŏn'gushil*, experiments with advanced Western-style composition.

Western culture may remain ascendant, but in both North and South Korea respect for indigenous music is slowly increasing. Nationalism contrasts the hedonism and rationalism of the West with emotional ties to things Korean. Ask Koreans what they appreciate in Western music, and they are likely to describe form, structure and order. But ask what appeals in Korean music, and typical responses will focus on feelings. Korean music tugs at the heartstrings; it alone reflects the air, the water and the soil of Korea.

Readings

Hahn Man-young, 1985. 'The origins of Korean music', *World of Music* 1985/2: 16-31

Keith Howard, 1989. *Bands, Songs, and Shamanistic Rituals: Folk Music in Korean Society.* Seoul: Royal Asiatic Society

  – 1995. *Korean Musical Instruments.* Hong Kong: Oxford University Press

Byong Won Lee, 1980. 'Korea', in *The New Grove Dictionary of Music and Musicians,* Stanley Sadie (ed.), 10: 207-208. London: Macmillan

  – 1987. *Buddhist Music of Korea.* Seoul: Jung Eum Sa Publishing Corporation

Byongwon Lee, 1993. 'Contemporary Korean musical cultures', in *Korea Briefing, 1993,* D. N. Clark (ed.). Boulder, CO: Westview Press: 121-138

Marshall R. Pihl, 1984. 'The Korean singer of tales', *Korea Journal* 24, no. 10: 21-31

Keith Pratt, 1987. *Korean Music: Its History and Its Performance.* Seoul: Jung Eum Sa

Robert C. Provine, 1984. 'Ajaeng', 'Changgo', 'Ching', 'Ch'ojŏk', 'Kkwaenggwari', 'P'iri', 'Sogo', 'Yonggo', in *The New Grove Dictionary of Musical Instruments,* Stanley Sadie (ed.), 1:36, 337-338, 355, 366; 2:443; 3:120-121, 157, 413, 886. London: Macmillan

Bang-song Song (trans.), 1980. *Source Readings in Korean Music.* Seoul: Korean National Commission for UNESCO

The Traditional Music and Dance of Korea, 1993. Seoul: Korean Traditional Performing Arts Centre

Recordings

It is not easy to find Korean music in European record shops, but the following are the main releases available on CD in 1996. In the list, romanisations have been left as they appear on the sleeves.

Corée: Musique instrumentale de la tradition classique. Ensemble Jong Nong Ak hôe. Ocora C558701 (70 minutes; ADD)

Korea: Ritual songs from the island of Chindo. Cho Kongnye/Kim Kirim (vocals) accompanied by other singers. VDE-Gallo VDE-756 (72 minutes; DDD)

Korea/Corée. National Center for Korean Traditional Performing Arts. Auvidisc UNESCO (57 minutes; AAD)

Shamanistic ceremonies of Chindo. Kim Dae Re with accompanists. JVC World Sounds VICG-5214 (69 minutes; DDD)

Music of the Kayagum. Soung Gumnyon accompanied by Chi Soung Ja. JVC World Sounds VICG-5018 (57 minutes; DDD)

Shimch'ongga. The Epic Vocal Art of Pansori. Jung Jung Min accompanied by Park Jong Sun. JVC World
    Sounds VICG-5019 (52 minutes; DDD)

Red Sun/SamulNori: Here Comes the White Tiger. ECM 521 734-2 (60 minutes; DDD)

6.3 Dance

Traditional dance

Dance has always been as popular as music in Korea. The two, indeed, have always gone
together, with dance the essential accompaniment of many pieces of music, from the stiff
movements characteristic of Confucian ritual and the restrained patterns of court dance to
the expressive actions of popular dance and the exuberant leaps of *nongak*, known
commonly as farmers' dance. Among Koguryŏ tombs, the Tomb of the Dancers in
Tonggou on the Yalu river, dated AD500-600, depicts a row of figures, both male and
female, on one wall. They are engaged unmistakably in dance. Their elongated sleeves,
covering their hands, are still an essential element in traditional Korean dance.

The presence of spectators in this tomb scene suggests that the dancers are performing
at court or in a noble household. By the 9th century, dances of exorcism, such as the
Dance of Ch'ŏyong, and dances associated with Buddhist chanting, brought from China,
had made their appearance in Unified Shilla Korea. In the following Koryŏ period (918-
1392), the displays of dancing at court, performed by women entertainers known as
kisaeng, were renowned for their lavish spectacle, in which music, singing and
movement all combined. Costumes and props were elaborate. The P'algwanhoe and
Yŏndŭnghoe festivals, with their strong Buddhist elements, celebrated yearly to entreat
heavenly protection for the nation, always contained dancing. In the 12th century
Confucian ritual dance joined the scene when the Chinese Song emperor Huizong
included dance scores along with the sets of instruments and music that he presented in
1116 to the Koryŏ court, in response to Korean appeals for guidance on Confucian rites.

The Chosŏn court (1392-1910) maintained the traditions of ritual and court dance. In
the 15th century, King Sejong (r. 1418-1450), who was a considerable patron of the
sciences and arts, ordered a revision and classification of all court music and dance into
three basic groups: *aak* (Confucian ritual), *tangak* (music of the Chinese Song and Tang
periods) and *hyangak* (indigenous or Korean music). A manual of 1493, the *Akhak
kwebŏm* (Guide to the study of music), described the music and dance of both the
Chinese and the Korean traditions. In 1759 the *Shiyong mubo* (Scripts of current dances)
for the first time gathered dance scores together. In the dance as well as the music
performed at court Chinese influence was strong, though it soon blended with native
Korean elements. Dances were classified as *tangmu*—Chinese style—and *hyangmu*—

Korean style. Both shared similar patterns of movement, with some variations in structure. This style of dance was exclusively under the patronage of the court. Costumes were based on court dress. Though lavish in its effect, court dance was extremely formal and allowed little scope for personal expression.

To these forms of traditional Korean dance—ritual, Buddhist and court—should be added popular dance forms, generally more vigorous and sometimes cruder that the first three. The dancing used in shamanist ceremonies of exorcism may call for ritual props and involve swirling and jumping on the spot. The dances accompanying the music of local percussion bands—*nongak*—demand much energy and skill: the participants play their instruments as they dance. Finally, masked dance drama, *t'al ch'um*, a combination of mime, dialogue, singing and dance, incorporates simple dance movements.

What is still performed

All of these traditional forms of dance are still performed, though court dances lost their original setting with the demise of the court. Confucian ritual dances can be seen three times a year in Seoul, when they are performed in two separate ceremonies to honour Confucius and once in another to commemorate the spirits of Chosŏn dynasty monarchs. To the accompaniment of grave music played on ancient instruments, a group of 64 dancers aligned in eight rows of eight bow to the left, right and centre and make slow movements with their arms and legs. In their hands they hold props that indicate they are representing first civilian officials, then military. The meditative and solemn mood encouraged by these ponderous movements has an almost mesmerising effect.

The Buddhist dance repertoire consists of four dances. Intended as expressions of various points of Buddhist teaching, they are commonly known as the butterfly dance, the cymbal dance, the drum dance and the dance of the eightfold path. Only one sect, the married T'aego monks, still performs these dances as part of religious ritual. One of the best places to see them is Pongwŏn temple near Yonsei University in Seoul. The butterfly dance and the two forms of the drum dance have been adapted and expanded to produce attractive and popular secular dances.

Shamanist dances have likewise become concert items, but still form part of the shaman's ritual that lies at the heart of the exorcism ceremony. The farmers' dance, which at one time had a role in village rituals and was performed only by men, now features largely as entertainment, often at folk festivals, when male and female dancers take part. *Kanggangsullae* is a circular dance associated with the harvest full moon. It is performed to singing, sometimes by women alone, sometimes by men and women. The masked dance drama has also lost much of its ritual connotation, but survives as a preserved form.

Court dance is nowadays seen only on stage. Its music and movements are preserved by the National Center for Korean Traditional Performing Arts in Seoul, established in the 1950s. Since the end of the 19th century a number of dances, for single or group performance, have been created out of older traditions. These include shaman's dances, drum dances and the popular fan dance.

A different approach to dance

For many Westerners the pleasure of watching dance or participating in it lies foremost in the physical skills involved and the use of the body to express personal emotion or interpret a range of feelings. Technical virtuosity is highly prized. Where Western ballet or modern dance has been taken over, Korean dancers will absorb some of the principles that underlie such dance. But the movements and spirit of Korean traditional dance are quite different.

The most characteristic pose is the suspended position, where the dancer balances on one foot with the other gently extended, while the shoulders softly rise and fall. As the tension and energy build up, the free leg rises a little higher, then is released in a downward movement. The foot comes down on the heel, with the rest of it following in a kind of caress of the floor. The arms are held lightly extended at shoulder height, with the hands pointing downwards or up and in. The shoulders move frequently in a pulsing movement that follows the cycle of inhalation and exhalation of breath. For a Korean dancer the centre of weight appears to be the area of the chest and lungs. From this perhaps follows the concept of the body as a single unit. No one section is allowed to operate in isolation from any other part. The body does not seek to reach a certain pose; rather it moves continuously through a series of positions. The recurring sequence in Korean dance is the creation of tension followed by relaxation. The stimulation of the emotions is intended, since the essence of dance is to convey an inner spirituality and joy.

One look at the costume of a Korean dancer will show where the emphasis lies. However splendid its texture may be, it is there to cover, not to display her body. The curves of the sleeves and skirt of her dress, usually the *hanbok*, reinforce the fluidity of her movements, rather than hinting at the form underneath. In effect, whereas Western dance extends the body outwards, through stretched, pointing arms and legs, Korean dance is directed inwards.

New forms of dance

Only in the early 1920s were new dance forms introduced into Korea. As in other areas of cultural activity—literature, painting and so on—some of the new concepts came in through Japanese practitioners. In 1922 Baku Ishii, a pioneer of modern dance in Japan, visited Seoul to present his *Dance Poem*. Several young dance students, notably Cho T'aegwŏn and Ch'oe Sŭnghŭi, were greatly influenced by him. They and others went on to create new forms that sought to incorporate the new techniques they had learnt with themes and motifs drawn from Korean dance.

Western ballet was introduced during the 1930s. After 1945 and liberation from Japan, ballet struggled to establish itself better in the South. In 1973 the National Ballet Company was inaugurated. The development of modern dance was stimulated by the work of Yuk Wansun, a dancer and teacher at Ewha Women's University in Seoul. She introduced the techniques of Martha Graham, with whom she had studied in New York, and achieved success in Korea with a modern dance drama, *Jesus Christ Superstar*. The department of dance she established at Ewha in 1962 has produced many dancers and dance teachers. It has, moreover, had the effect of giving academic status to dance, thereby raising the social standing of a profession once regarded as a lower-class occupation.

The dance scene in South Korea has been much more active since the 1960s, with the emergence of avant-garde dancers such as Hong Shinja, the creative dance movement, the establishment of a magazine, *Ch'um,* devoted to dance and the inauguration in 1979 of a National Dance Festival. Diversity and creativity are widely accepted and look set to continue.

North Korea

As with music, dance in North Korea since 1945 has been exposed to first Soviet, then Chinese revolutionary art norms, visible principally in the themes chosen—heroic actions against national and class enemies and praise for the North Korean leader Kim Il Sung— but also in the techniques absorbed. Ballet in particular displays strong Chinese stylistic influence. Dances derived from shaman dances and Buddhist drum dances are performed as concert pieces, but with movements and rhythms that diverge from the pattern of similar dances as they have developed in the South from these same sources. Organised mass dancing by children and young people on ceremonial occasions is as common in North Korea as it is in China. It is difficult to judge how far new trends in classical and popular dance have penetrated North Korean society.

North Korean dance circles have devised a system of notation, reportedly under the guidance of Kim Il Sung's son, Kim Jong Il. This notation, known as the *chamo* system, is based largely on letters taken from the Roman alphabet and on symbols representing parts of the body, such as the foot. Modifications to a letter or symbol expand the scope of the system. It can be applied equally to ballet, traditional Korean dance and folk dance from other societies, and thus makes a claim to universality. The system is said to be taught to school children, alongside lessons in music notation.

Whether under the influence either of this notation or of Chinese dance styles, or because isolation has produced a separate course of development, body movements and in particular hand gestures associated with Korean traditional dance are no longer the same in the North as those practised in the South, but tend to be more vigorous and angular.

References

Kim Kyoung-ae, 1995. 'Development of Korean dance since Liberation', *Koreana* 9, no.3: 56-61

Christine Loken, 1978. 'Moving in the Korean way: movement characteristics of the Korean people as expressed in their dance', *Korea Journal* 18, no.2: 42-46

The Traditional Music and Dance of Korea, 1993. Seoul: Korean Traditional Performing Arts Centre

U Chang Sop, 1988. *The Chamo System of Dance Notation*. P'yŏngyang: Foreign Languages Publishing House

Judy Van Zile, 1993. 'The many faces of Korean dance', in *Korean Briefing, 1993*, D. N. Clark (ed.). Boulder, CO: Westview Press: 99-119

7

VALUES AND ISSUES

7.1 The structure of dynastic society

Throughout Korea's dynastic history, a king stood at the helm of the state. He was the highest authority in the realm and ruled the country, at least in theory, as an absolute ruler. Unlike the Chinese emperor, however, the Korean king was never a 'Son of Heaven' a mediator between mankind and Heaven. Rather, the Korean king was always surrounded by a court of powerful aristocrats who effectively curtailed his authority. It is for this reason that the royal institution was comparatively weak throughout Korean history. This is not to say that there were no strong kings. An excellent example of an outstanding ruler is King Sejong, often called The Great, who during his time on the throne (1418-1450) presided over one of the most innovative and flourishing periods in Korean history.

According to the Confucian concept of rulership, the Korean king was supposed to be wise and just, a sage monarch who ruled through morality rather than force. Before and after ascending the throne, the king was constantly reminded of the high ideals of Confucian kingship by his teachers and advisers, all of whom had studied Confucian classics over many years. Such indoctrination was to safeguard against tyrannical rule. It did not always succeed in this aim, as the example of Yŏngsan'gun (r.1494-1506) shows. After a few tumultuous years on the throne, during which he carried out two bloody purges of officials, he was deposed and was never given a posthumous temple name by which kings were usually known to posterity.

The king, however, was not completely powerless where his officialdom was concerned. He could appoint and dismiss officials, remunerate faithful servants and punish wayward ministers. He also was the highest examiner of those prospective officials who had successfully passed the provincial and capital civil service examinations, which were based on the Confucian classics and were obligatory for all who sought a government post. Candidates finally had to demonstrate their abilities in the palace in the royal presence. The royal descendants were exempted from these examinations for four generations in order to prevent intrigue and family favouritism in government.

Korean public life was dominated by aristocratic families to such an extent that it is no exaggeration to say that the actual rulers of Korea were the aristocrats. In Korea's traditional society, social status was the major factor in determining a man's chances in life. Only someone of aristocratic status was admitted to the civil service examinations and thus had a chance to become a government official. In other words, political participation depended solely on high social status. Those who held office also had privileged access to the country's economic resources. It was not easy, however, to pass the civil service examinations. Many years of study had to prepare a candidate for this most momentous series of tests. Each official had a long education in the Confucian classics behind him, a circumstance that made scholarship a precondition for office-holding. The importance of this combination is acknowledged in the modern term 'scholar-official'.

The aristocracy was a relatively thin top layer of society. It consisted of few hundred powerful descent groups from which most of the successful candidates emerged. In Chosŏn times (1392-1910), the descent of an aristocratic group was patrilineal: it was traced through male links. It focused on an ancestor who usually had been a high official, and identified itself with a surname and an ancestral seat, for example, the Kim of Andong or the Yi of Chŏnju. In the course of time, such a descent group, often called lineage, developed into a complex social structure that consisted of a main line and various branch lines. To be able to trace kinship relations detailed records of the family tree were kept. These genealogies listed the names of the male members (daughters were listed under their husband's names) through generations and also recorded their major government positions and other memorable facts. These records, kept with great care in Korea until recent times, are an immensely important source for the social history of the country.

The most important communal action of a group based on the male descendants was the veneration of ancestors. On the anniversaries of the deaths of ancestors in four ascending generations (from father to great-great-grandfather), the direct descendants would gather to hold memorial services. Such occasions not only celebrated the fact of common descent, but also the communality among the kinsmen. The services therefore concluded with a grand feast during which special ritual food was eaten. (The habit of visiting ancestral tombs and shrines is still maintained in Korea.)

The aristocratic lineages of the Chosŏn period typically settled in so-called single-surname villages still preserved throughout the peninsula. Brothers and cousins sharing a common surname lived in close proximity. Each family occupied a walled compound accessible only through an imposing main gate. The men's quarters were immediately inside the gate, whereas the women were secluded in an inner residence to which no stranger had access. This living arrangement clearly shows the strict gender separation demanded by Confucian etiquette in which women were expected to keep the home and raise the children and were generally accorded lower status than the men The focal point of the village was the ancestral shrine. Here were kept wooden tablets inscribed with the names of particular ancestors, each functioning almost as a residence for the ancestor's spirit. The nearby hills served as the lineage's graveyard, the size and ornamentation of the graves indicating the social standing of those buried in them.

The daily life of the elite was regimented by the Confucian social code that defined a person's position within the family and lineage on the basis of his or her gender, age and relationship to past and present family members. The younger generation had to show deference and respect to seniors at all times. Only a truly respectful and dutiful son was believed to become a loyal subject of the king. The status of daughters was very low because they eventually married outside the family and thus were not recognised as permanent members of the families into which they were born. Marriages were carefully arranged as the elite typically exchanged women among itself to form formidable marriage alliances.

It belonged to the privileges of the elite to be fully literate. Literacy consisted of a knowledge of the Chinese classical literature, and all the writing was done in classical Chinese. Scholarship was held in high esteem. The Korean scholars were prolific writers of official and private records, and this is one of the reasons why we know today much more about the elite than the other social classes that made up traditional Korean society.

The elite could not have existed without the support of the two lower classes, the commoners and slaves. The commoners who constituted the majority of the population were mostly peasants. A commoner was easily recognisable by his simple cotton clothes. In contrast to the imposing houses of the elite, the peasants lived in straw thatched huts in rural villages. By tilling the fields, their own or, as tenants, those of the elite, they were the growers of a great variety of agrarian products, most importantly rice, barley and beans. Some commoners were artisans who produced daily utensils such as pots and pans.

The commoners were liable to taxation, compulsory labour in the community, and military service. Taxes were levied in the form of rice and cloth (produced domestically by the women). At regular intervals a commoner had to participate in public works such as road building and construction of government buildings and royal palaces. While this kind of work was usually done during the slack season, service in the military could be arbitrary. One man on duty had to be supported by two men off duty. Hated as the 'commoner's burden', military service was eventually turned into an additional tax with, at some points in history, every family having to provide a male person to serve in the military.

In the Confucian state the peasantry was regarded as the nation's mainstay, and thus commended to the king's special benevolence. Reality did not always correspond to ideology, however, and the life of the peasants was hard and rarely much above subsistence level. Nevertheless, some commoner peasants are known to have become wealthy, especially in the vicinity of towns where they could cultivate cash crops.

The commoners' role was, thus, predominately economic. They did not participate in the country's political life. Few of them could have received sufficient education to compete with the elite in the examinations. Some Confucian values nevertheless percolated down to them through simple literature illustrating aspects of a morally sound life, respect towards parents and obedience towards the state.

At the bottom of traditional society were the base people, the majority of whom were slaves. Constituting a large proportion of that society (some 30% in the 15th century), the slaves were called the hands and feet of the elite. As the property of the individual owners or government agencies they fulfilled an enormously important economic role. Some were the domestic servants in the large households of the elite, others worked in their masters' fields. They also staffed the various government workshops in which they produced the many items for daily use in the government and in the royal palace.

Slaves led a precarious existence which depended largely on the benevolence of their masters. As they could be bought, sold and inherited, it was difficult for them to maintain a regular family life. In order to keep the service requirements of commoners and slaves distinct, intermarriage between the two classes was impeded by law, but in the course of time mixed marriages became quite common. As a result of economic developments in the second half of the Chosŏn dynasty, slavery became increasingly unproductive, and government slaves were at last freed in 1801.

Readings

William T. de Bary and JaHyun Kim Haboush (eds), 1985. *The Rise of Neo- Confucianism in Korea.* New York: Columbia University Press

Ch'oe Yŏng-ho, 1987. *The Civil Examinations and the Social Structure in Early Yi Dynasty Korea: 1392-1600.* Seoul: The Korean Research Center

Martina Deuchler, 1992. *The Confucian Transformation of Korea: A Study of Society and Ideology.* Cambridge, MA: Harvard University Press

Roger L. Janelli and Dawnhee Yim Janelli, 1982. *Ancestor Worship and Korean Society.* Stanford, CA: Stanford University Press

James B. Palais, 1975. *Politics and Policy in Traditional Korea*. Cambridge, MA: Harvard University Press

- 1982-83. 'Land tenure in Korea: tenth to twelfth centuries', *Journal of Korean Studies* 4:73-205

- 1984. 'Slavery and slave society in the Koryŏ period', *Journal of Korean Studies* 5: 173-190

- 1984. 'Confucianism and the aristocratic/bureaucratic balance in Korea', *Harvard Journal of Asiatic Studies* 44, no.2: 427-468

7.2 Adapting to change in the 20th century

The transition to an industrial society is a crucial and traumatic time in the history of any nation. In the case of Britain, it took the better part of two centuries. Yet Western societies, including Britain, are still recovering from and looking for solutions to the resultant problems of mobility, the weakening of the family unit, rural depopulation, urbanisation and suburbanisation. South Korea has made the transition within a generation. Indeed, the speed with which it has accepted change is one of the most remarkable aspects of its recent history. The fact that it is still seeking solutions to some of the problems of transition is hardly surprising.

Seoul is today an enormous city with a tightly packed population of around 11 million, expanding suburbs and a belt of new, overspill towns. In 1990, a quarter of all South Koreans were recorded as living in the capital, while the combined area of Seoul, Inch'ŏn and the surrounding province of Kyŏnggi was home to 48.1% of the population. Other cities, though smaller, have grown similarly. Yet in 1955, well within the memory of older generations, three-quarters of the population lived in the countryside. By the year 2000, it is predicted, Korea's rural inhabitants will amount to just 12% of its total population. The proportion of land under cultivation—presently around 20% of total land area—continues to decline annually as more urban and industrial sites are created. These sites will in turn continue to attract rural workers away from agriculture, and the circle of rural population decline and urban growth will be reinforced.

Even before the migrations of the 1960s and later, Koreans had been moving around. In the 1930s, a number were drawn to urban centres as the Japanese colonial authorities began to develop manufacturing industry and laid down a rail and road system. During the same period the population was increasing, but emigration to the Japanese-controlled area of Manchuria in the northeast of China and to Japan itself absorbed the surplus. After the end of World War II, up to one million Koreans were repatriated from these territories. The Korean War drove many more from the North to the South. Without land, many of these displaced people settled in the cities.

The traditional pattern

The rural areas in the period immediately after the war might carry a dense population—around 1000 per square kilometre in some districts. Until the Land Reform Act, passed in 1949 but put into operation in the late 1950s, the majority of farmers worked the fields of landowners as tenants, and just over half of them owned no land whatsoever. The redistribution of land left it divided into many small farms. Some of these continued to be worked by tenants, but most were owned and cultivated on a family basis. The government's aim was self-sufficiency. Labour was provided by both the men and the women of a family. Tasks regarded as 'outside' tasks, such as building dikes for irrigation, ploughing, transplanting rice seedlings and harvesting rice, might in some places be assigned to the men, with women taking 'inside' work, such as tending the vegetable garden, raising silkworms, spinning and weaving cloth and processing raw foodstuffs, as well as bearing and nurturing children. Elsewhere, as in the Chŏlla region in the southwest, women would take part in rice transplanting (and are still seen doing this work in various parts of the countryside). Agriculture was barely mechanised. Standards of living and levels of education were generally low in the small communities in which rural people lived, often in relative isolation.

In such a society, the family was all-important as the basic social and economic unit. Its organisation and membership were clearly defined in the Civil Code, which ensured continuity through the requirement that succession pass from the existing head of the family to his eldest son. If there was no son, a boy, preferably a son of one of the father's brothers, could be adopted to fill this role. A daughter could never be heir to her father, since on marriage she left her family to join that of her husband. The unit formed by the father and his wife and their eldest son, who on his marriage was expected to bring his wife to live under his parents' roof, constituted the stem family. Younger brothers formerly also brought their wives to live in their parents' house for a number of years before moving out to form branch households. This extended household formed a joint family, which at its peak comprised three generations. In 1966, a revision of the Code required younger brothers to leave their natal household on marriage. The senior line of descent always passed through the eldest son. In return he alone had responsibility, reinforced by law, for supporting his parents in old age and he alone was qualified to perform ceremonies commemorating them after their death.

Such was the ideal of the traditional Korean family. For many households it was probably also more or less the practice. Migration out of the rural areas, which gathered momentum in the early 1960s, has altered the pattern, though it has not completely broken it. The eldest son is still regarded as the head of the family and his house, wherever it may be, forms a kind of family headquarters. Instead of his remaining with his parents, they may live on their own in retirement and, after widowhood, the surviving spouse will then move into the son's household. The three-generation household is less frequently encountered today.

The shift from rural to urban areas

Throughout the 1950s and 1960s, agriculture received little attention from government. Park Chung Hee, who seized power in 1961, resolved that industry, particularly export-led manufacture, should provide the generating force in South Korea's economic lift-off. (Only in 1971, with the inauguration of the *Saemaŭl undong* movement (New village movement; see chapter 3.5) did he examine the rural sector.) The need for labour in city-based factories was enormous. It was largely met by the influx of migrants from rural areas, many of them spurred by poverty and a lack of land in their villages. These newcomers, mostly young people within the most reproductive age group (18-25), helped to swell the population of cities. In 1960, the urban population comprised 28% of the national total. By 1975, the balance between the urban and rural populations was roughly equal (48.4% city dwellers, 51.6% rural residents). By 1990, the balance was nearly three-quarters urban (74.4%) to just over one-quarter rural. Another way of considering the question is to reflect that between 1946 and 1960 the urban population of South Korea more than doubled, from 2,832,000 to 6,997,000, but that the rural population remained almost constant. Between 1960 and 1985 the urban population jumped by a massive 20 million, to 26,443,000, whereas the rural population decreased by four million. During the post-war years, then, the growth in South Korea's population has occurred in its urban areas.

Until the 1970s, those who left the countryside were mainly young, unmarried men and women. Women were often in the majority. Younger sons formed part of the male contingent, but eldest sons also migrated. Where a head of family left, the whole family might have gone with him. The poorer sections of the community were more likely to be tempted to migrate, because of poor living standards, low income levels, limited economic prospects for themselves and inferior educational opportunities for their children in their home villages; though other reasons, such as changes in family size and composition, might also be influential. Particularly from the 1970s onwards, younger migrants might go in search of schooling. Those owning land in a village, who were still able to make a decent living from it, were probably less inclined to leave.

Migrants' experiences were often mixed. Their belief that their economic and social circumstances would improve at their new destination was not always fulfilled, as is evident from a survey of slum dwellers in Seoul in the early 1980s, which showed that nearly 60% had come directly from local rural villages. Lacking skills and education, at least two-thirds of these people could not obtain jobs in the capital. Nonetheless, despite improvised housing and poor amenities, migrants in general benefited from the higher incomes, wider range of occupational opportunities and chance of better education that urban living promised them and their children. The consequences for those remaining in their villages were also mixed. A drop in family numbers released more resources for those left behind, but it also meant that in the absence of the young and vigorous, a greater burden of farm work fell to the elderly. For example, in 1982, the rural working population aged over 50 comprised 23% of the total agricultural workforce, compared with 17% only a few years earlier, in 1975. The ratio of female to male agricultural workers also increased, thereby raising the dependency ratio in rural areas that had experienced net migration losses over a longish period. Latterly, from the late 1970s onwards, a greater number of elderly people have moved to cities, joining their sons and daughters who had migrated and settled there earlier.

Changes in family life

The other great changes that have overtaken the family in South Korea in the decades since World War II have been in its size and functioning. The traditional family was large, not just because two or three generations lived together under the same roof, but also because a married couple generally raised a fair number of children. The trend of large families continued until the 1960s. In the period 1955-1960, the fertility rate for Korean women, that is, the number of children a woman might expect to bear, was 6.3. Such a rate of population increase began to worry the economic planners, and as part of the first five-year economic plan initiated in 1962 birth control measures were promoted. The effect was fairly rapid: by 1973, the fertility rate had dropped to 3.9 children. By 1985, the average number of children born to a woman was two, spaced over an average of seven years. By the early 1990s, an average household size of 4.6 people suggested that families now comprise parents and unmarried children in a nuclear group, with no members of a third generation. The preference for sons nonetheless remains.

Various reasons have been suggested for the drop in family size apart from a willingness to use contraception. Marriage at a later age for both partners is one. Higher educational achievement by women and their desire to work outside of the home are other likely reasons. Added to that is the cost of putting children through school. Another factor that may also encourage smaller families is the cost of housing and the generally concentrated nature of the population of inner city districts. Many urban residents live in flats in high-rise blocks, either provided by the state or bought or rented privately. These flats offer convenience and security, but are not suited to very large families.

In the face of such changes in size and composition, the family in South Korea has undoubtedly taken on a different appearance, even if its basic structure survives. The position of eldest son and thus head of family is now seen as a dubious honour. Indeed, eldest sons are not popular as potential husbands, since the wife of such a man may find herself burdened with care of her parents-in-law and responsibility for arranging family ceremonies. Mother-in-law, on the other hand, seems to retain her power over her son's wife and is capable of controlling her activities and even her diet in the interests of family decorum and the younger woman's readiness for motherhood.

Readings

William W. Boyer and Byong Man Ahn, 1991. *Rural Development in South Korea: A Sociopolitical Analysis*. Newark: University of Delaware Press

Lauren Kendall, 1992. 'Changing gender relations: the Korean case', in M. L. Cohen (ed.), *Asia Case Studies in the Social Sciences*. Armonk, NY: M. E. Sharpe: 168-183

Kyong-Dong Kim, 1979. *Man and Society in Korea's Economic Growth*. Seoul: Seoul National University Press

E. S. Mason *et al.*, 1980. *The Economic and Social Modernization of the Republic of Korea*. Cambridge, MA: Harvard University Press: introduction and chapters 7, 11 and 12

Clark W. Sorensen, 1983. *Over the Mountains are Mountains*. Seattle: University of Washington Press

7.3 Korean women

The traditional view

Many would contend that a Korean woman's lot is not a happy one. The titles of three books in English on Korean women include, respectively, the phrases, 'Shamans, Housewives and Other Restless Spirits', 'Virtues in Conflict', 'View from the Inner Room'. Under the Koryŏ dynasty (918-1392), women enjoyed a measure of equality. But throughout the Chosŏn dynasty (1392-1910), they were forced to live under the constraints imposed by Confucianism, which are still reflected in the thought patterns of today. Confucianism is a closely reasoned schema for ordering and shaping society, in which the *illyun* moral imperatives separate the functions of husband and wife. In practice, in Korea it enshrined patrilinealism—descent through the male line—with relationships always divided between male *yang* above an unequal female *yin* (Kor.:*ŭm*). *Yang/yin* contrasts divide the cosmos, and go beyond sexual politics to include sun/moon, light/dark, dry/moist, and so on. In all cases, a balance was considered desirable between the two forces. In human society this meant that marriage was important. Since the required balance was not one of equals, marriage was essentially a kin transaction to acquire a woman's domestic and procreative services. Parents, relatives and marriage fixers (typically old women) chose suitable partners on the basis of family wealth, prestige and astrology, in the countryside often setting up arrangements whereby several sons and daughters would marry into the same family. Still today, over 50% of marriages in Korea are 'arranged'.

Picture the scene. An eligible bachelor was brought to meet the parents of a marriageable girl, perhaps together with a go-between. The daughter, head bowed, might serve a drink. This was the first sight the potential groom had of his bride, but propriety meant that the girl should not meet his gaze, continuing to look down. That was a typical 'first meeting' until the recent past. Today, where an arranged marriage is sought, a fixer provides photographs of potential spouses after first checking out their suitability. The couple might meet in a hotel coffee shop, where most discussion still takes place between respective parents.

The Confucian practice of patrilineal descent left women weak and vulnerable. Since male offspring alone ensured lineage survival, married women achieved status only as mothers. Still today, women's given names are often avoided; a girl, as the 'sister of X' (her brother), becomes a 'house person' (*chip saram*—wife), then the 'mother of Y' (her son). If a wife failed to produce a son, then it was accepted that the husband could take a concubine or a second wife. The family concern to perpetuate itself was of the utmost importance, for, without sons, who could carry out the ancestral observances required by Confucianism, which ensured continuing prosperity? Legal strictures in place since a 1921 revision of the Civil Code officially got rid of this disparity, but in Korea's countryside, old women can still be found who lived as concubines or second wives.

Girls were expected to be faithful and chaste (the terms *sujŏl* and *chŏngbu* applied). They should be exemplary women (*yŏllyŏ*). They were expected to be able to entertain guests and undertake household chores, roles which required little formal education. From the age of seven, strict segregation confined (and hid) women in the *an pang*, the inner rooms of houses. Women, through exogamy (which in the Korean case meant marriage outside their clan and the village of their birth), became part of a husband's family. There, they enjoyed no rights to inherit; indeed, this was the logic of the Confucian system. Keeping her virtue meant that even if a husband died his wife remained duty bound to his family. The remarriage of widows was scorned. Until the 1890s *Kabo* reforms (see chapter 2.3), women were not allowed to divorce; even then, although divorce was allowed if the husband agreed, a wife could not set up her own home. A divorced woman became a *kich'ŏ* an 'abandoned wife', not dissimilar to *hwanghyang nyŏ* ('returning woman'). This latter term had, since the 17th century, been reserved for women who made an unwelcome return to their natal home. (It had initially marked women sent away as tribute to China and Manchuria.) Disdain came from the perception that in marriage a woman should break all ties to her natal home. Long genealogical records, known as *chokpo*, were kept by families, tracing their history from its founder to the present day. A woman was marked down simply as 'wife of X family' in her own family *chokpo*, and her children appeared only in her husband's *chokpo*.

Korea also had a courtesan tradition going back many centuries. One early member of the profession of *kisaeng* (entertainment girl) was the poetess Hwang Chini (?-1544). *Kisaeng* were trained in the arts and manners for serving food and drink in institutes known as *kwŏnbon*. By the early 20th century many *kisaeng* had become little more than prostitutes. Some commercially produced picture books survive from this period, which detail the accomplishments of *miin*, the beautiful girls. Women who sang and danced in public had, though, fallen foul of the Confucian view of appropriate virtuous behaviour. Partly because of this, many *kisaeng* were recruited from the low echelons of rural society, particularly from the *ch'ŏnmin*, a socially outcast group of artisans, traders and entertainers ranked until the 1890s below farmers in the official hierarchy (see chapter 7.1). During the colonial period, girls began to work as cheap labour in new factories, both in Korea and Japan. The image of Britain's dark satanic mills would not be out of place; girls shared squalid barrack huts and worked long hours for little food. Parents and elders remained reluctant to let daughters undertake paid work outside the home; this conflicted with the old sense of propriety. However, the crisis of poverty and the low value placed on daughters conspired to attract the young.

As it is now

After 1945, change slowly began to occur. In North Korea, women were soon enlisted into the army of workers, much as in socialist states elsewhere, and a mirage of equality was quickly established. In South Korea, article 10 of the 1948 constitution guaranteed equality but, in respect to women, the state proved reluctant to allow this. The reason may have been a perception that to do so could engender conflict between law and social custom. Certainly, the Civil Code, promulgated in 1958 to take effect from January 1960, remained discriminatory: women acquired the right to inherit, but only half a son's entitlement; a mother and wife came third after sons and daughters; a woman had only limited parental rights, whereas a man could claim illegitimate children as his own; a woman could become household head only if there was no male heir.

In 1952, Tai-Young Lee became the first woman lawyer in South Korea. She dedicated herself to establishing women's legal rights, particularly in the area of counselling. Since 1956 her work has focused on her Korea Legal Aid Center for Family Relations, which has been at the vanguard of petitions to revise the family law. In June 1973, 61 women's organisations inaugurated the *Pŏmnyŏsŏng kajokpŏp kaejŏng ch'okchinhoe* (Pan-Women's Committee for the Expedition of the Revision of the Family Law), which became instrumental in persuading the government that change was essential. A revision was approved in December 1977. Now, in the absence of a will, sons and daughters could receive equal inheritance, except that the eldest son—whom tradition obliged to prepare and carry out appropriate ancestral observances—was to receive half as much again as his siblings. Married daughters received one quarter of their siblings' shares, and wives were now entitled to the same amount as the eldest son. Women also gained more parental rights, though the final arbiter remained the husband. And, if a woman returned to her natal home after divorce or bereavement, she lost her rights as a parent, a regulation which in effect meant that the husband's family kept the children of a broken union.

Clearly bias remained. In the 1980s, the increasing strength of women's groups, and campaigning journals which enjoyed wide circulation, led to further consideration of the Family Law. The most recent revision, in December 1989, addressed the issue of inequality, but continued to favour sons over daughters as family heads. There remain faint echoes of imbalance, which led the scholar Chungmoo Choi to remark: "Legal experts argue that [the revision] ameliorates only a certain *de jure* imbalance in practical matters and they expect that *de facto* discrimination against women may continue for some time."

In essence, the law has moved ahead of what pertains in Korea's conservative society. Why? Well, inequality is still widespread in everyday life. For example, one legacy of the colonial period in which the old and new collide is working girls, *yŏgong*. Old Korea considered paid work unsuitable for women, but in new Korea girls labour to supplement family incomes until—and prior to 1987 this was specified in officially sanctioned contracts—they either marry or get pregnant. *Yŏgong* have provided much of the labour for Korea's economic development, but as cheap labour they institutionalised a lack of training programmes and enjoyed few promotion opportunities. Thus, while women comprised over 40% of the South Korean workforce in 1991, they earned 52.7% of the average male wage. In 1991, the 50 top Korean conglomerates recruited 1200 women but 19,000 men to white-collar and management-track jobs. At the same time, domestic work was accorded so little monetary value that the average claim following the accidental death of a housewife was 276,250 *wŏn* (about £230). Again, women remained peripheral in the National Assembly until 1993; no woman, even if elected, was able to take decisions or develop her own policies.

A final comment. Until 1945, it was uncommon for girls to receive much education; they were excluded from Korea's only university. Although there were exceptions, parents saw little point in investing in the education of daughters who would soon be married off and leave their family. But in today's South Korea, a large number of women complete degrees. Education is valued; moreover, there is widespread belief that one can improve status through learning. Korean women are starting to move into prominent jobs; Lee In-ho, a professor of history at Seoul National University, was appointed ambassador to Finland in 1996, the first South Korean woman to hold such rank. Yet still few women occupy senior management positions: the old system of sexual mores will clearly need to change rapidly in the next few years.

Readings

Judith Cherry, 1989. 'Korean women's legal status: tradition and change', in Daniel Bouchez, Robert C. Provine, and Roderick Whitfield (eds), *Twenty Papers on Korean Studies Offered to Professor W. E. Skillend. Cahiers d'études Coréennes 5*: 45-51. Paris: Collège de France

Chungmoo Choi,1992. 'Korean women in a culture of inequality', in Donald N. Clark (ed.), *Korea Briefing ,1992*. Boulder, CO: Westview Press: 97-115

Martina Deuchler, 1992. *The Confucian Transformation of Korea*. Harvard: Council on East Asian Studies

Laurel Kendall, 1985. *Shamans, Housewives and Other Restless Spirits: Women in Korean Ritual Life*. Honolulu: Hawaii University Press

Laurel Kendall and Mark Peterson (eds), 1983. *Korean Women: View from the Inner Room*. New Haven: East Rock Press

Sandra Matielli (ed.), 1977. *Virtues in Conflict: Tradition and the Korean Woman Today*. Seoul: Royal Asiatic Society

Chunghee Sarah Suh, 1993. *Women in Korean Politics*. Boulder, CO: Westview Press

7.4 Education

Visit any home with school-age children in South Korea and you will become aware of the enormous place that education occupies in family life: long hours of study for older children and considerable financial costs for parents, since only the compulsory years of primary schooling are free. The more ambitious the parents the greater their involvement and the more intense the pressure placed on their children to do well at school. The goal of unrelenting effort and ever-recurring expenditure is admission to a good university, for beyond that can lie favourable career prospects and an advantageous marriage. Education, in short, is a way for the individual to get ahead.

The government's role

The willingness of parents to contribute as much as two-thirds of the direct costs of education, often through Parent-Teacher Associations, is of considerable benefit to the government. The greater part of the state education budget—about three-quarters—is devoted to the provision of free primary schooling. (In recent years, expenditure on education has amounted to about 20% of the national budget, equivalent to around 3% of GNP.) The needs of secondary and tertiary schooling are largely met by the private sector. For example, about 80% of all institutions of higher education are private. The running costs of education, moreover, are comparatively low. Class sizes have always been larger than those judged desirable in Western schools. In 1992, for instance, the average number of pupils in a primary school class was 40; at secondary level it was greater still, 50. In the same year, the average teacher-pupil ratio was 1:33 in primary schools and 1:23 in secondary schools. Teachers have long accepted fairly low salaries in return for tight classroom discipline and considerable social respect.

The government may not be prepared to fund education beyond a certain point, but it does involve itself in the direction, content and ethos of teaching. Education functions within a strong political framework. The right to education is enshrined in the constitution of 1948 and its 1987 revision and was expanded in the Education Law of 1948. The Charter of National Education, introduced in 1968, emphasised the moral purpose of education and its roles in nation-building and in fostering scientific and technological advancement. To this end, control over the entire system is vested in the government, working through the Ministry of Education and provincial and county boards. The curriculum for each stage, from primary school to university, is set by the government, and textbooks are vetted. Some subjects, such as the teaching of history, are considered particularly sensitive. The fierce anti-Communism of earlier post-war decades has now been muted, but military training for secondary school boys, instituted in 1969, continues (and these same boys are obliged to do national service after leaving school).

Parental pressure on places in the best schools has led in the past to heavy reliance on after-school cramming, an over-emphasis in the classroom on exams and considerable tension for children. The government has taken various steps to redress the situation. In 1968 the qualifying examination to enter middle school was abolished, and in 1973 entrance exams administered by individual high schools to 15-year-olds were modified in favour of a state-administered test. Both these changes encouraged more students to move up to higher levels. Private tutoring, which had flourished to supplement the lack of individual attention in class and thereby boost a child's chances of passing exams, was forbidden from 1980, but certainly persists. The sombre secondary school uniforms, based on the Japanese style of uniform, were abolished in 1983, though they are now reappearing.

Not all government measures have met with the agreement of families intent on securing the best chances for their children. Attempts to promote vocational high schools have been thwarted by parents who feel that academic high schools offer a better route to university. For the same reason, schools in Seoul are preferred to those in the provinces, and parents often do all they can to get their children educated in the capital.

Historical background

The tradition of Seoul's pre-eminence in education is an ancient one. Equally persistent has been the belief in education as a mark of status and culture. The earliest institutions in Korea for the teaching of Chinese language and Confucian classics are dated to the 4th century AD. The training offered at these and later colleges tutored male candidates—drawn almost exclusively from the aristocracy—for a protracted system of examinations, mainly in classical Chinese literature, that provided the route to government service. Only in 1895 were these examinations abolished as part of a series of profound reforms. Impetus for change came largely from Japanese advisors anxious to see Korea modernise, from Western missionaries (who from 1886 were permitted to set up schools offering a Western style of curriculum to both boys and girls), and from within the Korean government itself. From 1880, the government began intermittently to send teachers and students abroad on fact-finding visits and for instruction. In 1895, primary schools were instituted, followed shortly afterwards by middle schools. Local academies, which had provided elementary training in the Chinese classics, were forcibly closed, with the excuse that they threatened central control.

The Japanese, in their colonisation of Korea, maintained the school system but restricted Korean access to it. Primary education was widespread for Korean boys, but less provision was made for girls. Few children went on to further education. At the end of the Pacific War only 2% of the Korean population over 14 was found to have completed secondary school. Facilities for Japanese who lived in Korea were much better. The Japanese aim with the Koreans was to turn out loyal and productive citizens of the emperor, and these, they argued, would only need a basic education. By making Japanese the medium of instruction, by rewriting textbooks and confiscating those which dealt with Korean history and geography and, in 1938, by banning the study of Korean language and history in schools, they also hoped to eradicate Korean national sentiment. Some missionary schools were permitted to remain, but were kept under tight check.

When the Korean peninsula was liberated in 1945, the educational base was very low in both South and North. In South Korea, along with the organisation of formal schooling for children, illiteracy among 78% of the adult population had to be tackled. The US military administration of 1945-1948 in the southern half of the country began to institute a system of primary and secondary schools based on American models. This experiment did not survive the founding of the Republic of Korea in 1948. The Korean War (1950-1953) brought disruption and the destruction in whole or part of 70% of school buildings. Nonetheless, even during the war, compulsory literacy classes for those between 17 and 43 were introduced, and by 1970 the illiteracy rate had fallen to 11.6%. Education expanded throughout the later 1950s, though the shortage of schoolrooms often meant enormous classes and double or triple teaching shifts.

Organisation of schooling

Today, compulsory primary school starts at the age of six (seven in Korean reckoning), and may be preceded by one or two years of kindergarten, for which parents pay. In 1992, 40% of pre-school children attended kindergarten. Primary school lasts six years. Promotion through school is automatic, with no screening of pupils. Admission to fee-paying middle school is by lottery within the student's home district. All children are catered for, but choice is restricted. In this way, over-subscription of prestige schools is avoided. In 1993, all primary school leavers progressed to middle school.

After three years' middle school, students can take a state-administered high school qualifying test, with a choice between vocational and academic institutions. Admission to a particular school is again by lottery. In 1993, the follow-on rate from middle school was 98%. High school lasts four years, after which, aged 18, a student faces his or her big test of suitability for further education. Regulations governing admission to college were first introduced in 1968, when applicants were obliged to take a state qualifying test and then an examination administered by the university of choice. In 1981, the college exam was abolished in favour of admission based on a state test together with assessment of the applicant's school record. Seventy points were allocated to the test and 30 to the assessment. Further modifications were applied from 1994 that gave greater weight (40% or more) to school achievements and re-introduced a university-administered exam. The demand for college places remains insatiable. By 1991, the proportion of young people in the 18-21 age group in higher education stood at 42%. In 1993 a figure of 121 universities and colleges attended by over one million students was recorded.

Higher education comprises four-year undergraduate courses (six for medicine and dentistry). Junior vocational colleges run two-year courses. Although institutes have a measure of autonomy, they must submit to controls imposed by the Ministry of Education on student quotas, teaching qualifications and degree requirements and must include compulsory courses in Korean, at least two foreign languages, philosophy, cultural history, general theories of science and physical education. Military training is obligatory for male students.

Voluntary further education is provided through radio and correspondence schools, trade schools and evening classes.

The style of teaching in Korean schools tends towards lectures. Students typically recite information until it is known. Responsibility for progress relies on an individual's effort. Indeed, poor application rather than modest ability is judged to be the reason for low marks. All students are seen as capable of passing exams. Primary and secondary school pupils attend school for 220 days a year and put in long hours. High school students work for over 1200 hours per year (around 25% more than the average UK student) and may be in school from 7.30 am until 5pm, with a further four hours' study at school or a private institute in the evening. It is not uncommon to see pupils finally returning home at 10.30 or 11pm.

North Korea

The Korean enthusiasm for education is equally strong in the North, and results, in terms of provision of schooling and numbers enrolled, are as impressive as in the South. On liberation from Japanese occupation, 2.3 million illiterate people were recorded in the North, among whom women and peasants predominated. By 1949, it is said that illiteracy had been brought under control through a system of winter campaigns of 'Korean letters' schools and other types of schooling. Throughout the 1950s and 1960s adult schools existed side by side with universal education for children. The Korean War, as in the South, destroyed much of the educational infrastructure in North Korea: 72% of schools and 88% of classrooms were damaged. Schools were often reconstructed by people putting in extra hours after work. By 1956, compulsory primary education had been achieved, and compulsory secondary schooling by 1958.

Guiding principles of education

The content and ethos of education in the North are guided by very particular principles. In his *Theses on socialist education*, publicised in 1977 at a plenary meeting of the Central Committee of the Korean Workers Party, Kim Il Sung outlined the aims of education. These were to cultivate "revolutionary ideas, sound knowledge and a healthy body"—qualities essential for a good Communist. Education not in line with Communist ideas was "of no use at all". Schools must be punctilious in carrying out the correct educational programme, and teachers should display a proper ideological orientation. Kim set out four basic principles: Party guidance; the *juche* spirit of independence, which in the educational sphere meant learning first about "things of one's own country"; the incorporation of practice with education—knowledge for its own sake was useless; and state responsibility for the organisation of education. Elaborating on these basic aims, Kim went on to detail the methods and characteristics of the form of education he favoured.

While ideological instruction was to be paramount, it should be carried out by means of explanation and persuasion, he announced. A heuristic approach should be taken in teaching, that is, one based on processes of discovery, of discussion and debate and of question and answer. Education should include a measure of productive labour, though this should not predominate. Children's lives in and out of school should be filled with organised activities aimed at both social and political development. Membership of the Juvenile Corps and the League of Socialist Working Youth should be encouraged. School and family life should harmonise to produce an appropriate social environment. Even after the years of formal schooling, education should continue as a lifelong activity.

Framework of education

From Kim Il Sung's pronouncements and other sources, the framework of education in North Korea can be established. Schooling is compulsory for children between the ages of six and fifteen. (Presumably, as in the South, this is seven to sixteen in Korean reckoning.) A year's pre-school from four to five leads on to ten years' compulsory education, divided into four years' primary and six years' secondary tuition. Taken together, pre-school and the ten-year stint make up the 11 years' compulsory education introduced in 1972. Graduation is at 16, the minimum age for work.

Some students may go on to higher education, in specialised colleges offering two-to-three year courses or university, where courses last from four to six years. The basis for selection for such institutions is not clear, although Kim Il Sung's warning that Party considerations came into play in student enrolment at college level indicates that ideological reliability is an essential factor. A decade ago, in 1987, graduates of universities and specialised colleges numbered 1,353,000; but there are no recent statistics. Again in 1987, a total of 521,000 students were reported to be in higher education in North Korea. The ratio of male students to female that year was a little under 2:1. It is not known if this has changed. The only university in North Korea is Kim Il Sung University in P'yŏngyang, inaugurated in 1946. An education there provides a passport to a government or administrative job. Specialised colleges were eventually formed from relevant departments in Kim Il Sung University. A TV college was established in 1982. Arrangements for continuation classes for those at work are part of the educational system.

The state involves itself in the rearing of children from their earliest years through a system of nurseries and kindergartens operated on a daily, weekly or monthly basis. The importance of this "basic form of training Communists", as Kim Il Sung described it, was enshrined in a 1976 law. Although nursery is not obligatory and parents may rear their children at home, mothers are granted a fixed period of maternity leave, after which they are expected to return to work, thus making it extremely likely that they will entrust their child to a nursery. Indeed, one purpose of the universal provision of nursery care is to release women for work.

Information on the school curriculum is sparse, although emphasis on the *juche* spirit of teaching students to know their own country and society well can be taken to signify considerable periods of instruction in Party policy and traditions. Teaching in Korean language, history and geography, literature and music is compulsory and takes precedence over the history and geography of other countries. Technological subjects are taught primarily within a national context. The technical achievements of other countries are studied, but in a spirit of critical appraisal. Practical training in a subject takes up nearly half of the time spent on it. Some form of "productive labour"—presumably manual work—is part of the curriculum, as are daily exercise and instruction in music and the performing arts. Kim Il Sung's observation that the share of natural sciences and engineering in higher education should be markedly greater than that of the liberal arts is doubtless reflected in the balance of college courses.

In contrast to South Korea, where all but the years of compulsory primary education must be paid for, all education in North Korea is provided at state expense from nursery upwards. Students in higher education receive scholarships. Uniforms, textbooks, school stationery and other necessities are provided free. The funds for such expenditure are expected to be met through expansion of the economy. There is little way of knowing how far the above description of the educational process in North Korea still tallies with actual practice, or how far the scope of state provision for education is being maintained. The shortages of materials and foreign currency and general economic stagnation reported from North Korea in the past few years must presumably be having an adverse impact on the quality of educational provision in the country.

Readings

South Korea

Handbook of Korea, 1993. Seoul: Korean Overseas Information Service

J. E. Jayasuriya, 1983. *Education in Korea—A Third World Success Story.* Seoul: Korean National Commission for UNESCO

Noel F. McGinn *et al.,* 1980. *Education and Development in Korea.* Cambridge, MA: Harvard University Press

Edward S. Mason *et al.,* 1980. *The Economic and Social Modernization of the Republic of Korea,* ch. 10,'Education'. Cambridge, MA: Harvard University Press

OECD Economic Surveys, 1993-1994: Korea. Paris: Organisation for Economic Cooperation and Development

North Korea

Nicholas Eberstadt and Judith Banister, 1992. *The Population of North Korea.* Berkeley: Center for Korean Studies: 75-76

Kim Il Sung, 1979. *On Socialist Pedagogy.* Pyongyang: Foreign Languages Publishing House

Li Yong Bok, 1986. *Education in the Democratic People's Republic of Korea.* Pyongyang: Foreign Languages Publishing House

7.5 Nationalism

Koreans claim a 5000-year independent history as a homogeneous race, descended from the mythical Tan'gun (see Factsheet 2.1), who is said to have been born in the northern border mountain of Paektusan. This common ancestry, as it is proposed, means that Koreans North and South all believe re-unification is inevitable and regard all people of Korean descent, whether living in Kazakhstan, Uzbekistan, Japan, Europe or America, as Korean. Such a nationalistic view is wary of Koreans who enter into mixed marriages, and questions the import of foreign ideas and culture. Many Koreans claim that their strong national identity is a by-product of their struggle against Japanese colonialism, and south of Seoul a massive Independence Museum displays symbols of that struggle. This, though, does not tell the whole story.

Nationalism, wherever encountered in the world, is a modern, largely chimerical idea. The colonial period in Korea ended less because of an independence struggle than because Japan was defeated in 1945 by the Allies. The claim to independence judiciously ignores centuries as a suzerain state of China, the wholesale adoption of Chinese court culture, and numerous invasions by the Mongols and Japanese. *Kimch'i*, the pickled vegetables which seem so unique and integral to the Korean diet, have antecedents in Chinese methods of vegetable preservation and today include an essential ingredient, chilli, which is an American plant imported probably in the 18th century. Since the 1920s, shamanism, the indigenous folk religion, and the Korean language itself have been shown to have roots in Siberia (research was designed quite deliberately to demonstrate this, to find aspects of Korean identity removed from China and Japan). In North Korea, *juche*, the ideology of self reliance, ignores dogmatic allegiance to Soviet and Chinese socialism, while in South Korea, appeals to an indigenous identity ignore the rapid Westernisation which followed the Korean War.

What is nationalism? It is a political principle that found early expression in the French Revolution: "The only sovereign is the nation, man's first loyalty is to the nation, and the nation can alone make laws for its citizens." In nationalism, the state becomes congruent with the nation (two men are of the same nation if they share the same culture, land and associations). In biblical times, by contrast, the Israelites were followers of Yahweh with common ancestors, rather than a nation tied to a specific territory. In China or Korea, the character used for country, *guo* or *kuk*, describes the emperor or king speaking in an enclosed space. This, like the Israelites, suggests something other than nation, for under the Confucian system, the Chinese emperor and Korean king was head of state, above people who shared common ancestors.

The concept of nationalism first emerged in Korea during the 1890s. It appeared largely after the July 1896 formation of a *Tongnip hyŏphoe* (Independence Club), which led later and briefly to a political party known as the *Tongnip tang* (Independence Party). The Club argued five things that made it clearly nationalistic:

—*the concept of sovereignty*. The fourth of the Club's newspapers, the *Tongnip shinmun*, published on 15 January 1897, talked about independence and self-reliance of the nation. By November 1896, members of the Club had built an Independence Gate (the *Tongnip mun*, still standing) at the Seoul end of the road along which Chinese envoys used to travel. The newspaper also argued for the introduction of reforms in the legal code that would move control away from the king. It said that government officials should be servants of the people, not just subjects of the monarch.

> —*opposition to concessions*. The Club opposed privileges given, as a result of unequal treaties signed in the closing decades of the 19th century, to foreigners. These, it argued would undermine independence. Russia, Germany, America, Japan and the UK all wanted mining rights or coaling stations and port facilities.

> —*neutral diplomacy*. The Club argued against according preferential rights to any given country, rather like many of today's non-aligned nations.

> —*self-strengthening*. Korea was weak, because Koreans were weak. The people should be strengthened by gaining knowledge both of international affairs and of themselves.

> —*national culture*. Because Korea had followed China for so long, it needed to discover its own, independent, history (a five- volume history, the *Taedong yŏksa*, was prepared). Texts should replace Chinese characters with the Korean writing script, *han'gŭl* (see chapter 5.1). (In 1898, a national grammar was published, the *Kugŏ munbŏp*; before this, the Club had begun producing its own newspaper in the vernacular, the *Tongnip shinmun*.) Finally, a national anthem was needed (texts were published in 1896 editions of the *Tongnip shinmun*).

The Club folded in November 1898. After demonstrations against Russian interference and government corruption, a "plot" was uncovered in which leaders were said to have planned to proclaim a republic. Essentially, the Club had not produced a charismatic leader, and had consequently never spread beyond an urban elite to the peasantry; it never became a mass movement.

Nationalism was present in what became known as the 'Righteous Armies', groups which allied scholars (writers) to peasants (fighters). The first of these, the *Ŭlmi*, was set up at the beginning of 1896, after the assassination of Queen Min and the imposition of the Japanese-inspired reform programme (see chapter 2.3). It was conservative in its outlook and fought for independence and the preservation of Korean customs. More groups appeared in 1904 as Japan began moves to make Korea its protectorate. The 'Righteous Armies' became part of an armed struggle, engaging in bombing and armed confrontation. Further organisations sprang up in 1907, as Japan disbanded the Korean army. Guerrilla activity declined rapidly in 1910, as Japan asserted control. The nationalist struggle against Japan's colonial administration of Korea continued in a number of 'streams'. In Shanghai, the *Shinhan ch'ŏngnyŏndang* (Young Men's Society) called for public demonstrations. Other Koreans agitated for independence in America, and guerrilla groups were active in Manchuria and Russia (see chapter 15.4). In Japan, Korean students formed a secret society, in February 1919 producing a declaration of independence. In Korea, Christian groups explored Western ideas of freedom and education in meetings at Seoul's YMCA. Activists emerged within a new religion, *Ch'ŏndogyo* (the Heavenly Way). This was the religion that grew out of the *Tonghak* rebellion, and members were sent to meet with Koreans in Shanghai and Japan.

To Koreans, the most significant event in their nationalist development occurred on 1 March 1919, as a result of an alliance forged between these disparate groups. The February declaration in Japan was rewritten by Ch'oe Namsŏn, a *Ch'ŏndogyo* follower, printed, and distributed with the help of Christians and Buddhists. The death of the former Korean king, Kojong, provided a suitable event at which the Declaration of Independence could be announced: many people would be in Seoul, and the masses could be mobilised. So, at 2.00 pm, a student read out the declaration in Pagoda Park, Seoul. Along the streets running from the park, the shout of *"Tongnip manse!"* ("long live independence!") rang out. The leaders who had signed the declaration were in a restaurant, where they were promptly arrested by Japanese police. Marches and demonstrations began throughout the country. By the end of May, 1542 meetings had been held calling for independence, involving over two million people. 7509 Koreans had been killed, 15,961 wounded, and 46,948 arrested.

The declaration, and the size and ferocity of the meetings which followed it, caught the Japanese by surprise. Partly because of these upheavals, a new era began, moving from the first harsh period of colonisation to what became known as the *bunka seiji*, 'cultural rule'. Korean publications were permitted. Two newspapers, both of which survive to this day, began regular publication, the *Tonga ilbo* (East Asia Daily News) and *Chosŏn ilbo* (Korea Daily News). The inaugural edition of the *Tonga ilbo* announced it would "serve the masses" and promote the spread of "culturalism". Many journals were set up by youth, religious, social and labour organisations. These, in turn, encouraged Korean nationalism to move in two distinct directions. On the right, a moderate loose grouping emerged ,which came to be known as the *munhwa undong* ('cultural nationalist' is given in translation by the scholar Michael Robinson). The group utilised Kim Sŏngsu, the publisher of *Tonga ilbo*, as moneyman, Ch'oe Namsŏn, the publisher who had written the declaration, as publicist, the author and philosopher Yi Kwangsu as ideologue, and Chang Tŏksu as youth leader. Members established a new indigenous Korean literature and stressed myths such as the Tan'gun foundation legend and local cultural icons. They promoted the use of the Korean alphabet, *han'gŭl*, and tried to encourage self-sufficiency based on Korean production. They argued for gradual reform, for increases in education and capitalism amongst the populace. But in so doing, they showed themselves prepared to tolerate Japanese rule and found themselves discredited.

The claim to nationalism was made increasingly by those leaning more to the left, who preferred overt resistance to the colonial power. Radical Socialist and Communist groups developed. By 1945, five left-wing groupings were active: Koreans who had operated as guerrillas in Manchuria, those who had joined Chinese Communists in Yen'an and Soviet Communists around Khabarovsk, and local cells that gradually coalesced into the South and North Korean Workers' Parties.

The aftermath of 'liberation' was Soviet and American occupation, followed by the gradual emergence of two rival states (see chapter 3). Both needed outside assistance. Kim Il Sung in the North began with models for revolution: Stalin's Soviet Socialist Realism in art and culture as developed by Zhdanov but modified in Mao Zedong's speeches during the 1940s. Although marching one 'cultural nationalist', Yi Kwangsu, north to face trial for treason, the regime, too, soon abandoned Chinese characters in favour of the exclusive use of the Korean alphabet. Nationalism, now enshrined within the self-reliance philosophy of *juche*, meant the creation of a national, uniform identity based on an amalgamation of Korean and socialist models.

In the South, modernisation was equated with Westernisation. A number of factors led to the absorption of foreign models, amongst them the continuing presence of foreign troops, an education system inherited from Japan, and Christianity. The latter, with its appeals to the rights of man tied to European and American individualism, spread rapidly.

By the time South Koreans could pause to catch their breath, much of their overt identity had been lost. In a series of articles in the *Han'guk ilbo* (Korean Daily News), written between 1958 and 1962, the journalist Ye Yonghae sought to document what he regarded as dying traditions and introduced the idea of *In'gan munhwajae* (Human Cultural Assets), people who preserved old Korean arts and crafts. Ye lamented that most *In'gan munhwajae* were old, and nobody younger knew the traditions they had kept. In essence, he had taken up the mantle of 1920s cultural nationalists. Soon, in 1962, the incoming government of Park Chung Hee passed a law, the *Munhwajae pohobŏp*

(Cultural Asset Preservation Law), arguing that people must identify with their heritage if they were to retain any self-esteem and national pride as Koreans. The law allowed performance arts and crafts, *Muhyŏng munhwajae* (Intangible Cultural Assets)—in which the product could be displayed but the skill remained something studied and held by individuals—to be preserved alongside museum artefacts and old buildings. Today, there are 98 Intangible Cultural Assets, with some 175 Human Cultural Assets, each appointed to preserve, perform or make, and teach them in this government-sponsored preservation system.

To some extent, decline has been slowed or halted, and Koreans today recognise the value and importance of their own music, dance, rituals, crafts and even styles of food preparation. Whereas in the 1960s a middle-class urban family would have sent their children to piano lessons and played only Western classical music on their stereos, today they will probably have a CD collection including Korean folksongs and ancient orchestral music, and will accept that their offspring, as university students, spend countless hours playing traditional percussion music. To younger Koreans, nationalism has much to do with identifying with old indigenous customs. They prefer what they understand as the lifestyles of the masses of old, and so try to rediscover shamanism (rather than Christianity), rice wine (rather than just beer), and egalitarian *minyo* folksongs) and *nongak* (folk bands). This sort of nationalism spreads beyond customs, and has had much to do with riots and demonstrations against American culture in Korea. Donald Clark, writing for American students trying to understand this anti-American feeling in the late 1980s, described a typical scene:

> You have seen them on the nightly news: South Korean students hurling Molotov cocktails at phalanxes of helmeted riot police. While clouds of teargas swirl in the street, the narrator says something like this:

> "...Students fought police for four hours on the campus of XYZ university. [Cut to students burning an American flag.] Convinced that the CIA is pulling the strings, the students tried to occupy the sidewalk in front of the American Embassy. When they arrived, however, they were subdued by quick-response plainclothes police, who arrested them."

Nationalism in Korea, then, creates an image of a long-standing, unified, homogeneous Korea, divided by outsiders (the Allies) at the end of the Pacific War in 1945. On the negative side, because it rails against the wholesale adoption of Western culture, nationalism makes Koreans wary of globalisation. But on the positive side, nationalism has allowed Koreans to develop pride in who they are, and this, surely, has been fundamental to the building of the modern state which thrives today.

Readings

D. N. Clark, 1991. 'Bitter friendship: Understanding anti-Americanism in South Korea', in *Korea Briefing, 1991*, D. N. Clark (ed.). Boulder, CO: Westview Press: 146-167

Michael E. Robinson, 1988. *Cultural Nationalism in Colonial Korea, 1920-1925*. Seattle: University of Washington Press

Shin Yong-Ha, 1990. *Formation and Development of Modern Korean Nationalism*. Seoul: Dae Kwang Munhwasa

8

RELIGIONS AND BELIEFS

Buddhism, Confucianism and Christianity

The Buddhist temples, Confucian academies and Christian churches that dot the Korean landscape stand as visible reminders of the powerful role these three religions have played, and continue to play, in Korean civilisation. All three of these religions have become such an integral part of the spiritual as well as the architectural landscape of the Korean peninsula that they seem today to be just as Korean as the indigenous religion of shamanism which preceded them by many centuries. Yet all three were originally foreign religions that were adopted by the Korean people and then, over time, were adapted to Korean needs, values and beliefs, becoming Korean religions in the process.

Koreans first encountered Buddhism and Confucianism over 1500 years ago, when these religions were imported from China. Christianity came much later, penetrating the peninsula only a little more than two centuries ago. Yet all three have become so Koreanised that most Koreans no longer see them as foreign. Fuelling this adoption and Koreanisation of the imported religions has been a continuing search for harmony. In the case of Christianity, the goal is a life lived in harmony with the word of God. In the case of Confucianism, it is a life lived in harmony with our fellow human beings. In the case of Buddhism, it is a life lived in harmony with ultimate reality and with our own true inner nature.

8.1 Buddhism and 'ultimate reality'

'Ultimate reality' may seem too abstract a concept for anyone to organise their life around, especially when it is contrasted with the more concrete and down-to-earth guidelines found in the Confucian classics and in the Christian Bible. However, when Buddhists say that they are trying to live their lives in harmony with ultimate reality, what they mean is that they are trying to live always as though the world of everyday experience is not the real world.

To understand what Buddhists mean when they deny that the world of everyday experience is real, you need to understand what they mean by 'real'. They do not mean that if they stub their toes, they will not feel pain. Nor do they mean that a concrete wall is an illusion which they can stick their hands through anytime they want. 'Real', as Buddhists use that term, means unchanging and uncaused. Since we live in a world of constant change, and we as well as everything around us has been brought into existence by something else, we live in a world which ultimately is not real, at least in so far as Buddhists define reality.

This denial of the reality of the everyday world grew out of a search for an explanation of human unhappiness and suffering, and of the accompanying search for a way to end such suffering and unhappiness. The man who provided the Korean Buddhists, and indeed all Buddhists, with an answer to these problems was not a Korean but an inhabitant of South Asia around 2500 years ago.

Sometime during the 5th or 6th century BC, Sakyamuni, the man now known as the Buddha (a title that means the enlightened one, which was conferred on him by later generations), began trying to discover why it appeared to be impossible for him and for others to go through life without experiencing at least some pain and unhappiness. After years of wrestling with this problem, he decided it is life itself which is responsible. In others words, to live is to suffer.

He did not mean that people are unhappy from the moment they are born until the moment they die. He recognised that there are times when our lives are troublefree and we are glad to be alive. However, there are also times when we are disappointed and unhappy and even times when we feel physical pain. Such moments, ironically, are the inevitable consequence of our desire for pleasure and happiness. It is only because we seek pleasure that we are disappointed when we fail to obtain it. It is only because we want to feel strong and healthy that an injury or an illness feels so painful. In short, our desires are our downfall.

They doom us, moreover, to eternal suffering, since our desire to live can cause us to be reborn for another round of pain and suffering after we die. (The Buddha believed in reincarnation, as did most of those living in his society.) However, the Buddha believed that he had discovered a way for him and others after him to escape the cycle of birth, death and rebirth, and all the pain and suffering that entails. Since it was the desire for pleasure which caused unhappiness, if human beings could only eliminate their desires, they would no longer suffer. That meant eliminating not only the desire to feel good and avoid pain but also the deeper, underlying human craving for permanency.

Human beings want their moments of pleasure, as well as those objects and activities which give them those moments, to last forever. Since nothing in this world can actually go on forever, because of their craving for permanency men and women condemn themselves to frequent bouts of disappointment and unhappiness.

How could human beings eliminate all of their desires, including even the desire for life itself, and thus gain release from an eternity spent alternating between pain and pleasure? The Buddha's answer was that they have to stop taking life and the material world too seriously. They have to develop an attitude of detachment, in which they observe the world around them, with its trials and tribulations as well as its delights and gratifications, without demanding that it provide them with a consistency and a permanency it cannot provide. They have to realise that ultimately the world is not real.

This is the basic message of Buddhism. However, in the centuries between the Buddha's sermons and the arrival of Buddhist missionaries in Korea eight centuries later, much was added. As Buddha's followers gradually spread his message throughout India, southwards, up into Central Asia and over into China, they elaborated on the theological, philosophical and psychological ramifications of his musings.

Some of those elaborations appeared in *sutra*s, the scriptures of Buddhism, many of which offer the intellectually inclined a philosophical approach to cultivating detachment. Complicated analyses of the nature of the world and of the human mind were supposed to help those pursuing detachment to understand better the world of change and causation in which they were immersed so they could break free of the illusions of permanency and stability.

Other *sutra*s offered a different approach, that of devotion either to Buddha in one or more of his manifestations or devotion to some of his disciples who, having achieved a measure of enlightenment, had vowed to help the less enlightened avoid being reborn back into the world of suffering after they died. In many of these *sutra*s, Buddha, though he walked the earth at a particular place and at a specific time as the human being Sakyamuni, was portrayed as a human incarnation of ultimate reality, sharing transcendent Buddhahood with such others as Vairocana, the Creator and Lord of the Cosmos, and Amitabha, the Lord of Paradise. In yet other *sutra*s, the focus of attention was on *bodhisattva*s, beings who had earned release from the realm of suffering but, out of compassion for the less advanced, had postponed their own final emancipation in order to offer assistance to others who wished to reach that same goal. (One could regard them as analogous to saints in the Christian tradition.) Avalokiteshvara (Kwanŭm or Kwanseŭm in Korean), the *bodhisattva* of unlimited compassion in the here and now, and Maitreya, the *bodhisattva* who promised a better world in the future, were objects of particularly strong popular devotion.

After Buddhism reached China, a third approach to Buddhist salvation appeared, one which did not rely heavily on *sutra*s. Meditative Buddhism, known in the West by its

Japanese name of Zen (the Korean term is Sŏn), emphasised neither intellectual understanding nor devotion but the stilling of the mind. Meditative Buddhists practised sitting quietly and eliminating thoughts, particularly those thoughts which reflect the craving for permanency and encourage emotional attachment to the things of this world.

All three approaches reached Korea, with the intellectual and meditative approaches more popular among those who withdrew from the secular world into monastic communities, and the devotional approach more popular among the general population. These differing presentations of Buddhist doctrine are seen as complementary rather than contradictory, with each *sutra* or approach seen as pointing to only one of many ways in which the teachings of the Buddha can be interpreted. Buddhists believe that the eternal truths of Buddhism are to be found in the totality of Buddhist scripture, not in one specific text. That is why, when the Koryŏ dynasty, in the 13th century, wanted to preserve the most important scriptures of the Buddhist religion in a more permanent form than paper, they felt compelled to transfer texts on to more than 81,000 separate wooden printing blocks. And that is why monks in Korea's Buddhist seminaries today are required to study intensively not just one but many different *sutra*s as well as other Buddhist writings from past centuries.

How strong a religion?

Buddhism first penetrated Korea during the Three Kingdoms period, being welcomed into Koguryŏ in 372, Paekche in 384 and Shilla in 527 (these are the traditional dates and may not be accurate). At first it was a religion for the elite, supported by the government, but soon it began to gain popular support as well. Though official support for Buddhism began to wane after the Chosŏn dynasty replaced the Koryŏ dynasty in 1392, Buddhism survived in monasteries in the mountains of the peninsula and even flourished as part of the folk religion which prevailed in Korea's villages.

In the late 20th century, Buddhism has regained its vitality and its place as one of the most important religions in Korea. In fact, more and more Koreans are willing to call themselves Buddhists today than were willing to do so 70, 30 or even ten years ago. In the 1920s and the 1930s, when Korea was under Japanese rule, less than 200,000 Koreans in the entire peninsula identified themselves as Buddhists to government census takers. After the double traumas of Japanese rule and the Korean War, that number rose dramatically to almost 700,000 followers by 1962 in South Korea alone. Buddhists were nonetheless outnumbered by Christians, who claimed 1.3 million South Korean adherents that same year.

As the number of Christians has grown over the last three decades, the number of Buddhists has grown even faster. A 1991 survey found that the Buddhist population had surpassed the Christian population for the first time in modern Korean history. Of the 54% of the entire South Korean population who claimed a religious affiliation, over half (51.2%) called themselves Buddhists, compared to the 45% who said they were Catholic or Protestant. Those figures may be misleading, however. The growth in the numbers of those who identify themselves as Buddhists to census takers may reflect more their adoption of the Christian practice of proclaiming a specific religious orientation than a real growth in the numbers of those who frequent Buddhist temples, read Buddhist publications, or believe in Buddhist ideas and ideals. Buddhism has been such an integral part of Korean culture for so long that, until the Christian challenge, most followers did not feel they needed to identify themselves specifically as Buddhists. Now, however, as Korea nears the end of the 20th century, over one out of every four South Koreans proudly proclaims him or herself a follower of the Buddha. Korean Buddhism clearly cannot be dismissed as a religious relic of Korea's past, doomed to disappear into irrelevancy as Korea modernises.

8.2 Confucianism: a deeply rooted code

That census figures may not tell the whole story is also evident in the case of Confucianism. In 1991, government census takers found only around 440,000 Koreans, most of them older rural men, who identified their religious affiliation as Confucian. That is less that 1% of the total South Korean population of more than 44 million. Yet any Westerner who visits Korea will notice right away that much of the South Korean population seems to holds values, beliefs and attitudes that are quite different from those prevailing in Europe and America and which appear to reflect the Confucian emphasis on living in harmony with our fellow human beings, often at the expense of individual autonomy.

For example, in the early 1990s, 45% of all Korean parents rejected the notion that a son had the right to choose for himself whom he would marry. In accordance with Confucian tradition, they believed that parents not only had the right to veto their son's choice but also had an obligation to pick a bride for him (that is, if the son didn't find anyone first!) That belief in parental prerogatives was even stronger in the case of daughters. More than half would deny their daughters the right to choose their own husbands without parental interference.

Most Korean families, moreover, believe a departed parent or grandparent should be honoured on the anniversary of their death with some sort of ritual, usually a modified form of the traditional Confucian ritual often mistakenly referred to in English as ancestor worship. Koreans do not worship their ancestors but they do believe they should show respect for them.

Another characteristic Korean attitude often attributed to the influence of Confucianism is respect for education. Some surveys have shown that over 90% of Korean parents want their sons to have a university education. Only about 70% want their daughters to receive the same education. This is many more than did in the first half of this century but nevertheless reflects the lingering legacy of the Confucian bias in favour of sons.

What is Confucianism, that it has had such a strong influence on Korean attitudes and values? Like Buddhism, it entered Korea from China over 1500 years ago, although, unlike Buddhism, it is Chinese rather than South Asian in origin. Confucius (551-479BC) himself lived 1000 years before that, lecturing on ethics and tradition in China at around the time the Buddha was searching in South Asia for the solution to the problem of human suffering.

Confucianism was probably first imported into Korea by the same Buddhist monks who introduced Buddhism. At that time Confucianism, like Buddhism, was an integral component of the Chinese civilisation which Koreans were taking as the model for the transformation of their early tribal federations into kingdoms. Confucianism was seen as primarily an ethical and political philosophy, a this-worldly complement to the Buddhist focus on the reality beyond this world. Confucianism provided specific ritual and ethical rules governing relations between one human being and another, and it provided a canon of books which offered guidance for both interpersonal and political behaviour.

These included the ancient histories, ritual texts and poetry of China, as well as the collected sayings of Confucius and his most important disciple, Mencius (372-289BC). Koreans found in these books a reinforcement of certain ethical codes which they probably already valued, such as respect for social hierarchy, ancestors and tradition, and a belief that the overall good of the group is more important than the individual needs and wishes of that group's members.

Confucian ethics are centred around the pursuit of social harmony, primarily by assigning each member of society a particular function within that society. These social roles and responsibilities are epitomised by the Five Relationships and the ethical guidelines which govern these relationships. The most important relationship is that between a ruler and his subject, with the ruler enjoined to treat his subject benevolently and the subject enjoined to be loyal to his ruler. The next is that between a father and a son, with the father enjoined to be firm in raising his son and the son enjoined to be obedient and filial toward his father. The relationship between an elder brother and a younger brother is similar, with the elder brother given the responsibility of helping his younger brother become a responsible adult and the younger brother given the obligation of respecting his older brother. The relationship between a husband and a wife is also considered important, with the wife told to obey her husband and the husband to guide his wife well. The last of the five relationships is the only relationship of equality, that between friends. Friends are told that they should be honest with each other.

As can be seen from the Five Relationships, Confucian ethical principles are based on the assumption that society is organised hierarchically. Not all roles are equal in a Confucian society. Moreover, since a person's standing is defined by what role he or she plays (who must obey him or her and whom he or she must obey), seldom are two individuals considered equal. Relative social ranking is determined by differences of age (generally, the older you are, the more respect you are granted), sex (males are generally ranked higher than females), education (the more educational credentials you possess, the higher up the social ladder you are) and occupation (those engaged in mental labour are generally considered to rank above those engaged in physical labour).

Even today Koreans are constantly reminded that their identity comes more from the groups they belong to and the ranks they hold in those groups than from their own individuality. For example, when giving their names, Koreans list their family name first and then their personal name, emphasising that they are part of a family (a practice they share with the Chinese). Moreover, family titles often replace first names, with in-laws or acquaintances often addressing a mother as 'the mother of so-and-so' (so-and-so generally being the firstborn son), rather than using her given name. And younger siblings address their older siblings as 'older brother' or 'older sister', preferring the title to the given name. At the work place as well, Koreans usually address co-workers by their titles, such as 'Section Chief Kim' or 'Bureau Chief Lee', or, informally, as 'older brother' or 'older sister'. To use the personal name of a co-worker, especially of a superior, would be considered extremely impolite.

There are other ways as well for a person to show that he is aware of his place on the social ladder. For example, young people are not supposed to smoke in the presence of their elders or superiors. Bowing also shows respect. You bow more deeply to someone with higher status. Moreover, when you hand something to a superior, you use both hands, but you use only one hand when dealing with an inferior. And, when you speak to a superior in Korean, you use more polite language than you would use when you speak to a friend or to someone with a lower status than you. Even a child must remember to use more respectful language towards his parents, and they would not address him as an equal.

Confucian influence remains so strong that it would be quite unusual for a Korean to decide that he didn't want to go along with society and chose to be non-conformist, since to do so would not only subject him to public censure, but would cause problems for his family as well. How a person behaves can affect the reputation of his parents, his siblings and his children. In a society which values the family so highly, that is a powerful deterrent to anti-social behaviour.

A religion or an ethical code?

If Confucianism was merely concerned with such ethical principles as those outlined above, it would only be a moral philosophy, not a religion. Since it does not preach belief in a God or other spiritual beings and has no clergy or sacred scriptures, it does not resemble the religions that others are used to, such as Christianity, Buddhism or Islam. Therefore, some people deny that Confucianism is a religion. However, Confucianism underwent a transformation in China in the 12th century and developed into what Western scholars called Neo-Confucianism. When the transformed teaching reached Korea in the 14th century, it soon began to replace Buddhism as the dominant belief system on the peninsula and, for the next five centuries, operated as the functional equivalent of a religion. That is to say, it began to supply answers to questions it had ignored before, such as what ultimate reality is, the difference between life and death and the origin of evil, questions which all great religious have had to grapple with.

Neo-Confucian scholars were bothered by the Buddhist assertion that this world in which we live is not ultimately real. If this world is not real, then our moral obligations are not real either. That was an unacceptable conclusion for men who took their ethical responsibilities seriously. Therefore they looked for a way to provide philosophical support for Confucian ethics and to contradict the Buddhist definition of ultimate reality. They found their answer in a philosophy of *li* and *qi* (*ki* in Korean). They argued that, contrary to what the Buddhists teach, it is in fact change which is real, or rather, the patterns which those changes take constitute ultimate reality.

They admitted that the world in which we live is in constant flux and moreover, that everything that exists in this world depends for its existence on everything else in the world. However, for Neo-Confucians it is universality of change and causation which defines reality. After all, who can deny that it is realistic to expect that a son will someday change into a father? And who can deny that the fact that a man is called a son is caused by the fact that he has a father, and the fact that he is later called a father is caused by the fact that he has fathered a son?

Those patterns of change which determine when a man who was called a son begins to be called a father are *li*. *Li* is sometimes translated into English as 'principle' but it actually refers to natural patterns in nature and society, patterns which we should follow in our daily lives, just as a jade carver must work with the natural grain of a piece of jade if he wants to produce a carving (the original meaning of the word *li* is 'the veins in a piece of jade'). In the case of nature and society, it is *qi* which contains the patterns. *Qi* (*ch'i* is the older, Wade-Giles romanisation, as in *t'ai ch'i*) is usually translated as material force or as matter-energy, since is both shapeless matter and free-floating energy until it is given direction, shape and purpose by *li*.

This may seem quite abstract, but to the devout Neo-Confucians of the Chosŏn period, it provided the justification and the motivation for some concrete changes in their society. For example, they believed that the pattern which should govern male-female relations placed men above women. Therefore they began redesigning Korea's traditional family structure in order to reflect the *li* of patriarchy. Since they controlled the government during the Chosŏn dynasty, they were able to change the laws to prohibit women from performing the ancestor memorial rituals. Once they had done that, they changed the laws to reflect the assertion that, since daughters no longer had any ritual obligations, they did not need to inherit as much of their father's property as their brothers did.

There were other changes as well, such as allowing a man only one primary wife at a time and barring the sons of secondary wives from serving in prestigious government posts. Whether or not Neo-Confucianism was a religion, believers in Neo-Confucianism certainly acted with religious zeal in trying to transform Korean society to make it conform to their ideals and values.

This Neo-Confucian insistence on the ultimate reality of the world in which we live, and the accompanying Neo-Confucian devotion to promoting social harmony within a hierarchically patterned human community, overpowered Buddhism during the Chosŏn dynasty and formed the dominant ethical and philosophical perspective of Korea's ruling elite from the 15th to the 19th centuries. As the 20th century draws to an end, however, Neo-Confucianism no longer dominates Korean religious and philosophical life. A new teaching has risen to prominence, one that accepts much of the Confucian moral code but rejects the philosophical scaffolding which Neo-Confucianism had erected to support it. That new challenger is Christianity.

8.3 Christianity—late arrival and rapid growth

In the most recent government survey, close to 11 million Koreans called themselves Christians, only a million less than those who proclaimed faith in Buddhism. Today almost one out of every four South Koreans terms himself or herself a Christian, a remarkable statistic, since Christianity arrived in Korea a little more than two centuries ago and as recently as half a century ago could claim the allegiance of only slightly more than one out of every 50 Koreans.

These large numbers are particularly surprising considering the neighbourhood surrounding Korea. In neither China nor Japan do Christians make up more than 1% of the population. The only other nations in Asia and the Pacific with substantial Christian populations are either inhabited chiefly by immigrants from historically Christian nations of Europe or spent centuries under the colonial influence of such nations. Unlike Australia and New Zealand, Korea does not have a large number of citizens of European descent. Nor was Korea colonised by a European power, as Vietnam and the Philippines were. Yet Christians have become over the past few decades a significant part of the South Korean population. How did this happen?

The beginnings of Christianity on the Korean peninsula were inauspicious, and the first century was one of bloody persecution, not rapid growth.

It all began when a young Confucian scholar named Yi Sŭnghun (1756-1801) returned from Beijing, where he had accompanied his father on a diplomatic mission, and announced to his friends that he had been baptised a Catholic by a French priest who lived in the Chinese capital. At that point there were no Catholic missionaries in Korea, so Yi Sŭnghun began preaching his new faith on his own. Yi quickly converted quite a few other Confucian scholars. That was when his troubles began.

Male members of the Chosŏn Confucian scholarly elite were required to perform mourning rituals when their parents died. Catholics, however, were forbidden to perform or participate in such rituals, since authorities in Rome had ruled that such rituals were a form of ancestor worship and thus were banned as idolatrous. When the mother of Yun Chich'ung (1759-1791) died, and Yun, a convert to Catholicism, did not perform a proper Confucian memorial service for her, he and his fellow Korean Catholics were immediately attacked as perverted followers of an immoral religion. Yun was sentenced to death by the Neo-Confucian government in Seoul for his violation of Confucian moral principles, becoming Korea's first Christian martyr.

He was not to be the last. Thousands more were martyred over the next century, so many that Pope John Paul II travelled to Korea in 1984 to honour their memory by elevating 103 of those martyrs to sainthood, giving Korea more officially recognised Catholic saints than any other non-European nation.

When the first Protestant missionaries arrived in Korea in 1884, a hundred years after the first conversions to Catholicism, they escaped the persecution which Catholics had been forced to endure by presenting themselves more as modernisers than as missionaries. Within a decade of their arrival in Korea, American and Canadian Protestant churches had opened Korea's first modern medical facilities and schools. One of those schools, the first in Korea to provide formal education for women, later grew into Ehwa Women's University, and the first hospital they opened is now the Severance Hospital and Medical School affiliated with Seoul's Yonsei University.

Protestant missionaries were fortunate in that they first appeared in Korea at a time when the Korean government, under unprecedented threats to its sovereignty from both China and Japan, was beginning to realise that it needed Western technology. The king and his officials turned a blind eye to their proselytising activities in order to take advantage of their knowledge of the modern world and modern technology. Soon Catholics, too, were able to benefit from this new religious freedom, as did representatives of the Church of England.

Bishop C. John Corfe was the first Anglican missionary in Korea, arriving in 1890. Adopting the strategy pioneered by the Presbyterians and Methodists from North America, he quickly established the Anglican Church in Korea as a modernising force. Besides preaching the word of God, he and his fellow missionaries established orphanages, schools and hospitals throughout the Korean peninsula and, through them, began winning converts. The Korean Anglican Church has not grown as fast as other branches of Christianity in Korea, and its 58,000 members are but a small part of the almost 11-million-strong Korean Christian community. Nevertheless, Anglicans, with over 100 churches, are now a permanent part of the Korean religious landscape. In 1993, Bishop Simon Soung Soo Kim was appointed the first primate bishop of the Korean Province, which was granted its independence from the Church of England in April of that year.

Unfortunately, there is much disagreement among Korean Christians over how the word of God as revealed in the Bible is to be interpreted. In the consequent lack of harmony in the Korean Christian community, Catholics disagree with Protestants, Presbyterians disagree with Methodists, and Presbyterians disagree with other Presbyterians. The latter, who comprise almost 60% of all Protestants in South Korea, can choose from 74 different denominations, each claiming to represent true Korean Presbyterianism! At least eight of those groups claim over 100,000 followers each. If a Korean Christian doesn't feel comfortable with one of the Presbyterian interpretations of the word of God, he can turn to the Korean Methodist Church, the Jesus Korea Holiness Church, the Korea Baptist Convention, the Salvation Army, or the Full Gospel Church, to list just the major Protestant groups. Competition among all these varieties of Christianity has fuelled much of the remarkable growth of Protestant Christianity since 1960, from less than 500,000 baptised Christians in 1962 to a little more than 8 million in 1991.

The proselytising fervour of Korea's Protestants is one reason that almost one out of five South Koreans is now a Protestant. Another may be the rapid urbanisation and industrialisation of the Republic of Korea, which has torn millions of Koreans out of villages where they had been surrounded by family and friends and placed them in an impersonal urban environment. Churches provide an oasis of friendship and community in that desert of strangers. This could account for the far greater number of conversions to Christianity in the cities than in the countryside, and explain why the rate of growth for Protestant churches has recently slowed as the pace of urbanisation has slowed. A third factor could be that Christianity has been identified in Korea with the West, and with the modernisation and nationalism which interaction with the West has brought Korea this century. Since Christianity is often seen by South Koreans as part and parcel of the modern world, a modern world which is often indistinguishable in their eyes from the Western world, the more education South Koreans receive, and the greater the extent to which they hold modern or Western ideas and values, the more likely they are to be Protestant.

Many of the same factors which have fuelled Protestant growth since the end of the Korean War have ignited a rapid increase in the number of Korean Catholics as well. In addition, Catholic welfare organisations were some of the most effective in helping Korean War refugees with food, clothing, and housing in the 1950s. In gratitude, many Koreans began to take the Catholic version of Christianity more seriously and a church with only a little more than 200,000 believers in 1954 began to grow rapidly. Spurred by two visits by Pope John Paul II (in 1984 and 1989), growth accelerated in the 1980s. By 1993 there were three million Catholics in South Korea, almost 6% of the population.

Christianity now has clearly joined Buddhism and Confucianism as a formidable and permanent presence in Korea and as an integral part of modern Korean culture. Just as it is impossible to imagine traditional Korean culture without its Buddhist and Confucian elements, it is impossible to picture contemporary Korea without its Christian churches and pastors. The three religious traditions, each in its own way, address a deeply felt Korean need for harmony, however defined, and are therefore likely to continue to coexist and to shape and animate Korean culture and civilisation for the foreseeable future.

Readings

Robert Buswell, 1992. *The Zen Monastic Experience : Buddhist Practice in Contemporary Korea.* Princeton: Princeton University Press

Donald Clark, 1986. *Christianity in Modern Korea.* Lanham, MD: University Press of America

James H. Grayson, 1985. *Early Buddhism and Christianity in Korea*. Leiden: E.J. Brill

  – 1989. *Korea: A Religious History* . Oxford: Clarendon Press

Peter Harvey, 1990. *An Introduction to Buddhism*. Cambridge: Cambridge University Press

Michael Kalton, 1988. *To Become a Sage*. Cambridge, MA: Harvard University Press

8.4 The Yŏŭido Full Gospel Church

Paul Yonggi Cho, the founder of Yŏŭido [the church often uses the spelling 'Yoido'] Full Gospel Church, is well known to evangelical Christians worldwide. His books, on "walking" with the Holy Spirit, on prayer and church development, are widely translated. In Seoul, he presides over what is claimed to be the largest church in the world, a church with over 700,000 members organised into more than 10,000 home groups, some 500 pastors and an outreach that by 1989 supported 289 missionaries worldwide.

The church began in 1958 in a tent after the devastating civil war. After a crusade in which many Koreans joined his congregation, a dedicated building was erected for the 800 members. This became the Full Gospel Central Church in 1962. Cho, recently released from military service, was ordained. Numbers grew, and by 1964 four services were needed. By 1968, with a membership of 8,000, space had become critical. A new site was chosen, and in 1973 a new building was dedicated with a main sanctuary seating 10,000 on the island of Yŏŭido. one block away from the National Assembly. In November 1981, membership stood at 200,000. By 1986, over 500,000 were members.

One of Cho's books is called *More than Numbers*. Here he argues that church growth reflects two things: a dedicated cell group of up to 15 individuals, sharing common backgrounds and goals, who can actively promote their Christian faith, and a message related to real needs.

In the midst of the remarkable story, many Christians in Europe and America neglect this latter point. But how does the message relate to "real needs"? Essentially, the Full Gospel Church promotes what it calls a "gospel of fullness" based on five gospel messages and three blessings. Three of the messages would be well known to fundamentalist Christians: salvation, an active and ever-present Holy Spirit, and the promised second coming of Christ. But two offer a slightly unexpected focus, since they concentrate on healing and blessing. These are less common in the churches we are familiar with, but are recognised by many American TV evangelists (the church became part of the American Assemblies of God in 1984). It is here that the three blessings come in; according to church publications in English, they are: "thy soul prospereth", "thou mayest prosper" and "thou mayest be in health". The justification is that Jesus preached that "the Kingdom of God" has already arrived for believers.

Prosperity and blessings are a core teaching, expected by pastors and congregations alike. Both, though, have a long history in Korea, and can be traced back beyond the importation of Christianity to the indigenous religion of shamanism. In the early 1970s, the Full Gospel Church opened a retreat known as Prayer Mountain outside Seoul in Osan. Much as in a shaman's mountain shrines, this was where practices devoted to healing were focused, and where exorcisms took place (in contrast to Europe, exorcisms in Korea tend to identify the spirit with a human ancestor, not with a devil).

The church is widely respected by Christians the world over. It offers rousing and convincing preaching, and a large and reassuring substitute to the traditional clan and village ties of Koreans, both in the huge congregations and the small, familiar, personalised home groups. But if you are ever on the island of Yŏŭido on a Sunday, expect traffic jams and the jostle of thousands of people trying to catch the next service.

Readings

David Yonggi Cho, 1993. *More Than Numbers.* Seoul: Seoul Book Center

Lee Soong-Kyo *et al.*, 1989. *Ordeal and Glory through the 30-year History of the Full Gospel Church.* Seoul: Yoido Full Gospel Church

8.5 Shamanism

Early visitors to Korea such as Isabella Bird Bishop in the 1890s found the very air infested with animistic and 'shamanistic' noxious spirits. Missionaries expressed abhorrence at what they regarded as an ignorant, primitive practice. C.A.Clark's comment, made originally in 1932, was typical. To him, shamanism was "far too superstitious and baseless a cult to endure in the light of a modern scientific world". More recent government policies on religion concur with this negative image: in the North shamanism is banned, while in the South statistics omit mention of it. A 1978 survey found a total of 27,367,978 followers—from a then population of under 40 million—of Buddhism, Confucianism, Christianity and their local offshoots, but mentioned 'indigenous beliefs' in only the vaguest terms. The reason for this may be that many Koreans consider shamanism less a religion than a superstition.

Keeping shamanism under wraps reflects history. Confucian texts written during the Chosŏn dynasty (1392-1910) denigrated shaman rituals as *ŭmsa*, a term that implied something obscene or vulgar. In 1431, court women were banned from visiting the corrupting houses of shamans. The *Kyŏngguk taejŏn,* a legal code adopted in 1474, prohibited calling down heretical gods and ordered shamans to live outside the walls of Seoul. However, Queen Min, at the end of the 19th century, frequently invited shamans into the palace; she, for one, thought they could bring potential benefits.

The consensus among Koreans scholars is that some indigenous beliefs do constitute a religion. Such beliefs remain widespread, even if they are on the decline. Many Koreans believe non-human spirits ensure peace in the world beyond. Many call on direct ancestors for help both in this world and the other. There is a large pantheistic canon, and a corpus of practitioners organised in a number of associations. The largest of these is called—reflecting widespread persecution in the recent past and the fact that many of its members are refugees from North Korea—the Korean Federation of Associations for Victory over Communism and Respect of Beliefs. It claims a membership of over 40,000 spread between 215 branches, serving an estimated two million Koreans.

The term 'shaman' comes from the name given by the Tungus of Siberia to ritual practitioners considered to act as intermediaries with the spirit world. The classic text, by Mircea Eliade, is *Shamanism: The Archaic Technique of Ecstasy,* originally published in 1954. In this author's interpretation of Russian ethnographies, the shaman adopts an ecstatic state—some would define this as a trance—to journey to the realm of the spirits, seeking help as a healer or prophet and aiding the soul of a newly deceased person. The journey is perceived as a flight or as possession. The shaman also binds society together by preserving historical knowledge and by performing community exorcisms. 'Shamanism' is the label for these practices, and is used by extension for similar activities among Arctic and Ural-Altaic groups. Eliade found shamans among the Lapps, Inuit, American Indians, the Ainu of Japan and the Koreans, in many parts of south-east Asia, and elsewhere, existing as a result of diffusion and cultural survival, Traditional shamanism is not the same as New Age shamanism. The latter emphasises an individual attempt to delve into one's soul, discovering helping spirits as one goes. In contrast, a shaman does not choose his or her vacation and, in rituals, serves others, not him or herself.

The exact components of Korean shamanism remain a matter of debate, partly because Koreans apply the term to anything not explicitly Buddhist, Confucian or Christian, lumping together all practitioners of a broadly defined religion in which many local differences exist. Many Korean shamans don't go into an ecstatic state, and few know anything of a journey.

A Korean shaman is one of four types:

—*tan'gol* inherit their authority from their family and are found in the south. They are said to lack any conscious knowledge of spirits and base their claim to be efficacious on their skill in music, dance, and recitation.

—*shimbang* are hereditary specialists in Cheju, who typically do not experience ecstatic states.

— *mudang*, found in central and northern Korea, become shamans after the descent of a spirit. Often, the spirit causes an unexplained illness, and later becomes a helper as the *mudang* matures and begins to practice.

—*myŏngdu,* mostly found in the southern provinces, claim to be possessed by a dead child who is often related in some way.

It is clear that there are ecstatic and non-ecstatic types. The first, who experience possession by the gods, gain their authority by proving this possession through walking on blades, trying to cut themselves with knives and performing incredible balancing feats. Korean scholars, however, see both categories as coming from a common source. In part, this reflects an overlap in ritual practice and the spirits venerated, but in the main it has grown from historical and nationalistic concerns. Back in the 1920s, Koreans wanted to show that their culture came from Siberia, not from China (the former power) or Japan (the colonial ruler). Shamanism provided the link and, not surprisingly, as in Siberia, the archetypal shaman was considered ecstatic.

The basic division is between *tan'gol* and *mudang*.

Tan'gol

Until the 1950s, and in some places later, *tan'gol* held exclusive rights to practice rituals in a given area, normally based on local geography, and would live at the edge of a village. He or she would keep a list of clients, the *tan'golgi*, who each gave a retainer twice annually in the form of barley in spring and rice in autumn, which fee entitled them to call on the shaman whenever the need arose. The whole system was controlled by a local fraternity, the *shinch'ŏng*, the 'place of spirits', to which *tan'gol* paid dues and where training was offered. A *tan'gol* could cede or sell the rights to practice in his or her area. The few shaman families kept control by intermarriage. Most of the shamans were women, with inheritance passing from mother to daughter-in-law. The Korean system of patrilinealism, though, meant that the rights to practice were retained by husbands, who accordingly often acted as helpers and musicians to their wives.

Tan'gol were consulted over relatively minor matters, and could provide small rituals to promote health, wealth and happiness. But their main role was to provide a ritual known along the southwest coast as *Ssikkim kut*. This was for the dead, and was usually intended to help the spirit travel from its home to the other world.

Pak Pyŏngch'ŏn, born in 1933 and since 1980 appointed by the South Korean government as a Human Cultural Asset (*In'gan munhwajae*: see chapter 7.5 for an explanation) for his great knowledge of *Ssikkim kut*, comes from Chindo island off the southwest coast:

> You would be proud if you were the third generation of a musical family, or the third generation of artist. But my family have been *tan'gol* for more than 10 generations. I was born into a family where my grandfather was really famous, both as a *tan'gol* and as a musician. We controlled the largest Chindo *tan'gol pan*. In my house, we knew shamanism really well. When I was young, and supposedly sleeping, I heard all the ritual songs. When I ate, I had food left from ritual altars. When I played, my toys were drums and gongs, the instruments of a ritual. My family followed the rules of the shaman fraternity. My father was influential in the association, and I learnt much from him. I learnt much from my mother, who was a well known *tan'gol*. And I learnt from many other relatives. I got to know so many words and so many rituals: I knew my inheritance.

Mudang

Shamans from throughout the Korean peninsula have today congregated in Seoul, where they deal mostly with clients from their own region. Urban life, though, shifts concerns away from the farm and soil. In Seoul, then, shamans tell fortunes and ensure individual and family prosperity by offering small rituals in their own personal shrines. Public rituals have changed, with the introduction of rites directed at the 'engine spirit' of a new car and the guardian spirit of a refrigerator. Many shamans now perform before television cameras, rather than keep themselves hidden.

Since many people live in high-rise apartments, house spirits can be testy and difficult, and neighbours tend to get annoyed if a shaman tries to conduct an all-night ritual. Hence, shamans may take the spirits out of a client's house to a mountainside, or just call them to their own shrine and there conduct the rite. The rules of urban life mean that territory is less defined than in the countryside; simply, clients go to a particular shaman who comes recommended or who has built a good reputation.

There has also been a recent shift towards training institutes, where budding shamans can learn their craft. The old system required an initiate to undergo a period as apprentice to a senior shaman. One modern teacher, who is also both a practising shaman and Vice-President of the Federation, is Pak Ino:

> I was born in 1936. The descent of the spirits occurred 36 years ago [he was speaking in 1991]. When I turned 18, I became mentally ill, completely. I was sent to hospital three times. First I spent three months there, then two, then one. I was completely crazy. I refused, I kept refusing the call from the spirits. Misfortune struck. My mother died. I was about 20 years old. I continued to refuse. My father went blind and turned into a seer. Eventually, I could stand it no more, and gave in. I received words in a prophecy, and accepted what the spirits wanted from me.

It was because I refused that I was collared. In our family there were no shamans, but each year we paid for a ritual to be conducted on our behalf. Before, I had opposed it. When I saw any ritual going on, I wanted to break everything.

Who is my master spirit? For me it is, I think, General Yuch'ŏllyŏn, but I'm never really sure. I also have spiritual parents, shamans who helped with my training, and they are still alive.

(Source: unpublished article by Alexandre Guillemoz. 'What do Seoul *naerim mudang* learn?')

Pak is male, but well over 80% of Korean shamans are women. This is particularly curious, since in Siberia most shamans are men. All rituals in Korea, though, appear to have the same basic function: to restore or keep peace in the spirit world. To do this, shamans offer gifts to spirits, looking for help in return, and they make sure no spirit is left here on earth to bother the living. So, if a client breaks a leg, they might well go to a doctor for treatment and medicine. But then the shaman will be called to find out which spirit has caused them to break their leg, and a ritual will be given to appease that spirit.

Readings

Charles A. Clark, 1961. *Religions of Old Korea*, chapter 6. Seoul: Christian Literature Society of Korea

Mircea Eliade, 1972. *Shamanism: Archaic Techniques of Ecstasy*. Princeton: Princeton University Press

Mihaly Hoppál and Keith Howard (eds), 1993. *Shamans & Cultures*. Budapest: Akádemiai Kiadó/Los Angeles: International Society for Trans-Oceanic Research

Keith Howard, 1990. *Bands, Songs, and Shamanistic Rituals: Folk Music in Korean Society*. Seoul: Royal Asiatic Society

Laurel Kendall, 1985. *Shamans, Housewives, and Other Restless Spirits*. Honolulu: Hawaii University Press

Laurel Kendall, 1988. *The Life and Hard Times of a Korean Shaman*. Honolulu: Hawaii University Press

Chai-Shin Yu and R. Guisso (eds), 1988. *Shamanism: The Spirit World of Korea*. Berkeley: Asian Humanities Press

8.6 The Unification Church

The world knows its members as the 'Moonies'. For its followers, though, the true name of their church is The Holy Spirit Association for the Unification of World Christianity. This is commonly shortened to the Unification Church; in Korean, *T'ongilgyo*. The colloquial 'Moonies' derives from the name of the Church's founder, the Reverend Sun Myung Moon [Mun Sŏnmyŏng]. Like many of the new syncretic religions that have emerged in Korea over the past half-century, the Unification Church is led by a forceful, charismatic figure. The Reverend Moon's zeal, however, has led him to proselytise overseas and to extend his activities in non-religious directions.

Moon was born in 1920 in Chŏngju in what is now North Korea, into a Christian Presbyterian family, and studied electrical engineering at Waseda University in Tokyo. At the age of 16, he claimed, he saw the Supreme Being in a vision and received from him a mission to reform the Christian church. He embarked on this task in 1945, when he started a reform movement in the area around P'yŏngyang, the traditional centre of Korean Christianity. Imprisoned by the Communist authorities in 1945 for dissent, he was released by UN troops in 1950 as they swept north in the early stages of the Korean War. He made his way to Pusan in the south of the peninsula and in 1954 launched his church. The first overseas missionary was sent in 1959 to the United States, and from then on the Unification Church grew rapidly.

Its greatest expansion, in fact, has been outside of Korea, as its missionary work was extended from the US to Japan, Europe, the Middle East and Latin America. Moon himself visited Britain in 1978. In the 1970s he moved his headquarters from Korea to the US and opened a seminary in New York State. By the 1980s, the Unification Church was linked with business enterprises ranging from the production of ginseng to newspapers and even the manufacture of small arms (an interest it has since given up). In the cultural sphere it supported the Little Angels Dance Troupe and sponsored seminars on themes of universal peace and dialogue. Towards the end of the 1980s its world membership was numbered in millions.

Moon, however, has been frequently the target of comment and often of criticism. His extensive business interests have been queried, and his personal finances were investigated by the US authorities, who in 1983 imprisoned him on charges of tax evasion. In his native country attitudes towards him have varied from cautious tolerance, since he has generally taken a strong anti-Communist line, to hostility in face of claimed financial improprieties. Elsewhere, the Unification Church is alleged to have employed such methods as 'brain washing' in recruiting and keeping its members. This was said to be among the reasons for the British government's decision not to allow the Reverend Moon to visit the UK in 1995. The most eye-catching among Moon's present activities is his solemnisation of mass weddings in Seoul, when thousands of men and women, paired up by Moon and his wife, are married in vast ceremonies. A couple may never have met each other before, but their union is regarded as eternal.

Marriage, indeed, plays a central role in the doctrine of the Unification Church, since through marriage couples may reach perfection and God-centred families can be formed. While the church acknowledges that Jesus was sent to redeem mankind, it holds that he failed in his mission, since he died without marrying the perfect woman, and thus achieved only spiritual salvation for the world. Physical salvation is also required, to wash away the human sin transmitted to man by Eve, who was corrupted through sexual union with Satan in the form of the serpent. A Lord of the Second Advent must come to complete the work of Jesus by effecting this physical salvation. While Moon has not claimed he is this Lord, his attitudes and those of his followers suggest that he may regard himself as such. His wife, who plays a large part in the leadership of the church, has been identified as the Mother of the Universe. Moon's teaching, contained in the Divine Principle, consists of his interpretation of the Bible, together with other material appended by him.

In its origins and doctrine, the Unification Church, despite its international following, is influenced strongly by Korean beliefs. The vision Moon claims to have had at 16 of a great spirit, which propelled him towards the formation of his church, is reminiscent of the 'sickness' that a shaman experiences at the onset of her or his powers (see the preceding section). The view of marriage as a completion of human experience and a rite of passage leading, for followers of the Unification Church, to a perfect state, is akin to the Confucian insistence on marriage as the balancing of opposites and the achievement of maturity.

The present worldwide strength of the Unification Church is estimated at around 500,000. British membership is said to be about 600.

Readings

James H. Grayson, 1989. *Korea: A Religious History.* Oxford: Clarendon Press: 247--250

- 1991. 'The impact of Korean Protestant Christianity on Buddhism and the new religions', in *Papers of the British Association for Korean Studies,* 1: 57-73

The Guardian, 2 November 1995

8.7 North Korea—little room for religion

The difficulty of extracting any information about North Korea that is not filtered through official channels makes it hard to get a picture of the present state of religious practice in the DPRK. Visits by foreign religious delegations, such as that undertaken by the Canadian Council of Churches in 1988, do nonetheless throw some light.

The current constitution (1992) guarantees freedom of religious belief. This right also includes the right to construct buildings for religious use and to perform religious ceremonies. Such a guarantee suggests a measure of tolerance and would appear to be more liberal than the 1972 constitution, now superseded, which permitted freedom of religious belief but at the same time the freedom to disseminate anti-religious propaganda. Two churches, one Catholic, one Protestant, were open for worship in

P'yŏngyang in 1988. At Mount Myohyang, in the northwest of the peninsula, Pohyŏn temple, founded in the 9th or 10th century, was restored in 1976 and now has a few caretaker monks installed in what is effectively a museum. Buddhist temples have survived in other areas, notably in the Kŭmgang range (known also in English as the Diamond Mountains), but some only as cultural monuments. Religious life clearly does survive, but it would be hard to speak of independent religious activities, which are not likely to be encouraged. Both party and government in North Korea remain intolerant of any opposition to their authority. A non-sanctioned religious group might serve as a focus for independent thought and action and as such could not be permitted. The same clause in the 1992 constitution granting freedom of belief makes it clear that no one may use religion as a means of destroying the state or social order. Nor can religion be used as a way of introducing foreign influence, thus no foreign missionaries are admitted.

From 1945 to 1950, in the years when the Communist regime of Kim Il Sung was still establishing its hold in the North, places of religion remained open and religious activity was permitted, provided religious leaders kept out of politics and caused no trouble. (The experience of Mun Sŏnmyŏng, founder of the Unification Church, bears this out: see the preceding section.) There were about 500 Buddhist temples. P'yŏngyang was known as a centre of Christian activity, even though the Christian population in northern Korea as a whole was small. The city was said to contain 300,000 Protestants and over 2000 churches on liberation. The persecution of religious personnel, however, was already under way. By 1950 the Protestant church in North Korea, for example, was said to number about 100,000 believers and have 1400 church buildings. Policies of land reform and nationalisation of industry, introduced in 1946, had the further effect of depriving temples and churches of their land and property and left them without financial resources. At the same time the North Korean authorities were organising religious groups into national federations as a means of controlling their activities. These associations were allowed nominal participation in national life as members of a 'united front' of non-Communist political parties and popular organisations. (This way of neutralising other groups was often employed elsewhere by Communist parties once in control. China is another example.) Thus the Korean Buddhist Federation, the Korean Christian (i.e. Protestant) Federation and the Korean Confucian Federation came into being during 1945-47. *Ch'ŏndogyo* ('doctrine of the heavenly way'), a religion native to Korea that developed out of the *Tonghak* movement (see chapter 2.1 and 2.2), had some popular support in North Korea and was allowed to exist as well, probably because of its indigenous roots and anti-foreign sentiments. (The Korean Ch'ŏndogyo Young Friends Party is one of the few political parties tolerated by the Korean Workers Party, though it has no effective power).

The Korean War (1950-53) and the years following it brought a much harder line on religion. Temples and churches destroyed in the fighting were not rebuilt and those that survived were put to secular uses. Buddhist monks, condemned as "social parasites", were forced to work and both they and Christian clergy continued to suffer discrimination and even death. (Richard Kim's novel *The Martyred,* dealing with incidents immediately before the outbreak of the Korean War, catches the agonised spirit of that period.) Foreign priests were similarly targeted. When North Korean troops invaded the south during the civil war, they detained or killed Christian clergy and took others north, including foreign church workers. Among British clergy who were forced to march north were members of the Anglican church and the Salvation Army. The participation of foreign missionaries in the Korean Christian churches was particularly suspect to a regime that attributed the wartime devastation of its country to foreign attack and subsequently resisted all Western influence.

The drive against religious activity was accompanied by an ideological campaign to discredit religion. Kim Il Sung, in an essay entitled *Why We Must Oppose Religion,* published in 1959, criticised it as the "enemy of science and development" and an obstacle to the establishment of socialism and Communism, and called on his readers to "eliminate all remnants in our hearts of superstitious and unscientific religion". By the first half of the 1970s, however, it appears that the North Korean government felt some purpose might be served by reviving the religious federations, which had become very inactive, for propaganda activities in its initiative to improve links with the outside world. (This was the time of initial contacts between North and South Korea.) Thus, in 1974, the Korean Christian Federation sought admission to the World Council of Churches (WCC), but was rebuffed because it would not supply information on its numbers and organisation in North Korea. From 1986, however, North Korean delegates have been attending WCC gatherings and various national religious meetings, where they meet clergy from South Korea. In 1987 and 1988, North Korean Catholics were able to establish contact with representatives of the Vatican. In 1988, the Korean Catholic Association was founded to promote co-operation with Catholics in foreign countries. The Korean Buddhists Federation has likewise renewed contact with foreign Buddhist organisations and in 1986 attended the World Council of Buddhism in Nepal, where delegates met Buddhists from South Korea.

The Canadian Council of Churches delegation of 1988 indicated in its report that North Korean Protestants, thought to number about 15,000, maintained their religious life through 'house churches' or sections, each consisting typically of some ten believers with a leader, who generally met in a member's home. About 500 such groups are said to exist, including 50 in P'yŏngyang. Church workers are reported to number about 300 and to include around 20 mostly elderly pastors. The usual rites of communion, baptism, marriage and funeral services are carried out. The KCF has reprinted an edition of the Bible and a hymnal. Since 1972, theological training for new church leaders has been permitted. No public proselytising is undertaken, and recruitment is solely through personal contact.

The Catholic church in North Korea is probably even smaller. By 1988, only about 800 believers had been identified in two to three provinces. The Canadian delegation found that, as with their Protestant counterparts, Catholics worshipped primarily within the family and in small groups meeting privately under lay leadership. Most believers had been educated in their faith by family members. Preparations were under way for the training of priests. By their own admission, North Korean Catholics in 1988 knew only an older style of worship that included, for instance, hymns in Latin.

In their conversations with the Canadian delegation in 1988, the Korean Buddhists Federation claimed 10,000 adherents served by 300 monks. Most of the latter were elderly men. There were also said to be over 60 'active' temples, some inhabited by monks. A training institute functioned in the north of the country, at which some young men were studying. In rural areas signs have been reported, including stone cairns and rags tied around trees, that suggest the possibility of continuing shamamist observances.

Contacts between religious believers from South and North Korea is a delicate matter. International gatherings offer relatively neutral ground for contact, but even meetings under such conditions can be considered suspect. An unauthorised visit to North Korea by South Korean church workers in 1989 led to the latters' imprisonment on their return to South Korea. A personal representative of Cardinal Kim of South Korea has, however, been able to visit the Korean Catholic Association in North Korea several times on behalf of the Vatican.

Readings

Asia Watch, January 1986. *Human Rights in Korea.* New York and Washington, D. C.: Asia Watch Committee

Richard Kim, 1969. *The Martyred.* Seoul: Si-sa-yong-o-sa Publishers

Kong Jong-won, 1983 (third edition). *Earth without Heaven: How Religion Was Extinguished in North Korea.* Seoul: Korea Religious Research Institute

'Report of the Canadian Council of Churches Delegation to the Democratic People's Republic of Korea, 4-13 November 1988', in *Currents* 10, no.4 (January 1989)

Rinn-Sup Shinn *et al.,* 1969. *Area Handbook for North Korea.* Washington, D.C.: American University, Foreign Area Studies

Nena Vreeland, Rinn-Sup Shinn *et al.,* 1976. *Area Handbook for North Korea.* Washington, D. C.: American University, Foreign Area Studies

9

THE PHYSICAL ENVIRONMENT

9.1 The Korean peninsula

Korea is a peninsula. It juts out from the world's largest continent toward its largest ocean and links the continent with the rim of islands skirting it. Consequently its geography has both continental and maritime features. From north to south the Korean peninsula measures almost 1100 km. The range of climate and vegetation is accordingly great, from the subtropical, broadleaf evergreen forests of Cheju island to the dark, coniferous forests of the Kaema plateau in the northern part of North Korea.

Including its many islands the Korean peninsula covers an area of 219,530 sq km (North Korea 120,538 sq km and South Korea 98,992 sq km). This is about the same as mainland Britain. Korean schoolchildren once learnt that Korea is shaped rather like a rabbit, with its ears being the part of North Korea that is on the mainland, north of the actual peninsula; today they are taught it looks like a tiger.

From the mouth of the Yalu (Korean: Amnok) in the west to the mouth of the Tumen (Korean: Tuman) in the east, Korea's boundary with the countries of the Asian mainland is 1041 km long (1025 km frontier with China and 15 km with Russia). The southeastern tip of the peninsula is only 206 km from Japan, from which it is separated by the Strait of Korea.

9.2 Types of terrain

Geologically speaking, Korea is part of mainland Asia, and its geological development is closely related to that of China. Korea's main geological features, four massifs and three foldbelts, continue on across the Yellow Sea in eastern China. Their general SW-NE trend is known in Korea as the 'China direction'.

The massifs are composed mainly of grey gneiss. In the foldbelts there are thick deposits of massive dark grey limestones. They are the raw material for the cement industry, an important industry in both North and South Korea. Also of economic importance are coal deposits, some of which are as much as 2 m thick. In South Korea they are mined in the central T'aebaek range and in North Korea in the basins of the Taedong and Ch'ŏngch'ŏn rivers.

Korea's geological history went through various periods of orogeny (mountain formation) with intrusions of magmatic rock. Connected with these intrusions are a large number of mineral deposits, including iron ore (magnetite and haematite), gold and tungsten. Many of the deposits are so small, however, that by international standards Korea is fairly low in mineral resources. The mineral deposits are also quite unequally distributed. North Korea is able to produce almost all of its primary energy from its own coal and also produces the iron ore it needs. Its most important export article is the gold mined in Pukchin (North P'yŏngan Province). South Korea, on the other hand, is forced to import almost all of the raw materials its industry requires. The only important export article is the tungsten mined near Sangdong (Kangwŏn Province), which accounts for 5.9% of world production.

The late Cretaceous period (around 70 million years ago) saw the beginning of a new phase in Korea's geological development, a phase dominated by plate tectonics. Along the western rim of the Pacific ocean the Pacific plate, which dips under the continental Eurasian plate, cracked open in the area that is now the East Sea. Basalt from the earth's crust intruded into the cracks, causing local spreading of the sea floor. In the course of the Tertiary era (from 63 million to 1 million years ago), what had previously been the edge of the continental plate was shoved into its present location to become the Japanese islands as we know them today.

On the western side of the widening East Sea the same forces bent the new rim of the plate upward and initiated the so-called T'aebaek orogeny. This new phase of formation consisted in a tilting of the block that forms the Korean peninsula. The eastern side of the block is being tilted up, and at the same time the western and southern side is being depressed. Consequently, the east coast is very steep, while the west and south coasts drop off more gradually. The crest of the tilted block runs more or less N-S, in the so-called 'Korea direction', following the curvature of the east coast and close to it. Its highest peaks are in the T'aebaek range (1500-1600 m).

The T'aebaek orogeny was associated with intrusions of basaltic material. They continued on into the Quaternary (the present geological period) as part of the volcanic activity around the East Sea. In South Korea volcanic activity was pretty much restricted to the two volcanic islands of Ullŭng off the east coast and Cheju off the south coast (with 1950 m-high Mt Halla). In North Korea volcanic rocks are much more prevalent. They cover an area of 22,000 sq km around Mt Paektu, the 2749 m-high volcano on the border between North Korea and China.

The tilting of the Korean peninsula led to increased erosion. Deep valleys were cut into the block and it was divided up into separate mountain ranges. One of the most lasting impressions a foreign visitor to Korea retains is of a never-ending succession of ridges and valleys. The erosive activity of the streams depended highly on the type of bedrock they encountered. Where the bedrock was less resistant, wide basins developed with mouths opening up toward the west and south coasts. These basins are separated from each other by mountain ranges composed of harder rock, which spread out like fingers from the T'aebaek range and its northern extension, the Nangnim range, generally following the old 'China direction' (SW-NE).

The many mountains and the steep relief greatly affect agricultural land use. Fifty-nine percent of the territory of South Korea is mountainous, and in North Korea the percentage is even higher. The highest mountains are concentrated in the northern and northeastern part of the country, but some of the ranges radiating out from them extend as far as the west and south coast. Although the mountains are not actually very high, they are extremely steep. Agriculture is therefore confined to the narrow valley bottoms and the lower, gentler parts of the slopes. In mountainous regions less than 10% of the total area is farmed and little of this area can be used for growing rice. The most important factor limiting agricultural land use lies thus in the steep slopes of its mountainous terrain. Only 21.2% of the territory of South Korea is farmed (64% of the farmed area consists of rice paddies) and only around 17.5% of the area of North Korea (approximately 30% of this as rice paddies).

In South Korea about 18% of the territory is hill country. The hills form a kind of transition between the mountains of the east coast and the alluvial plains of the west coast. Along the large rivers hilly country also extends far into the mountains. Rice terraces cover the valley bottoms and climb up the side valleys, branching off like fingers into the hills. On the gentler slopes and backs of the hills dry field crops are grown. Only the higher, more deeply eroded hilltops are forested. The amount of cultivated land and the proportion of paddies in the hill country is about the same as the national average.

The most important agricultural areas are the alluvial plains along the middle and lower reaches of the large rivers and the coastal plains along the west coast, where land reclamation projects had already begun during the Japanese colonial period. These level areas with their fertile soil, where extensive irrigation systems can be set up, are particularly suited for rice growing. In such areas the amount of cultivated land and the proportion of paddies are usually far above the national average.

Because the alluvial plains played such an important role in agriculture, economically and culturally the Korean peninsula developed very lopsidedly. The alluvial plains on the lower reaches of the Taedong, Han, Kŭm and Yŏngsan rivers, which open up toward the coast and in many cases merge to form a coastal plain, became Korea's 'rice basket'. This was intensively settled, while the rugged mountain coast and the densely forested plateaus of the northeast remained sparsely populated. The frontier did not advance into these regions until the beginning of this century as population pressure increased.

9.3 Climate

The factor that influences Korea's climate most profoundly is the annual reversal of the air pressure gradient between the northeast Asian mainland and the northwest Pacific and the accompanying north-south shift in the polar front.

In winter, the polar front (the boundary between continental polar and maritime tropical air masses) lies south of Korea. The winter monsoon, driven by the high pressure area over Siberia, brings extremely cold, dry continental air to Korea. This causes the January mean temperature in Chunggangjin (in the extreme north) to drop to -21.1° C. Even in Seoul it is -4.6° C. Only the south and southeast coast have much higher winter temperatures (January mean temperature in Pusan +2.0° C), partly because of the lower latitude, but mainly because they are protected from the cold winter winds by the Sobaek range and are warmed by the Tsushima current. The frost-free period here is 226 days, 56 days longer than in the northern part of South Korea (in Seoul it is 170 days).

In spring (April to May), the high pressure area over Siberia dissipates, and the weather is occasionally already affected by the fringes of extratropical cyclones, whose tracks approach Korea with the polar front on the latter's way northward. When the polar front draws nearer, around the end of June, the early summer rainy period begins. It is known as *changma* in Korea. This rainy period is preceded by approximately two weeks of showery weather, which is very important for flooding the rice paddies and allowing the rice to be transplanted on time. The actual amount of rain that falls in summer varies widely. In years in which the North Pacific high is too strong and the polar front passes Korea too fast (and with it the extratropical cyclones that bring the rain), not enough rain falls to flood the paddies. That is why it is so important to increase the area that is artificially irrigated.

The polar front moves northward, bringing North Korea its single period of maximum precipitation in August. In South Korea, the early summer rainy period makes way to a period with much less precipitation around the end of July or beginning of August. South Korea is now under the influence of the summer monsoon, which brings high temperatures (August mean temperature in Seoul 25.5° C) and high humidity, but much less precipitation.

As the polar front returns, wandering cyclones again take the place of the stable high pressure of summer. This transition is known in Korea as the beginning of the late summer rainy period (second half of August). This rainy period, called *nŭt changma* in Korean, lasts for an average of 25 days and brings a definite second summer precipitation maximum. In late summer, tropical cyclones may also affect Korea's weather. These typhoons bring torrential rains that regularly cause flooding and devastating mudslides.

By the middle of September the polar front has shifted so far south that the high pressure area developing over Siberia can begin to influence Korea's weather. This brings a short, sunny autumn, unanimously considered Korea's most agreeable season. Around early or mid-November, as the winter monsoon begins to flow, the long cold winter again sets in.

Climatically, most of North Korea and the northern part of South Korea (the provinces of Kyŏnggi and Kangwŏn) belong to the cool temperate zone, with cold, dry winters and hot, humid summers. The natural vegetation is summergreen deciduous forest with a great variety of species. For the most part, though, the natural vegetation has had to yield to agriculture or been replaced by secondary forests. With the high summer temperatures and precipitation maximum, paddy rice farming is the most important type of agriculture, wherever the land is flat enough to allow this. The low winter temperatures mean that the vegetation period for winter grain is so long that it coincides with the summer rice-growing period. Consequently, winter grain can only be grown on dry fields, and the paddies lie fallow in winter.

The southern part of Korea belongs to the warm temperate zone. Its northern boundary is defined as the line representing an average temperature of -5° C in the coldest month (January). This line is an important boundary for agriculture, because it represents approximately the northern limit of double cropping. South of this boundary it is possible to grow a winter crop of barley or wheat on the drained paddies. The higher winter temperatures and the earlier onset of the vegetation period also allow the farmers to grow a very profitable extra crop of early spring vegetables.

On the south coast and on Cheju island the mean January temperature is above freezing and even the mean minimum temperature is above -3° C. The natural vegetation here consists of subtropical broadleaf evergreens. Since around 1970, farmers have taken advantage of the warmer climate to grow vegetables in unheated vinyl greenhouses. On Cheju island, citrus fruit plantations have been rapidly expanding.

In the northern part of North Korea the winter is so long that it is impossible to grow a second crop on the dry fields. In this area, defined as the region with at least four winter months with mean temperatures below 1° C, only one summer crop of rice (especially in the western part of North P'yŏngan Province) or one dry field crop, maize, potatoes, buckwheat, foxtail millet or kaoliang, is grown. In the extreme northeast and on the Kaema plateau the summer temperatures are so low (mean temperature of the warmest month below 22° C) that these areas belong to the cold snowy forest zone with extremely cold winters and cool summers. This climatic zone extends far southward into South Korea in the higher elevations of the T'aebaek range. The natural vegetation of this zone is coniferous forest. Until the 1960s, these mountainous regions were not used agriculturally, aside from small patches cultivated by slash and burn techniques ('fire-field farming'). More recently the people living in these areas have started to take advantage of the cooler summers of these higher elevations to grow such crops as tobacco and certain kinds of vegetables.

9.4 Population development

South Korea

From 21.5 million in 1955 the population of South Korea increased to 43.5 million in 1990, the result of a simultaneous increase in the birth rate and drop in the death rate in the years since the Korean War (average life expectancy rose from 34 years in 1934 to 71 years in 1989). By 1960-1961 the excess of births had reached 30 per 1000 inhabitants, one of the highest figures in the world. A population explosion like this jeopardized any attempts to increase agricultural production to the point where it could feed the population or start an economic upswing. Accordingly, when the government started its first five-year plan (1962-1967) it also initiated an intensive and extremely successful family planning campaign. By 1990, the birth rate had dropped to 15.6 per 1000 inhabitants, and the excess of births was only 9.8 per 1000 inhabitants. When it comes to family planning, two different Confucian traditions clash. On the one hand, the wish to have a son to carry on the family line and perform the ceremonies for the ancestors is so great that it sometimes leads to large numbers of children. On the other hand, the only way for a family to rise in the Confucian hierarchy of society is to send its children to a good school or university. This is only possible with a small number of children. A trend towards later marriage has also helped to lower the birth rate, as young men do their three years' compulsory military service and job opportunities for women are improving. (For further discussion of demographic changes see chapter 14.1.)

In 1955, three-quarters of the population of South Korea (75.5%) lived in the countryside. Industrialisation triggered a massive migration to the cities, mainly towards the large centres with over a quarter of a million inhabitants. In 1990, 74.4% of the population lived in towns and cities. Of this urban population, more than 83% was concentrated in the large metropolitan centres of Seoul (and its satellite towns, Puch'ŏn, Suwŏn, Sŏngnam, Anyang, Kwangmyŏng and Ansan), Pusan, Taegu, Inch'ŏn, Kwangju,

Taejŏn, Ulsan, Chŏnju, Ch'ŏngju, Masan, Ch'angwŏn, P'ohang, Chinju and Mokp'o. At the same time the population of medium-sized and small towns stagnated, so that the gap between urban and rural living standards increased.

The rural areas have been losing population particularly rapidly. The new jobs created in industry and in the simultaneously expanding services sector began to siphon off the excess labour. Most of the children of farm families began to move to town, looking for jobs in industry, and for the first time the remaining household members were able to switch from their traditional subsistence farming to market-oriented farming. Since the late 1960s not only single family members have been leaving the countryside; entire families have been migrating to the cities and towns, especially from the high mountains. As a result, the number of farm households has also been decreasing (from 2,587,000 in 1967 to 1,767,000 in 1990). (The impact of such changes is discussed further in chapters 7.2 and 14.2.)

With an average density of 438 persons per sq km, South Korea is one of the most densely populated countries in the world, apart from a few city states. (For comparison, the Netherlands has 363 inhabitants per sq km.) When account is taken of the fact that only 21.2% of the territory is cultivable, but 15.3% of the population still make their living by farming, South Korea's agricultural population density (316 persons per sq km of cultivated area) is exceeded by only very few parts of the world, such as Java and Bangladesh.

The asymmetry between the east and west coast is still apparent in the demographic distribution. The rural population density decreases from 300 persons per sq km in the heavily peopled alluvial plains of the west coast to 79 persons per sq km in the higher mountains along the east coast. The population density in the hill country lies between these two extremes.

North Korea

In 1990 the population of North Korea was estimated at 21,770,000. With an average of 177 inhabitants per sq km, North Korea is much less densely populated than South Korea. The rural population is concentrated primarily in the strip along the west coast that includes the provinces of South and North Hwanghae and South and North P'yŏngan, where the population density lies between 124 and 184 persons per sq km. The east coast provinces of Kangwŏn and South and North Hamgyŏng, with their much narrower strip of arable land, have population densities between 69 and 97 persons per sq km. The two mountainous northern provinces of Ryanggang and Chagang (new provinces created by the current North Korean regime), where agriculture is limited to a few small clearings and the climate makes rice growing practically impossible, are extremely sparsely settled (49 and 31 inhabitants per sq km respectively).

Until the beginning of the 20th century North Korea had never been very densely settled, and the only cities were on the west coast: P'yŏngyang, with its port city of Namp'o, and Kaesŏng. The only city on the east coast of any importance was Wŏnsan, which had a good connection to Seoul via the Ch'ugaryŏng rift valley. During the colonial period, as the Japanese began to exploit Korea's mineral resources and water power and to develop industry, the strips along the west coast and especially along the east coast began to urbanise. Large numbers of persons from the overpopulated agricultural areas of the south migrated north to work here. The Korean War brought heavy population losses, and two million persons fled to the south. After the War, North Korea concentrated on developing industry, and the process of urbanisation continued apace. In 1985, 64% of the North Korean population lived in towns and cities. Thirteen cities had populations of more than 100,000, among them P'yŏngyang, Hamhŭng-Hŭngnam. Ch'ŏngjin, Wŏnsan, Kimch'aek, Sariwŏn and Kaesŏng.

9.5 Transportation

South Korea

In 1970, South Korea began constructing a network of motorways that was to cover the whole country. By 1990, it comprised 1551 km and formed the backbone of a good road network, which had been greatly expanded in parallel (56,715 km, of which 71.5% was paved). Road construction has not been able to keep up with rapid motorisation, however. In 1990, 66.3% of passenger traffic and 21.1% of goods traffic was conveyed by road. In passenger traffic the excellent public bus network plays an important role. The railway system (6435 km, of which 8.1% is electrified) in 1990 handled 22.1% of passenger traffic and 30.9% of goods traffic. It is planned to build a high-speed train link between Seoul and Pusan.

Shipping is the most important means of transportation of goods, with 47.8% of the total. In particular bulk goods are transported mainly by ship along the coast. The most important ports for parcelled goods are Pusan and Inch'ŏn. Their capacity is surpassed today, however, by specialised industrial ports for bulk goods (ore, coke, oil), such as P'ohang, Ulsan, Yŏch'ŏn and Kwangyang. South Korea now has ferry connections to Japan (Pusan-Shimonoseki, Pusan-Osaka, Yŏsu-Hakata) and China (Inch'ŏn-Weihai, In'chŏn-Tianjin). Inland navigation is nonexistent because the water level of the rivers fluctuates so highly. There are three international airports, Seoul-Kimp'o, Pusan-Kimhae and Cheju. Construction has begun on a new airport near the island of Yŏngjong northwest of Inch'ŏn. Domestic air service accounted for 3.0% of the passenger traffic in 1990.

North Korea

The backbone of North Korea's traffic network is the railway (5045 km). Of this 60% is electrified, but its capacity is not very high, because most of it is single track and the rolling stock is very old. The road network (23,000 km, of which only 7.5% is paved) is in very poor condition apart from the two stretches of motorway from Namp'o via P'yŏngyang to Wŏnsan and from P'yŏngyang to Kaesŏng (460 km all told). Private cars are not permitted, and the only motor vehicles are lorries and official cars imported for government and party cadres. Since the early 1990s, road traffic has been curtailed even more because of fuel shortage, and lorries are increasingly being re-equipped to allow them to run on wood. The inhabitants are not free to leave their home county without a special permit, consequently there is practically no domestic travel and no regular domestic air traffic. All connections with South Korea (including postal services) have been suspended since the partition of the country in 1953. The most important sea port is Namp'o. Although work has been underway since 1980 to make the Taedong river into an east-west waterway, inland navigation is not yet of any significance.

Readings

Patricia M. Bartz, 1972. *South Korea*. Oxford: Clarendon Press

Eckart Dege, 1991. *Kleiner Reiseführer Nordkorea*. Kiel: Verein zur Förderung regionalwissenschaft -licher Analysen e.V.

 – 1992. Korea: *Eine landeskundliche Einführung*. Kiel: Verein zur Förderung regionalwissen schaft -licher Analysen e.V.

Nicholas Eberstadt and Judith Banister, 1992. *The Population of North Korea*. Berkeley: Center for Korean Studies

Hermann Lautensach, 1945. *Korea, eine Landeskunde auf Grund eigener Reisen und der Literatur*. Trans. and ed. Katherine and Eckart Dege, 1988, as *Korea: A Geography Based on the Author's Travels and Literature*. Berlin: Springer-Verlag

Shannon McCune, 1956. *Korea's Heritage: A Regional and Social Geography*. Rutland, VT, and Tokyo: Tuttle

A. Schinz and E. Dege, 1990. 'P'yŏngyang—ancient and modern—the capital of North Korea', *GeoJournal* 22, no.1: 21-32

10

THE URBAN SCENE

10.1 Seoul: development today

Until the end of the Japanese colonial period, urban development kept pace with the growing population. In the chaotic political and economic conditions after the devastation of the Korean War, people poured into the capital, to the point where the infrastructure could not keep up with the growing numbers. During the Korean War the population had dropped to 650,000. By 1953 it had increased again to one million and since then it has continued to increase steadily, until by 1990 it had reached 10.6 million. More than 70% of these new inhabitants had rural origins. Seoul was by far the most important goal of rural migration to the cities.

In the early stages it was Seoul's traditional function as political and cultural centre and the economic role it had developed that acted as a magnet. As industrialisation gained momentum, its economic role became more and more important, in particular its value as an industrial site. In 1966, when only 13% of the total population of the country lived in Seoul, 39% of the industrial jobs were already concentrated there. The average per capita income was then already 88% higher than that for the country as a whole. The appeal of the amenities of urban life also figured, and Seoul's traditional role as a university town also attracted the elite. Unless a person had studied at one of the 37 universities in Seoul, he could hardly count on moving up into a senior position in the administration or business. Consequently, almost two-thirds of the students in the entire country studied in Seoul.

This uncontrollable influx caused enormous social and infrastructural problems. Accommodation could not be built fast enough to keep up with the population explosion. Most of the housing stock (96% in 1970, when the city already had 5.5 million inhabitants) consisted of small, one-storey, one-family houses with tiny inner courtyards resembling traditional rural houses. In 1975, 42% of the families in Seoul did not have a home of their own and had to live as subtenants. In spite of the tremendous building boom it has not been possible to reduce this housing shortage. The figures for 1975 show that in that year one-quarter of the population of Seoul had a living space of less than 3 sq m per person. Compared with other large cities in the world, the area of Seoul is quite small (London is more than two and a half times as large). The city area also encompasses many mountains so steep that no houses can be built on them, and even cultivated fields, so that in 1985 only 45% of the area was actually covered with urban buildings, of which housing formed 70%. The population density (17,557 persons per sq km in 1990) is accordingly high. Some older inner city wards have population concentrations as high as 100,000 persons per sq km, a density that allows only 9 sq m per person.

During the phase of extremely rapid urbanisation in the 1960s, slums (known in Korean as *p'anjach'ŏn*) began to sprout up on steep slopes and in low-lying areas that were endangered by flooding. By 1970 one third of the housing consisted of makeshift houses (*p'anjajip*) in *p'anjach'ŏn*. In the mid-1960s, the city government started redevelopment measures. The inhabitants were moved into blocks of flats constructed in the locations of the former slums. This created more problems than it solved, however, because it cut social ties. Immigrants from the same province tended to cluster together in the same *p'anjach'ŏn*. In the early 1970s, the city government started a new method. It transferred title to the land to the inhabitants and provided the areas with urban infrastructure, hoping this would be a stimulus for the residents to improve their own living conditions. Such programmes appear to have been successful, and formerly disreputable *p'anjach'ŏn* have turned into normal city wards. By 1978, the number of *p'anjajip* had already dropped to 4% of the total housing stock.

In 1966, a master plan was devised to control the development of the city. It was changed in 1971 to fit it into the national development plan. The main priorities were to decentralise population and industry at the national level in order to stop the city from growing, to develop new residential areas in order to ease crowding and to shift certain municipal functions out of the city centre.

One of the most effective instruments for doing so, apart from dispersing industry, was the proclamation of a green belt encircling the entire city, in which all types of construction are totally prohibited. This caused the price of land in the city region to rise so astronomically, even in the newly developing suburbs 10 to 15 km from the city centre, that many potential immigrants moved to smaller regional centres or one of the new satellite towns being developed around Seoul instead of to Seoul itself. The population growth levelled off and eventually the new industrial centres developing on the southeast coast and even a number of provincial centres were growing faster than Seoul. In 1986, the point was reached where for the first time more people were registered as moving out of Seoul than into it. By that time Seoul had a population of just under 10 million.

Since the mid-1960s, the population of Seoul has not only quadrupled, there have also been enormous shifts of population within the city boundaries. The development of a Central Business District, begun in Japanese times, continues unabated, as the residential population is replaced in the old city centre by shops, banks, offices and the other buildings typical of a large modern metropolis. The districts at the edge of the old city centre, developed by the Japanese, are among the most densely populated parts of the city. The population development has been most dynamic in the suburbs to the east and south of the city. Between 1970 and 1985 alone, more than three million persons found homes in the new housing areas south of the Han river. The proportion of the population living south of the river increased from 17% in 1960 to 48% in 1990. Seoul was originally founded in a basin lying between mountains, at some distance from the river, but is now a city straddling the river.

With the development of the nuclear family as a norm, the emancipation of women and the shortage of servants, a totally new type of living has become more and more popular in Korea—a freehold flat in a high-rise building with all the amenities of modern life, such as central heating, lift, refuse chute and a door with a burglar-proof lock. The proportion of such flats rose from 4% in 1970 to 35% in 1990. Especially south of the Han, new city districts were developed, such as Yŏŭido, Panp'o and Chamsil, with extensive areas given over to blocks of flats in up to 15-storey-high buildings. Some of the flats are quite luxurious.

In spite of this rapid construction, Seoul still has a tremendous housing shortage. In 1990 the average occupation rate of homes was 193%, i.e. almost two families were living in every home or flat, every other family as a subtenant. In the densely populated districts at the edge of the old city centre the rate is much higher. There are even areas where it is more than 600%. Astonishingly, even in the new upper-middle-class housing developments at the eastern and southern edge of the city the rate is also higher than average. Many new house owners have overextended themselves and sublet rooms to help pay the mortgage, though this is more easily done in a one-family house than in a flat.

Meanwhile the city is full. The entire area within the green belt has been constructed over. The only direction in which it is possible to build is up. Consequently the typical one-storey houses are being replaced by high-rise buildings. As a response to the continuing housing shortage, the government began constructing satellite cities around Seoul but outside the green belt, each for half a million inhabitants. By the early 1990s the first of these were ready for occupancy.

The most important employer and the undisputed centre is today the Central Business District. It occupies a small triangle in the southwestern part of the old city centre. In this small area are concentrated the head offices of almost all of the country's large industrial and commercial firms, a large number of banks, large department stores and international hotels. Among the most recent to be developed was the 42-storey Lotte Hotel with its 14-storey department store beside it. Construction has not only gone higher and higher; it has also gone underground. Under most of the streets in this area are arcades with shop after shop selling luxury goods, such as jewellery, antiques, watches and expensive cameras. The arcades are connected with each other and have direct entrances to the underground stations and the lower floors of the large department stores and hotels. The eastern part of the Central Business District is the entertainment district of Myŏng-dong with its bars, restaurants and luxury shops.

Until 1995, to the northwest of the Central Business District was the former government axis, leading to the Capital building, an impressive neo-Renaissance-style building constructed by the Japanese between 1916 and 1926 as the seat of the governor-general. After liberation it was the seat of the South Korean government, then served as the National Museum, but has now been torn down so as to restore the view of Kyŏngbok Palace behind it. Originally this axis was lined by ministries and embassies, but since the government moved to a site in the south of Seoul and the Sejong Culture Centre was constructed here, it has become more of a cultural district.

North of the Central Business District is Chong-no, one of the most important shopping streets in the city since the Chosŏn period. It extends as far as the East Gate, with shops specialising in certain kinds of goods concentrated in its different blocks: jewellery shops, shops stocking traditional Korean dresses, bookshops, shops selling religious paraphernalia, chemists dispensing Chinese medicine, etc. Similar specialisation characterises the shopping district south of Chong-no, where on either side of the Ch'ŏnggye-ch'ŏn thoroughfare also extending to the East Gate, shops fill entire buildings and market halls.

Two new centres, both south of the old city, have begun to take over some of the functions of the city centre and thus relieve some of its congestion. One is Yŏŭido, where Parliament and the press have moved. The other is Kangnam, to which many municipal offices and the offices of many private firms have moved. Many hotels, restaurants and shops have been established here, creating a true, second city centre. A large 11-storey bus terminal for long-distance buses was built here to take the place of the many terminals that used to be spread throughout the whole city. It is connected to the underground network and has ramps leading directly onto the motorway. Institutions that required a lot of space and traffic were moved to the edge of the city, such as the central markets for fishery and agricultural products and the National University. The areas they vacated were turned into parks. Strategic reasons, as well as those of town planning, have played a part particularly in the relocation of government offices, education and research establishments and industry south of the Han river. Seoul's location, within 50 km south of the Demilitarized Zone between South and North Korea, makes it vulnerable to attack from the North. Memories remain of the difficult exit from Seoul in face of the North Korean invasion of 1950.

Seoul's traditional monocentric structure has thus turned into a polycentric structure, a development initiated with the city development plan of 1971. Before this could happen, however, the city's transportation network had to undergo a radical change. Fourteen new arterial roads radiating out from the city centre and three new circular roads have been constructed. To do so, many tunnels had to be built through the mountains. Namsan (South Mountain), the southern limit of the old city centre, has tunnels piercing it in three different directions. Bridges across the Han River, which is 1-1.5 km wide at this point, are also particularly important. Since the mid-1970s alone, 12 new bridges have been built, raising the number to 16. Today the river is no longer an obstacle to traffic.

In spite of this large-scale road construction, traffic congestion remains chronic. Motorisation is increasing at a rate the planners would never have dreamed of a short while ago. In 1985, 256,000 private cars were registered in Seoul, along with 130,000 lorries, 44,000 buses and 37,000 taxis. By 1990, the total number of registered vehicles had risen to 1.2 million, 824,000 of them private vehicles. Buses (with 7.7 million passengers per day) and taxis (2.6 million) have reached the limits of their capacity. Construction of a combined underground-suburban fast train system has therefore been particularly important. The first section, opened in 1974, connects the cities of Suwŏn and Inch'ŏn with Seoul via suburban fast train and continues underground in an east-west direction under the city centre. In 1985, three further lines were opened, two diagonal lines and one circular route connecting the Central Business District with the new centres south of the river. By that year the system was transporting 1.5 million passengers per day. In the 1990s it is planned to build four more lines, which are to connect the eastern and westernmost suburbs, the satellite town of Sŏngnam and the international airport in Kimp'o with the city.

The goal of all of these efforts is to develop Seoul into a metropolis that not only is the economic and cultural centre of the country itself, but also can play its role in the network of international cities in which the global exchange of raw materials, capital, industrial products and information takes place. As a newly industrialised country lacking raw materials and capital, Korea particularly needs to be securely integrated into this global network. The awarding of the 1988 Summer Olympics to Seoul acted as a great stimulus in the redevelopment of the city.

One of the most visible results of these efforts, apart from the extremely modern stadiums, is the rejuvenation of the Han river. In the dry months of winter, when extensive gravel banks were laid dry, it used to look like a tremendous sewer. Now that the water level is kept constant by a system of dams, it is a broad, park-lined expanse of water in the middle of the city, criss-crossed by sailing boats and passenger boats. Where 87.2% of the city's sewage used to flow into the river untreated, new sewer systems and sewage treatment plants with a daily capacity of three million tons are now capable of treating all sewage.

10.2 Old and new housing

In Korean cities people traditionally lived in very much the same manner as in the country, except that houses were even more crowded together than in the villages. Above the sea of one-storey houses, usually with thatched roofs even in the cities, only the city gates, the seat of the governor and the Confucian school stood out. In the capital the royal palaces with their mighty tiled roofs dominated the surrounding district. The first modern structures began to appear during the Japanese colonial period. A few surviving buildings in a Japanese or 'Europeanised' style can still be seen. Even today the basic form of the Korean farmhouse is evident in urban houses. Characteristic is the high wall that surrounds a single family house and a yard, however small. The living area is still divided between rooms with the traditional *ondol* underfloor heating system and an unheated, wooden-floored entrance room that corresponds to the large veranda of the farmhouse and has sliding glass doors that open on to the yard. This division makes it possible to shift the focus of family life from the heated living rooms into the cool, well-aired entrance room in the heat of summer.

In South Korea rapid urbanisation not only caused the cities to expand; it also led to overcrowding. Since the 1960s, urban detached houses have often been built with a groundfloor that ostensibly contains a garage and rooms for servants. In reality it is often rented out or houses a small business to help the owner pay the mortgage. Even in higher-class neighbourhoods one can often hear knitting machines rattling or discover a small shop behind a garage door.

The first blocks of flats were not constructed until the 1970s. The first were part of slum redevelopment projects, simple blocks for low-income families built by the city government. Soon private construction companies also began to build large complexes of freehold flats in high-rise buildings with up to 15 storeys. The flats have retained the traditional division between rooms with underfloor heating and a large, wooden-floored entrance room with sliding doors that open on to a balcony. In the entrance hall Western-style upholstered furniture is often found today. The kitchen has changed. Its floor is now on the same level as the other floors, and there is no wall separating it from the entrance room. It serves as kitchen and dining room in one. The courtyard has been replaced by a glassed-in balcony along the kitchen wall. Here all the messy jobs are done that the housewife traditionally did in the courtyard, and here the large clay *kimch'i* pots stand. Thus the outward appearance of Korean cities has been 'Westernised', but the traditional Korean way of living has been retained for the most part.

In contrast to South Korea, the North Korean cities have no problems with runaway urbanisation. Population movements are tightly controlled and are related to economic conditions. When the cities were rebuilt after the devastation of the Korean War, with a lot of assistance from friendly socialist countries, their appearance changed considerably. Only very few city wards still have the dense, one-storey single family houses that are so typical of South Korean cities. North Korean cities have street after street of prefabricated eight-storey blocks of flats and do not differ much from the newer parts of the former East Berlin, Moscow or Novosibirsk. The exception is the central part of P'yŏngyang with its monumental palaces, revolutionary monuments and broad streets.

Readings

A Handbook of Korea, 1993. Seoul, Korean Overseas Information Service: 474-488

Rudiger Machetzki and Manfred Pohl (eds), 1988. *Korea*. Stuttgart: Thienemann

OECD Economic Surveys, 1993-1994, Korea. Paris: Organisation for Economic Co-operation and Development: 121-130

11

THE RURAL SCENE

11.1 Settlement patterns

Korean villages are generally densely clustered settlements. The individual farmhouses are separated from each other by narrow alleys. The preferred location for villages is at the southern foot of the hills at the edge of the rice plain. During the winter this location is sunny and well protected from the icy north winds. Only in the mountains of the north and east, where arable land is extremely sparse, are dispersed farmsteads found. Often they are lined up along a creek or the side of a valley.

Larger villages may have a grocery store, perhaps a barber, a pub and a rice mill. Apart from this there are neither stores nor craftsmen in Korean villages. These are concentrated in townships representing the lowest level of local administration, where they may be found in an astonishing number and degree of specialisation. These central places are also the venues for periodic markets, held usually every five days. A special square is reserved for this purpose. Some markets are open-air, others have stalls. People flock to the market in small groups, each of the same sex, from the surrounding villages. There they are able to supply almost all of their needs for food, textiles, shoes, household goods and farm tools. Only for such durable purchases as sewing machines or TV sets is it necessary to go to the closest county seat.

Schools are also concentrated in a few locations. Every morning small troops of children from the surrounding villages can be spotted heading through the early morning mist rising from the rice fields, or in winter across the frozen rice paddies in the pale early morning sun, towards the centrally located school. It will consist of sprawling white-washed buildings beside a large, dusty yard. Whereas primary and middle schools can generally be reached by foot, high schools are usually located in the county seat, and the students have to take a local bus to get there.

In North Korea the structure of the villages has changed considerably. In many places the old straw-roofed houses have been replaced by small white buildings with red tile roofs. North Korea has been trying to diminish the traditional and still existing gap between urban and rural lifestyles by building multi-storey schools, day-nurseries, infirmaries, cultural centres and cinemas in the villages.

11.2 Agriculture

South Korea

Since the 1960s Korea has been industrialising at an increasingly rapid pace. This has been accompanied by equally rapid urbanisation, and the two processes together have had a profound effect on agriculture. Changing social and economic conditions have caused the agricultural population to view physical and economic factors in new ways. New agricultural regions have developed. The new regional structures have not, however, obliterated the old divisions between east and west coast, alluvial plains and mountains.

Between 1955 and 1990 the proportion of the total population employed in agriculture and fishing decreased dramatically from 61.9% to 15.3%. Nevertheless, agriculture is still the economic basis for a significant portion of the South Korean population. As a rule only some of the members of a family have left the countryside (though entire families may go). Consequently, farm size has not changed very much. Given the density of population in the small area that could be cultivated (21.2% of the total area), individual farms have always been very small, with an average size of only 1.22 ha. Only 1.7% of farms have more than 3 ha; almost two-thirds (61.8%) have less than 1 ha, and more than one-fourth (27.8%) less than 0.5 ha. As intensive as Korean farming is, such farms are of course too small to support a family. Extra income has to be earned, from day labour or traditionally from such crafts as rope making, basketry, making mats and straw bags. The main goal of such small farms is subsistence. For instance, in 1974 two-thirds of their agricultural income consisted in the value of the foodstuffs consumed in the household.

In the past years quite a number of medium-sized and large farms have succeeded in making the transition from subsistence farming to market-oriented farming. Several factors have contributed to this. Since younger family members have been moving to the cities and towns, the average family size in the countryside has decreased, from 6.3 persons in 1964 to 3.8 persons in 1990. With fewer people eating, more foodstuffs can be sold on the market. A number of technological innovations have also helped to increase considerably the yield per hectare. Irrigation systems have been expanded so that in 1990 73.4% of the area planted to rice was irrigated (compared with 54.6% in 1961). This has greatly lowered the risk inherent in rice-growing in a country with such variable summer precipitation. The use of chemical fertiliser has increased since Korea developed its own fertiliser industry (from 73 kg NPK/ha between 1958 and 1962 to 473 kg/ha in 1990) and this has also helped to improve yields on the leached-out soils.

A further factor has been the development of new rice varieties. The state-run experimental station in Suwǒn, in co-operation with the International Rice Research Institute, crossed tropical (*Indica*) varieties with local (*Japonica*) varieties and succeeded in developing new high-yield hybrid rice varieties that respond well to the increased use of nitrogenous fertiliser. In 1971, the first variety, '*T'ongil*', was introduced. It had a 37% higher yield per ha than traditional strains. Other new hybrid varieties were developed, and by 1977 54.6% of the total area cultivated with rice was planted to such new varieties. To spread these new rice strains and modern agricultural methods in general more effectively, a programme of integrated rural development was initiated, which came to be known as *Saemaǔl undong* ('new community movement'; see chapter 3.5 for a fuller discussion).

As a result of all of these innovations, South Korea succeeded in increasing rice yields by 50% in only two decades (from an average of 3.02 metric tons per hectare between 1961 and 1965 to 4.58 between 1986 and 1990). This meant that in good years South Korea had the highest rice yields in the world, and for the first time in its history no longer depended on rice imports. The government buys up most of the rice harvest at set prices, which are considerably higher than world market prices, and thus subsidises the country's farmers. Meanwhile, an entire year's harvest is stored in government warehouses. The rice surplus is not only due to increased production, however. The Korean diet has also been changing. Where previously rice was by far the most important staple food, nowadays increasingly more bread is being eaten, made of imported wheat. Furthermore, Koreans have started to eat more meat, and to feed the animals more and more feed grain is being imported, so that in spite of increased rice production, by 1990 South Korea was importing 58.9% of its total grain supply.

Since the third five year plan started in 1972, the Korean government has made increased efforts to improve the lot of the agriculture population, mainly through the application of price supports for rice. The result has been to increase the disparities between small subsistence farms and large market-oriented rice growers and between different agricultural regions. This has only served to accentuate the traditional gradient between the lowlands of the south and west coast and the mountainous east. The alluvial plains of the west and south coast with their particularly high proportion of rice paddies (more than 70% of the cultivated area) have turned into the agricultural region that is producing the greatest surpluses. They have of course profited especially from the increased yields, and the decreasing population pressure has also played a role in this region, which was previously particularly densely populated.

As a result, the agricultural landscape has changed very much in the past two decades. Where previously the rice paddies spread out like huge mosaics that had developed over the course of centuries, their knee-high dams exactly fitting the contours of the land, now the fields are strictly rectangular, 100 m long and 30 m wide, with new irrigation canals and wide paths. The old ox-drawn plough that had not changed in centuries has been almost entirely superseded by power tillers, of which there were 751,000 by 1990. As part of the *Saemaŭl* movement the rural population re-enforced the banks of rivers and canals and built roads and bridges, so that now practically all villages can be reached by car or power tiller, where previously many could only be reached on foot. The traditional Korean villages were almost inconspicuous with their brown mud walls and grey straw roofs, nestling at the foot of the hills above the rice plains. Nowadays their bright coloured *Saemaŭl* roofs stand out between the green of the rice paddies and the reddish brown of the hills. The *Saemaŭl* movement did much to raise the standard of living in the countryside. Wells, sewage canals, communal washhouses, village centres and a central water supply were built. Except for some of the most remote islands and mountain areas, by 1984 electricity had been supplied to 98% of all farming and fishing households. TV antennas could often be seen sprouting out of the roofs as soon as a village was electrified.

These actively developing regions with agricultural surpluses contrast with a much more passive region in the high mountains of the T'aebaek range north of the Scoul -P'ohang line and the central part of the Sobaek range. For the most part this region was not cultivated until the early part of this century, when rapid population growth forced landless farmers to try to eke out a living by slash and burn techniques of agriculture in remote, high mountain regions. The slopes are so steep that often less than 10% can be cultivated. For a long time it was considered a depressed area. Rice can only be grown in the narrow valley bottoms, and rice paddies make up less than 20% of the cultivated area. For climatic reasons farming was pretty much restricted to growing maize and potatoes, red beans, soy beans and foxtail millet on dry fields on the steep slopes in summer. Double cropping is not possible. Thus most of the mountain farmers barely managed to survive. For this reason the government encouraged migration out of these areas. Farming was prohibited on slopes that were steeper than 20° and reafforestation was carried out on a large scale. The government paid each farm family that moved out of the mountains a reward equal to one year's income.

Many of the remaining farmers have switched to market production meanwhile, cleverly taking advantage of the climatic conditions. For instance, farmers in the high mountains of the northeast grow Chinese cabbage and radishes for the urban markets in the hot summer months, when these vegetables, highly important for the Korean cuisine, do not grow well in the lowland. Many farmers in the mountains also grow tobacco on a contract system with the Office of Monopoly and have begun to raise beef cattle on pastures on moderately steep slopes that would be in danger of erosion if used for crops.

Between the former depressed mountain areas and the alluvial plains with their food surplus, there is a broad area of hill country, covering mainly the foothills of the T'aebaek and Sobaek ranges and the Naktong river basin. With its balanced proportion of paddies and dry fields, it is an area particularly suited for subsistence agriculture. Nowadays, many farmers have turned to market-oriented production and are growing special crops, largely in vinyl greenhouses.

The innovation of special crops has contributed a great deal to regional diversity in Korean agriculture. With the rising standard of living, the demand for such crops has increased and many farmers have turned to the market. They have benefited from the expansion of the road network. All of these factors have helped to make this development particularly dynamic in the past two decades. For example, the farmers in the Kimhae plain in the delta of the Naktong river started to specialise in growing vegetables in winter in greenhouses constructed of bamboo poles and vinyl sheeting. This change did not come about until the highway from Seoul to Pusan was completed and it became possible to transport delicate vegetables (cucumbers, tomatoes, lettuce) rapidly to the markets of Seoul. Very abruptly the centre of commercial vegetable growing shifted from the area around Seoul, where greenhouses have to be heated in winter, to the south coast, 400 km away but with a much more favourable climate. As the highway network expanded, other areas also began to specialise in growing vegetables in greenhouses, and other centres are now found in the southeast in the valley of the Naktong river, in the southwest between Kwangju and Naju and even as far north as Taejŏn, Ch'ŏnan and Suwŏn, where the greenhouses are carefully covered with straw mats at night. Fruit was another special crop that spread as new highways were built on which it could be transported to urban markets. The traditional centre of apple growing was Taegu. From here orchards with apples, pears and peaches spread into various parts of the hill country that had hitherto been cultivated rather extensively. Centres are now around Yesan and Nonsan in South Ch'ungch'ŏng Province, P'yŏngt'aek and Ich'on in Kyŏnggi Province and Chŏnju in North Chŏlla Province.

Other special crops that play an important role in certain regions are ginseng, a traditional East Asian medicinal plant that is grown around Kŭmsan and on the island of Kanghwa, and tobacco, grown in North Ch'ungch'ŏng Province and processed at Sint'anjin. In the hill country of the upper Naktong river basin, mulberry bushes are grown to feed silkworms.

In spite of increasing rice yields, South Korea has not managed to become self-sufficient in grain production, its originally stated goal. In addition to rice, Western-style baked goods, meat, vegetables and fruit are being eaten. It is much more profitable to import wheat for baked goods and other grain for fodder and use the limited arable land for growing lucrative special crops. As a result, grain dropped from 74.0% to 41.9% of the total value of all agricultural crops between 1961 and 1990, while vegetables increased from 11.6% to 16.8% and fruit from 1.8% to 6.7% in the same period.

While the production of rice was increased by expanding irrigation systems (to 51.6% of the cultivated area in 1990), cultivation of other types of grain, especially winter barley, decreased sharply (from 29.8% of the cultivated area in 1970 to 8.2% in 1990). With this, double cropping has also decreased. Another crop that is no longer much grown is potatoes, particularly sweet potatoes, which were considered the 'poor man's rice'. Pulses have held their own, especially soybeans, the most important protein source in the former mostly vegetarian diet. Vegetable growing has increased greatly (from 6.4% of the cultivated area in 1970 to 11.5% in 1990). The most important vegetables are Chinese cabbage, radish, red pepper and garlic, the main ingredients of the indispensable *kimch'i*. Fruit growing has also increased greatly. In 1970, only 1.9% of the cultivated area was devoted to fruit growing; in 1990, 5.5% was. The most important kinds of fruit are apples, peaches, grapes, pears and persimmons, which are grown in plantations in the hill country. Tangerines are grown in Cheju island. Tangerine growing has increased particularly rapidly. In the past decade the area planted to this fruit has expanded by a factor of ten and is now second only to apples.

Livestock raising has increased rapidly as eating habits have changed (from 9.4% of the value of agricultural production in 1961 to 27.2% in 1990), but it still is very much subordinate to crop growing. Dairy farming was practically unknown in traditional Korea. As the urban population to a certain extent adopts Western eating habits, farm households are beginning to engage in dairy farming. It is geared very much to the urban market, however, and is therefore pretty much restricted to the immediate environs of the urban agglomerations. Large-scale cattle farms are run by big, well-funded concerns in such peripheral regions as the higher elevations of Cheju island and the mountains of Kangwŏn Province (where farm households have also now begun to raise cattle for beef). Otherwise family farms kept cattle mainly as draught animals. Pigs, raised by on average one-third of rural families, are still the main source of meat. The amount of meat eaten per person per day has risen from 13 g in 1966 to 40 g in 1989 (9 g of beef and 31 g of pork), but is still very low by comparison with the industrialised West (e.g.USA 200 g per day).

By the early 1990s quite a number of farmhouses had been abandoned and fields left fallow, as the older generation could no longer tend them. The size of farms may in fact increase in the not too distant future as many families turn away completely from farming and the remaining households take over their land. In an entirely new development, former rice paddies, now that South Korea is overproducing rice, are being used to grow vegetables in vinyl greenhouses. Until very recently no Korean farmer in his right mind would have thought of using paddy land for anything but rice, but today vegetables are even more profitable.

North Korea

North Korea is so mountainous that the cultivated area, at only 17.5% of the total, is even more limited than in South Korea. The continental climate, with its long, severe winters, also restricts agricultural use. Double cropping of rice paddies is impossible, and winter grain can only be grown on dry fields in the southern provinces of South and North Hwanghae and South P'yŏngan and a narrow strip along the east coast. After the division of the peninsula it was a big problem to feed the population. During the Japanese period rice had come from South Korea and other grains from Manchuria (the name then given to the northeast region of China). The North Koreans completely transformed their agricultural structure, however, reclaiming a lot of land. In contrast to South Korea, they have in good years been able to feed their population with the products they harvest themselves. However, in poor years North Korea too has to import grain. This has become increasingly difficult with the country's chronic shortage of foreign currency. By 1995, a combination of bad harvests and currency shortage had depleted food reserves to the point where North Korea has had to seek international assistance.

The most important part of the transformation of agriculture was the collectivisation of the small individual farms. There was some resistance to this, because many of the farmers did not want to give up the holdings they had received in the land reforms of 1946. Nevertheless, by August 1958 collectivisation was completed. In the same year the many small collective farms were combined to form agricultural co-operatives at the village level, each with around 300 families and 450 to 500 ha of cultivated land.

Land reform and the subsequent collectivisation have changed the traditional rural social structure fundamentally. The villages and Confucian-based family ties between individuals lost their importance, and the work brigades of the agricultural co-operatives became the new cells of rural society. North Korean producers' co-operatives are characterised by a high degree of integration. They not only control the entire agricultural production; they are also in charge of practically all aspects of life in the community, trade, supply of goods, finances, schools and health care. The individual farm families are combined in work brigades, which receive daily instructions from the co-operative's leaders, whose head is also the head of the village People's Committee.

State agricultural technicians help the co-operative's leaders with all technical questions, be it plans of what to cultivate, construction of irrigation systems, or use of machines, fertiliser and pesticides. This system guarantees that innovations are put into practice rapidly. The close liaison between functionaries and the co-operative's farmers is organised according to the 'Ch'ŏngsan-ri method', named after a village in South P'yŏngan that Kim Il Sung visited for two weeks in 1959 to study means of avoiding the blatant mistakes that can occur when government cadres give instructions without knowing the problems at the grassroots. The 'Ch'ŏngsan-ri method' obliges the functionaries to work together with the farmers and guide them and gives the farmers more say in the decision-making process.

All large investments lie in the hand of the state, be they in construction of irrigation systems, housing or community facilities, or purchase of agricultural machinery. The agricultural co-operatives, for their part, are obliged to deliver set quotas, determined annually, to the state. Only the surpluses can be used to pay the farmers. This gives the government direct control of agricultural income and consumption and ensures a sufficient supply of food for the urban population.

Collectivisation created the basis for large-scale agricultural innovations. Extensive irrigation systems increased the irrigated area almost tenfold. Massive application of chemical fertiliser also helped to raise agricultural production. Since the small collective farms were combined to form large co-operatives, great progress in mechanisation has also been made. In the fertile plains along the west coast, heavy tractors dominate the agricultural landscape. They are used almost entirely for transportation and ploughing. Machines for transplanting or harvesting rice are so rare, that even today North Korean agriculture is extremely labour intensive. This is evident from the fact that 42.8% of employed persons are engaged in agriculture, a very high proportion for an industrialised country. Moreover, at peak times (transplanting rice seedlings by hand, harvesting by sickle) the urban population and the military have to be mobilised to help the farmers.

The main goal of North Korean agriculture is, as in South Korea, to produce enough grain. In 1984, 71% of the cultivated area was devoted to grain. Orographical and climatic conditions made it possible for only 35.2% of this proportion to be planted with rice. However, because rice yields are higher, the rice crop made up approximately one-half of the total grain harvest. Rice cultivation is concentrated in the western coastal plain, where the provinces of South Hwanghae and South and North P'yŏngan produce almost 70% of North Korea's rice. Because rice cultivation has increased so much, maize and millet, which used to be the most important staple foods in North Korea, have been relegated to second and third place. Maize is grown particularly in the northwest, where it extends up to an altitude of 800 m. In the hill country along the west coast, especially in the province of South Hwanghae, wheat is the most important dry-field crop. On the small fields scattered around in the mountains of the northern provinces the crops are restricted for climatic reasons to millet and kaoliang, which together still took up 23.5% of the cultivated area in 1984.

Vegetable growing was also expanded considerably by the introduction of artificial sprinkler systems and vinyl greenhouses. In campaigns to use the hill country that is too steep for ploughing, orchards and mulberry plantations (for silkworm culture) were also expanded. Increased cultivation of hills that used to be covered with secondary forests has worsened erosion, however, filling the rivers with silt and ultimately leading to disastrous floods in the rice plains and regular destruction of large parts of the harvests.

Livestock raising is still underdeveloped in North Korea. It is carried out mainly on centrally run state farms and 130 regional ones. Farms near the cities specialise in dairy farming or industrialised poultry farming for eggs and meat, whereas the farms in remote areas, as along the lower reaches of the Tumen, concentrate on beef cattle. Their purpose is also to test and introduce modern agricultural techniques.

11.3 Fishing and marine cultures

Food production in South Korea includes the surrounding seas. Because warm and cold ocean currents meet off Korea, conditions are excellent for a great variety of fish, including such tropical species as sardines, mackerels and hair tails (sabre fish) and such cold-water species as Alaska pollack, herring, cod, halibut and shrimp. Coastal fishing still contributes 54.7% of the total value of South Korea's fishery production, which at 3.2 million tons has already surpassed the pre-war production of the entire peninsula. At present coastal fishing is in a stage of transition from small wooden rowing boats or sailing boats run by part-time fishermen to full-time professional fishing with motor-driven craft. Deep-sea fishing has also developed into an important industry, and over 780 Korean fishing vessels now fish the important fishing grounds of the world. A large proportion of the catch is processed on board factory ships and directly exported.

Another important export item, particularly to Japan, is marine cultures cultivated in the shallow waters of the many bays and sounds. The main products are seaweed, laver (thin dried sheets of algae), oysters and clams. Since 1962, traditional methods of gathering marine products have been giving way to carefully tended, artificially seeded cultures, following Japanese examples. Marine cultures thrive only within a very limited temperature range. The nets and ropes on which they grow have to be constantly moved to keep them in the water layers with the correct temperatures. They are therefore extremely labour intensive, but they require little capital and are an ideal way for the coastal inhabitants to earn extra income in the winter.

Readings

Eckart Dege, 1982. *Entwicklungsdisparitäten der Agrarregionen Südkoreas*. Kiel: Kieler Geographische Schriften 55

Kyong-Dong Kim, 1979. *Man and Society in Korea's Economic Growth*. Seoul: Seoul National University Press: 143-206

Pak Ki-Hyuk and Sidney Gamble, 1975. *The Changing Korean Village*. Seoul: Shinhung Press

Clark W. Sorensen, 1983. *Over the Mountains are Mountains*. Seattle: University of Washington Press

12

THE BIRTH OF AN ASIAN TIGER

The chapters that follow are concerned with the recent development of the economy of the Republic of Korea (ROK). Since the end of the Pacific War, the economy of the Democratic People's Republic of Korea (DPRK), for reasons discussed in chapters 3.4, 9.5 and 11.2, has developed along very different lines from that the ROK.

12.1 The speed of industrialisation

The rate of economic growth in the Republic of Korea during the generation following the ceasefire between North and South in 1953 is one of the fastest and most sustained among non-petroleum exporting nations anywhere in the world. In the years of recovery following the Korean War, the ROK attained an average annual GNP growth rate of 7.5%, increasing to an average of 9.6% between 1960 and 1976. Even in the worldwide recessions of the late 1970s, early 1980s and the 1990s, Korea has maintained an annual rate of GNP growth unequalled by most developed or developing countries. Average annual household income rose from US $82 in 1961 to $6498 in 1991. The overall performance of the Korean economy since 1953 compares favourably with that of more advanced industrial giants such as the United States, Germany and even neighbouring Japan. Along with Hong Kong, Singapore, Japan and Taiwan, South Korea ranks as an 'Asian tiger' in terms of its economic strength.

The rate of growth has not, of course, been uniform throughout the Korean economy. The most spectacular progress until recently was in the industrial sector, with an annual average growth rate of approximately 14% until the mid-1980s. Thus, the industrial share of Korea's GNP doubled from 16% in 1962—at the outset of Park Chung Hee's first five-year plan—to 31% in 1981, just 20 years later. The share of the service sector increased from 47% to 51% during the same period, but has recently increased further as Koreans have become more affluent. By contrast, the agricultural sector declined over these 20 years, from 37% in 1962 to 18% in 1981 and less than 10% in 1991 (though agricultural production doubled during the same period).

Causes of economic progress

A number of factors help to explain this rapid transformation.. Perhaps of paramount importance is education. The significance traditionally attached to education in Confucian societies has ensured a continuing supply of capable businessmen and entrepreneurs as well as of scientists, engineers and technicians. The introduction of vocational studies was initially a legacy of the Japanese occupation, and was ultimately based on German precedent. Also part of the legacy was a ready pool of trained and experienced miners and factory workers, many of whom had been deported to Manchuria or Japan during the occupation, but who brought their skills back to Korea with them.

While seeking to develop the Korean economy for their own benefit, the Japanese left a good infrastructure of transport and communications, which served as the basis for the modern network of roads, railways and ports. It was during the Japanese occupation that Pusan, now Korea's second largest city, was developed because of its proximity to Japan; and the Seoul-Pusan railway was built. Originally, the line extended beyond Seoul to P'yŏngyang, Manchuria and Beijing and was an integral part of Japanese colonial expansion. To the south of Seoul, the city of Taejŏn—barely more than a village in pre-Japanese days—was developed by the colonising Japanese as a major railway junction and depot. Thus, although the period of occupation was and remains anathema to most Koreans, the economic development which ensued after the Japanese departure from the peninsula did to some degree owe its origins and its rapidity to Japanese foundations.

Another factor in stimulating economic growth in the ROK was the north-south division of the peninsula at the 38th parallel, which was designated as the ceasefire line between the Communists and the United Nations forces in 1953. This division brought about widespread economic disruption and dislocation. Two-thirds of the Korean population and two-thirds of the paddy acreage remained in the South, but the North retained most of the peninsula's mineral resources. More seriously, most of the peninsula's electricity had previously been produced by northern hydropower. These very deficiencies, however, acted as a spur to effort in the South.

In 1953, the fledgling ROK was faced not only with the need to reform its government, following half a century of disruption, but also with the problem of rebuilding its entire economy. An obstacle to economic reconstruction was the requirement for a large military budget in the light of the constant fear of renewed civil war. However, because of the continued presence of US troops in the South, this defence burden (estimated roughly at 5% of GNP) has been considerably tempered. This has enabled the ROK to diversity its economy and export potential, in contrast to the DPRK, which spends an estimated 20% or more of its GNP on defence and relies heavily on the export of raw materials and military expertise to balance its budget.

A BBC radio programme in January 1996 in the series *Asian Gold* suggested that anti-Communism on its own did not represent a political or economic creed sufficient to account for the birth of this political 'Asian tiger'. Perhaps not, but when combined with the very real strength of anti-Japanese sentiment, expressed as a determination to compete in the Japanese export market, the two negatives together have created a powerful positive incentive. This, when added to the resolve of Koreans and their leaders, has brought the Republic from a war-torn, impoverished state in 1953 to that of a fully developed economy less than half a century later. Geo-political factors have played a crucial part in the rapid development.

Other stimuli to growth

From the end of the Korean War in 1953 until the military coup of 1961 that brought General Park Chung Hee to power, economic policy was of necessity predominantly inward-looking. It was mainly concerned with rebuilding the housing stock, infrastructure and industrial facilities that had been destroyed by war, with controlling inflation, and with maximising inward foreign aid. The South Korean government was not entirely independent. All major economic policies from 1952 were determined jointly by it and the US aid mission to Korea, so American interests were initially as important as Korean ones in making economic decisions. At least in the early years of post-war reconstruction, this caused few problems to South Koreans and was generally regarded as highly beneficial, given that the major objective of both governments was to make the ROK economically as well as politically secure—an objective it could not easily have achieved alone.

A sweetener for the continuing American military presence and for American participation in Korean policy decisions was the extent of US economic aid to South Korea, without which successful reconstruction might have been much slower. Between 1953 and 1960, South Korea was heavily dependent on aid from two principal sources: the United States and the United Nations Korea Reconstruction Agency (UNKRA), itself heavily dominated—as were the United Nations forces remaining in Korea—by the US. In addition to financing rebuilding projects, grants from these donors facilitated the import of goods for both domestic and industrial use and in due course enabled a policy of import substitution to be initiated, albeit on a small scale first, in some consumer goods industries. By 1957, when the South Korean government became preoccupied with price stabilisation, the United States announced its intention of reducing aid, though this nevertheless continued in various forms until the mid-1970s.

By the end of the 1950s, the extensive post-war aid had largely done its work. With substantial completion of the reconstruction programme, the South Korean government changed direction in terms of both economic policies and leadership. The younger generation demanded a more pro-actively Korean style of government, while industrialists became anxious to extend import substitution to a wider variety of products, which South Korea was by then capable of producing. From that time the ROK was determined to play, at the expense of price stabilisation, a more self-deterministic and assertive role in the world economy.

12.2 The course of industrialisation

The period of most sustained rapid growth, and accompanying social change, was from 1961 to 1975. These years saw the transition of the South Korean nation from a mainly agricultural to an industrial society. Indeed, the government's emphasis from the early 1960s on export-oriented industrial growth led, initially, to a neglect of the countryside which was not corrected until the 1970s (see chapter 3.5).

The new military government of Park Chung Hee adopted, in 1961, the first five-year economic development plan. It aimed at achieving an annual GNP growth rate of 7.1% between 1962 and 1966, by creating the basis for self-sustained growth independent of external aid. Beginning with a reform of the exchange rate in 1961, the economic programme was initially concerned with fiscal changes to the budget and to the currency and tax systems. The government also began to seek foreign loans and encourage investment from overseas. Gradually it sought to increase exports, and conversely to restrict imports, from the early 1960s. Among the first import-substituting industries were iron and steel, shipbuilding, petrochemicals, textiles and machinery. All of these were later to develop into export industries in their own right.

The first five-year plan was even more successful than anticipated, despite a slow growth rate during the first year. As a consequence, it was followed by a series of such plans. Although there were obvious differences from one to the next—according to the stage and rate of economic development—they all shared one similarity: a commitment to labour-intensive, export-led industrialisation during this period.

By the mid-1970s, the success of South Korea's economic policies was clear. The Korean economy was noted not only for its rapid GNP growth rate, but also for its export of manufactured goods which, by 1973-75, comprised over 80% of total exports. Chief among Korean manufactured exports were textiles, wood and rubber products, metals and metal products, and machinery. In heavy industry, Korean shipbuilding was beginning to dominate world markets.

12.3 The financing of industrialisation

The linchpin of industrial growth in Korea was heavy investment, initially from overseas and in particular from the USA. In the immediate post-war period, individual entrepreneurs and businesses were generally in no position to invest their own capital in modernisation and expansionist activities. (The period required for capital formation is of necessity a long one.) The Korean government was thus largely dependent on external grants and loans in the early stages of its industrialisation programme. The balance changed, however. While almost 50% of general government expenditure and 70% of Korea's imports were financed by grants from abroad during the years 1953-60, the proportion of foreign capital in the country's total investment programme fell to less than 40% in the following 15 years of rapid industrial expansion as other forms of investment became of increasing significance. Of these, the most notable was domestic saving, which appears to have played as important a part in national capital formation as government investment during the later 1960s and 1970s, following the interest rate reform of 1965. Improved standards of living among a growing proportion of the population in the wake of industrial advance may have produced surplus funds to invest in savings.

The government's contribution to national investment was greatly stimulated by an increase in taxation, which rose from around 10% of wages and salaries in the early 1960s to about 14% ten years later. Indirect taxes, such as those on consumer goods, services and fuel, together with taxes on property and capital, continued to comprise a large proportion of government income. Tariffs on imported goods, including oil, were high, although the protection of most Korean manufacturers declined from 1955 to 1975. For a long time, however, the government gave businesses greater incentives to export than to produce goods for domestic consumption.

The third major contributor to Korean savings and capital investment was the corporate and business sectors. Companies have been the single largest element in Korean economic growth since 1961, illustrated by a compound GDP growth rate of over 13% per annum between 1961 and 1975. During this period they contributed approximately half of all national savings.

12.4 The structure of Korean industry: rise of the *chaebŏl*

As already noted, the growth of the Korean economy from 1961 to 1975 was particularly marked by the production of manufactured exports. Even with government subsidies and incentives indicated by the five-year plans and other policies, it is unlikely that the manufacturing sector could have grown so rapidly were it not for the underlying nature and structure of the firms involved, which were capable not only of implementing decisions, but of making them independently. Korean industry prior to 1961, relatively small-scale though it was, was far removed from the domestic industries and even the individually-owned factories that normally characterise an economy in the early stages of its development.

The rapid expansion of manufacturing until the mid-1970s was due primarily to the growth of firms already in existence. Between 1962 and 1964, the total number of businesses grew by less than 40%, but tripled in terms of the workers they employed, and increased an average of nine times in terms of production. Moreover, the larger a firm, the more rapidly it tended to expand.

How did this happen? Put simply, the growth of Korean firms is an example of vertical integration. In the automobile industry, for example, Korean companies such as Hyundai and Daewoo needed not only to build vehicles. At one end of the scale they also needed to make the nuts and bolts to put them together, and at the other to construct the roads for them to run on. They also needed to import rubber for tyres and oil for fuel, necessitating involvement in both shipping and shipbuilding. This is how the *chaebŏl,* or conglomerates, developed. Other notable examples include such firms as Lucky-Goldstar (now LG), Samsung and Lotte. By the mid-1970s, around 30% of Korean GNP was being produced by roughly 35 firms. Production was very much dominated by half a dozen firms.

This economic structure, while remarkable to Western observers, is not at all unusual in developing countries and especially in East Asia, where comparisons between the Korean *chaebŏl* and the Japanese *zaibatsu* are sometimes made. Indeed, while the most marked differences between Japanese and Korean conglomerates are said to lie in management and government control, it remains a fact that some of the Korean *chaebŏl,* such as Samsung (see Factsheet 5.2), have their roots in the Japanese era. The close relationship between the *chaebŏl* and the Korean government was crucial to the development of the economy. Given that the nation's economic structure was dominated by relatively few firms, close government direction, if not actual control, was relatively easy. The *chaebŏl* were in a far better position than smaller firms to benefit from government inducements to export on account not only of their size but also of the variety of their activities. The construction industry, for instance, dominated by firms such as Hyundai and Daewoo, was to become one of Korea's most successful exports.

Readings

A. H. Amsden, 1989. *Asia's Next Giant: South Korea and Late Industrialisation.* New York: Oxford University Press

J. Cherry, 1993. *Republic of Korea.* London: Cassell

K. S. Kim and M. Roemer, 1979. *Growth and Structural Transformation.* Cambridge, MA: Harvard University Press

E. S. Mason *et al.*, 1980. *The Economic and Social Modernization of the Republic of Korea.* Cambridge, MA: Harvard University Press

13

THE TIGER MATURES

13.1 The era of diversification

As a result of the international oil crisis and the subsequent steep increase in the price of oil in 1974, Korea—which was and remains heavily dependent on imported oil— found itself with a $2 billion budget deficit and trade restrictions on exports such as textiles and footwear imposed by its major overseas competitors, especially the United States. In the wake of the oil crisis, which affected all oil-importing industrial nations, the world economy went into recession. South Korea was one of the first countries to emerge. By 1977 it had succeeded, for the first time since the war, in achieving a trade surplus. It did this in part by diversifying exports to include the non-manufacturing sector, especially construction.

Ironically, some of the major markets for Korea's booming construction industry were Middle Eastern nations whose oil policies had caused the crisis in the first place. Not only Korean companies, but large armies of Korean workers began to go overseas to fulfil construction contracts in Middle East countries such as Saudi Arabia and Southeast Asian states such as Malaysia and Indonesia.

A new era in South Korean industrialisation began in this way. By virtue of the variety of activities incorporated in their structure, the *chaebŏl* were in a strong position to lead the movement to diversify in order to compete in world markets. While export-led manufacturing, including textiles and footwear, continued to comprise a major part of the nation's GNP, the industrial base gradually and increasingly shifted toward heavy industry. With the growth in both domestic and overseas construction contracts came an increase in activities such as shipbuilding and automobile manufacture. And with these came the increasing need to produce steel at home rather than import it from neighbouring rivals such as Japan.

In the 1970s and the 1980s, the growth rate in the steel industry was faster than that of the Korean economy as a whole. Whereas in 1970 South Korea had produced just 0.1% of the world's steel, by 1990 it was the sixth largest producer in the world. Production is dominated by POSCO (the P'ohang Steel Corporation), which opened its first integrated iron and steel plant at P'ohang, on the southeast coast north of Pusan, in 1973. By the early 1980s this firm alone was the world's twelfth largest steel producer (it is today the second largest).

As had been the case 20 years earlier, political events in the late 1970s were to have an impact on the course of South Korean economic development. So, too, were other developments in the world economy. In 1979, exports declined for the first time in 20 years, and the GNP growth rate fell to 6.5%—its lowest since the first oil crisis. There were various reasons for this. The ROK was at an economic crossroads, having started to lose its competitive edge in manufacturing exports as a result of high inflation, which led to a 29% increase in wages in the latter part of the decade. Countries such as Taiwan and Singapore, in contrast, managed to keep their labour costs low. Meanwhile, Korea had not yet established a leading role in the heavy industries in which it was investing substantially. In 1979, Park Chung Hee was assassinated, and in 1980 a poor rice harvest at home and the second oil crisis abroad produced a negative GNP growth rate for the first time since the government's industrialisation programme began.

13.2 The need for consolidation

It was clear that the need to stabilise the economy after two decades of rapid growth was paramount. Fiscal measures were introduced in the fifth five-year plan under the new president, Chun Doo Hwan, which eventually reduced the annual rate of inflation—over 25% in 1980—to one-tenth of that figure within six years. Domestic markets were expanded by reducing or eliminating import tariffs; and regulations restricting foreign investment began to be eased in an effort to stimulate local industry.

A the same time, measures were introduced to curb the expansion of the *chaebŏl*, which in some cases were felt to be virtual monopolies of whole sectors of industry. Incentives were offered to small and medium-sized firms to help them gain a stronger foothold in both domestic and foreign markets, and in 1981 the Anti-Monopoly and Fair Trade Act was passed. The need to curb conglomerate growth was illustrated by the collapse of the Kukje group in 1985, which sent shock waves through the entire economy. It was felt that Kukje, like other giant corporations, had expanded too rapidly into areas unconnected with its original interests, resulting in heavy debts and eventual bankruptcy.

Although stabilisation was a key feature of the fifth five-year plan, slowdown was not. The search for new products and new markets continued as before. During this decade Korea became a 'high-tech' economy, adding electrical and electronic goods to its list of manufactured products. The domestic market expanded as Koreans themselves increasingly became consumer oriented. In an effort to improve the country's image in the world and to prove itself as a developed nation, the ROK hosted the Asian Games in 1986 and the Olympics in 1988, thus further boosting local industry and infrastructure in Seoul and its environs.

13.3 The emergence of a developed nation

The growth of the domestic market since the 1980s has added a new dimension to the South Korean economy. Not only have Korean producers adjusted their range of goods for domestic consumption, but the import of luxury goods has become a lucrative alternative for many companies previously engaged in export. The expansion of imports in the early 1990s led to substantial trade deficits and to increased friction with rival overseas producers. Previously, South Korean manufacturers had to compete with American products in the USA, Japanese in Japan, and so on, which was only possible while production and labour costs were sufficiently low to offset the import tariffs of those countries. From the late 1980s, the situation began to reverse. Foreign goods had to compete on the Korean market, and Korean import restrictions made that all but impossible.

In order to maintain good relations with its trading partners, therefore, the ROK has been under pressure—from groups at home as well as overseas—to liberalise its tariff structure and open up its domestic market to foreign competition. This affects two aspects of the economy in particular. One is the *chaebŏl*, whose monopolies are threatened by the local presence of foreign competitors, and particularly those whose labour and production costs are now lower than Korea's. One way in which the *chaebŏl* are confronting this is by building production plants in other countries, such as Britain, to reduce their own costs. Another is by intensifying their sales activities in Europe and other trading blocs in order to diversify their markets away from their older trading partners of Japan and the USA. The other aspect is the agricultural sector. One of the major obstacles facing the recent Uruguay round of the GATT talks was the opening up of South Korea's rice markets to foreign producers. Experts predicted that this would result in a 25% decline of the nation's rice farmers, who form the greater part of a rapidly declining economic sector. Meanwhile, the import of almost all agricultural products apart from rice and beef is due to be liberalised by 1997.

Side by side with efforts to seek harmonious trading relations with other nations through bilateral or multilateral agreements such as GATT, the quest for international recognition as a major world economy is being pursued. In its application to join the Organisation for Economic Cooperation and Development in 1996, the ROK is seeking to strengthen its ties with, and take its place among, the world's economically advanced nations.

13.4 The ROK and its trading partners

North-South relations

South Korea's economic development during the decades that have elapsed since the Korean War has inevitably affected its relationship with the DPRK. Most recently this has changed from one of intense economic and political rivalry to one of unilateral aid as the North Korean economy apparently deteriorates. In recent years, with the changes in its own economy, the ROK has learned that its new-found economic security is not guaranteed. It has also learned, from the German experience, that reunification—still a much sought-after goal—is likely to be attained at a high price to the South in terms of the aid and investment that will probably have to be injected in to the Northern economy. In a sense, the ROK may have to do for the DPRK what the USA and the United Nations did for South Korea between 1953 and 1961.

This does not lessen the ROK's desire for reunification. Recently, however, more emphasis has been placed on economic co-operation between North and South—as in the case of improved telecommunications on both sides of the DMZ and international projects such as the Tumen Delta development—and less on the single government of a unified Korea. This is due partly to the uncertainties of the North's economy and the potential burden of economic reunification to the South, but also partly to changing relations with the ROK's other neighbours.

South Korea and East Asia

After the Korean War, tension ran high in the ROK not only from fear of another invasion from the North, but also because of uncertainties elsewhere. Hostility towards Japan was still paramount, but so too was distrust of both the Soviet Union and China. The reversion of Hong Kong to China in 1997 and the effect this will have on Hong Kong's subsequent ability to continue to perform as one of the 'Asian tigers' will undoubtedly influence Korea's economic future, although the impact is impossible to predict. China has designs on another 'tiger'—Taiwan—with equally unpredictable consequences for its development and that of neighbouring countries.

With regard to Russia, tension between it and South Korea has eased considerably in recent years. Even before the Soviet Union ceased to exist, the possibility of economic co-operation with the ROK was under discussion. Indeed, in the late 1980s South Korea was already involved in capital investment and loans to its former enemy, especially with a view to tapping the rich natural resources of Siberia. The Tumen Delta project, which aims at developing a marsh and forest area bordered by Russia, China and North Korea into a free market zone, has attracted attention from South Korea and from Japan as an investment of both technology and capital. It is through joint economic projects like this that political tensions in the region are most likely to be eased, if not altogether resolved.

Indeed, it is almost harder to imagine the ROK working with Japan than with any of the other countries involved in the Tumen Delta development. As well as the ages-old animosity that has existed between the two nations, Japan—currently the strongest economy in East Asia—has perhaps more to lose than any other country from the possible reunification of North and South Korea. The strong industrial base of the South, combined with the natural resources of the North, might enable a united Korea to outstrip Japan's economic performance in the next century. It is thus essential for Japan to maintain interest in the region, which would give it as well as the ROK not only a base in the landmass of northeast Asia, but also a terminal for overland trade with Europe.

Korea and Europe

Korea is now better connected with the outside world than at any previous stage in its history. For the first time since World War II, it is possible for passenger aircraft to fly from Seoul over Siberia and Russia to Scandinavia and Europe. Travel times have been vastly reduced, an important factor in the development of business between the two regions.

For the past decade or so, South Korea has been anxious to increase its trade and its links with Europe. The desire to avoid being part of either a Japanese or an American economic empire and more specifically the wish to counter trade imbalances with Japan and recent protectionist practices in the USA, have prompted it to diversify its trade away from the United States and Japan.

Economic relations between the ROK and Britain, first formalised by diplomatic treaty in 1883, have considerably broadened in recent years. By the late 1980s Britain ranked twelfth among the ROK's trading partners, while the ROK was twenty-eighth among Britain's. The UK has had a trade deficit with South Korea since 1973, which has widened considerably during the past two decades. In particular, Britain has lost out to South Korea in major industries such as shipbuilding and steel. The principal British exports to the ROK are chemicals, machinery, plant, scientific instruments and leather, while the UK imports Korean textiles, clothing and footwear and, more recently, automobiles. Korean electronic goods are now manufactured as well as sold in this country. British firms have tended to lag behind those of France, Germany and the Netherlands in the export of consumer goods to South Korea, although banking and insurance concerns such as Lloyds and Barclays have played a significant part in the opening up of the domestic South Korean market to overseas investment. The ROK has been accused in the past by the EC of 'dumping' goods—especially in the shipbuilding and electronics industries—and of undermining copyright and patent agreements. It still has to overcome long-standing ignorance and misconceptions among Europeans. As in the case of the Tumen Delta project, where Koreans would work together with other nationalities, projects such as the Samsung plant in northeast England, with an injection of about $1 billion, may go further than mere trade agreements to ease such mistrust.

Readings

E. C. Hwang, 1993. *The Korean Economies: A Comparison of North and South.* Oxford: Oxford University Press

D. Kim and N. Sopiee (eds), 1979. *Regional Cooperation in the Pacific Area.* Seoul: Seoul National University Press

Tony Michell, 1988. *From a Developing to a Newly Industrialised Country: The Republic of Korea, 1961-82.* Geneva: International Labour Office

B. N. Song, 1990. *The Rise of the Korean Economy.* Oxford: Oxford University Press

14

THE STING IN THE TAIL?

A perspective on South Korean economic development

This chapter looks at some economic and social consequences of progress. The development of the South Korean economy over the past 35 years has brought about impressive social as well as economic achievements, such as a general rise in living standards, high rates of employment, and improved educational standards and facilities. Yet there have also been considerable costs. The rapid growth of the population, with its improved health and greater longevity, has placed a burden on land and resources. The population has also become highly mobile, and accelerating urbanisation has both increased the strain on urban infrastructure and more than halved the numbers employed in agriculture. Overseas emigration, especially to the United States, has become a characteristic of the ROK. All this has resulted in an erosion of the traditional extended family system and Confucian social structure, leaving a gap in social welfare planning where the government—interventionist in economic affairs to a degree that would not be tolerated in most Western industrial nations—has previously had no role and which it has been slow to fill.

14.1 The demographic revolution

Since the Korean War, the population of the ROK has more than doubled. In July 1993, the total population stood at 43.7 million. Because of the mountainous nature of its terrain, there is relatively little room for such a large population. After Bangladesh and Taiwan, it is the third mostly densely populated nation in the world, with 440 persons per square km. The annual rate of population growth reached a peak of 2.6% in the 1960s, but has since declined to around 1.0% in the 1990s.

Such rapid population growth is due to two principal factors: a decline in the death rate and an increase in the birth rate. The fall in South Korea's death rate from 33 persons per 1000 in 1955 to 15 per 1000 in 1965 and 7 per 1000 by the early 1980s, initially attributed to the cessation of war, is due to generally improved living standards throughout the country during this period and a result of better and more extensive medical care. From 1955 to 1975, the number of licensed health personnel (doctors, nurses and pharmacists) quadrupled; and an increase in compulsory health insurance to include most workers has helped to remedy the previous under-utilisation of hospital facilities. Average life expectancy has increased to 67 for men and 75 for women in 1990 from 51 and 54 respectively in 1960. Rural infant mortality fell from 106 per 1000 live births in 1953 to 12 per 1000 by the late 1980s. In recent years the ROK's death rate has been relatively stable.

The birth rate too has changed, but in a very different way. In the years following the Korean War, and especially during the 1960s and early 1970s, it soared. The increase was initially due to a post-war baby boom which, combined with the high rate of infant mortality at the time, encouraged couples to have families of 6 or 7 children. The desire of a Confucian society to produce male heirs compounded the increase in births by encouraging women to continue their families until a son was born. In the two decades or so following the war it was not uncommon to find families consisting of four or more girls, with their youngest sibling a boy.

Contraception, promoted by government campaigns to encourage couples to limit their family size, has led to a slowdown in the rate of population growth. Abortion, too, is frequently practised. Since it became possible to determine the gender of a foetus it is feared that females may be sometimes aborted in favour of males. This may be already imbalancing the sex ratio of the Korean population. Later average age at marriage for both partners, and especially women, also tends to reduce the rate of population growth. The number of unmarried women as a proportion of all women aged between 20 and 24 increased from 72.1% in 1985 to 80.7% in 1990. This is mainly due to the growing numbers of women in the urban workforce, especially in the service sector—itself the most rapid growing part of the economy. Young men for their part have to fulfil compulsory military service.

The fact that a society in transition from an agricultural to an industrial economy undergoes rapid population growth based on an increasing birth rate and a declining death rate is attested by the experience of many other countries, such as Britain during the 19th century. Put very simply, the argument is that the population increase accompanying industrialisation stems from the need to create a supply of labour. This in turn stimulates industrial growth as the larger population needs to support itself. In the case of Korea, it is at best only partially true. Obviously, South Korea's industrial labour supply in the 1960s was not the result of post-war baby boom, which matured a decade later. It is easier to define the relationship between industrial and demographic maturity. As standards of living improve, so people tend to have smaller families. And as the population growth rate slows down, so the age structure changes. Mature industrial nations such as Britain, the United States, France, Germany and Japan have ageing populations, in which the ratio of retired people to those in employment is ever-increasing. Although Korea still has a young population—the average age in the late 1980s was only 27 years—the proportion of older people is constantly growing, and the distorted sex ratio in favour of males will drastically affect the birth rate in the next generation. (See chapters 7.2 and 9.4 for further discussion.)

14.2 Migration and urbanisation

South Korea is not only the third most densely populated country in the world; it is also one of the most urbanised. According to the 1990 census, nearly two-thirds of the South Korean population lived in cities of over 50,000 inhabitants, and nearly half the total population lived in the six largest cities, each with over one million inhabitants. In the United States and Western Europe, the proportion of the population living in cities with over 50,000 inhabitants grew at the rate of about 1% annually between 1950 and 1975. In other less developed nations, the rate was between 2% and 3%. During the same 25-year period in the ROK, however, the rate of urbanisation was over 4% per annum. One-quarter of the nation's population currently lives in Seoul.

The initial reason for South Korea's rapid urbanisation was, of course, rural-to-urban migration during the 1960s and the 1970s, a result of the location of the nation's growing industries in the cities. This in turn affected the urban birth rate, since such migration tends to be age selective and favours those in the younger, economically active and therefore reproductive age groups (20-45). Seoul was the greatest beneficiary. The location of central government there since 1394, together with the city's political, educational and cultural pre-eminence, had always attracted people to the capital (see chapter 10.1). However, initial policies to establish satellite cities around Seoul (such as Sŏngnam, Puch'ŏn, Anyang and the ancient fortified city of Suwŏn) made congestion worse, not better. While they may have slowed the rate of population growth in Seoul itself, the capital is like the hub of a wheel, to which all the spokes are connected. More and more workers commute into Seoul from satellite cities and, as a result of the increase since the late 1980s in private car ownership, traffic congestion lasts from early morning until late at night.

The ROK's second and third largest cities are respectively the southern port city of Pusan and the textile city of Taegu. Also experiencing recent rapid growth are other older cities such as Inch'ŏn (the port for Seoul), Taejŏn and Kwangju. However, their rate of growth has slowed since the early 1980s as some of their traditional industries have begun to decline. New areas have been designated for industrial growth, such as Masan and Ch'angwŏn on the south coast, which have become centres for engineering works.

On the southeast coast, Ulsan is now one of the world's foremost shipbuilding sites, dominated by the Hyundai Corporation, which also has a vehicle plant there. Also on the east coast is the port of P'ohang, the home since 1973 of POSCO. Taedŏk, near Taejŏn, has become a focal point for government-sponsored research and development; and Taejŏn itself was the centre of the 1993 Expo, aimed not only at stimulating investment in R&D but also at diverting tourism away from Seoul.

Factors other than locational convenience have sometimes influenced the selection of sites for development. A good example of this is Kumi, just under 50 km north of Taegu. Although on the main railway line between Seoul and Pusan, it is surrounded by mountains which often prevent the dispersal of pollution and smog. Its proximity to the industrial city of Taegu exacerbates pollution in the entire region, which is still a major farming area. Kumi, however, was the birthplace of Park Chung Hee, and he was anxious to stimulate economic growth in his native town.

One other aspect of Korean migration must be considered: that of overseas emigration. In the 1960s and early 1970s, around 40,000 South Koreans emigrated every year. This figure has declined in recent times, partly because of improved living conditions at home and government incentives for return migration. But as late as 1992, over 10,000 South Koreans emigrated in one year, of whom more than 7000 went to the USA (see chapter 15.4 for further discussion).

Net emigration loss effects a population in two ways: it reduces the size of that population—which is why it may be encouraged if population growth is too rapid—and it causes 'brain drain'. The majority of overseas emigrants leaving their native country voluntarily tend to be young but also extremely well qualified: doctors, university professors and so on. On the other hand, it may stimulate not only the movement of persons but also of capital, goods and services between two nations. The ideal is certainly not to check emigration but to try to counterbalance it by encouraging immigration. There is some evidence that this is beginning to happen in the Korean case, although Korea has retained—indeed, is proud of—its racial homogeneity and tends to attract foreign nationals as temporary workers rather than as permanent settlers.

14.3 Labour and industrial relations

The rapid growth of the South Korean workforce since the end of the Korean War has, from the employers' point of view, been beneficial since it meant that throughout the period of rapid industrial growth there was an abundant supply of labour. The laws of supply and demand have helped to determine that until fairly recently, when other factors began to affect the labour market, the price of labour has been cheap. Legislation preventing unions from altering this situation prevailed in most sectors until the late 1908s; and relations between employers and their workforce were often confrontational.

From then onwards, however, South Korean labour has become increasingly expensive. The years from before the Asian Games (1986) until after the Seoul Olympics (1988) saw an economic boom, which brought in its wake improved living standards as well as substantial wage increases and subsequent inflation. In addition, the growth of the high-tech and service industries meant that it became increasingly difficult to recruit workers in some sectors such as mining, construction and manufacturing. Accordingly, employers have increasingly sought to recruit workers from abroad. Construction companies engaged in overseas contracts had already employed both local and migrant labour for many years, in addition to Korean workers. In 1991, restrictions on the import of foreign labour to the ROK were lifted to allow small and medium-sized companies to recruit up to 6% of their workforce from overseas, compared with just 1% previously, and to retain them for one year instead of three months. Further liberalisation followed, as did a crackdown on illegal migrants. The majority of overseas workers in the Korean workforce are from China, Russia and former Soviet territories, and Southeast Asia (especially the Philippines). Ethnic Koreans wishing to return home are now given priority in recruitment drives.

Working and living conditions of the labour force, both Korean and foreign, have long given cause for concern in some Korean industries. Although the wages of foreign workers are generally better than those in their home countries, they were extremely low by modern Korean standards. During the period of rapid industrialisation the majority of South Korean workers were equally poorly paid. Many workers lived in dormitories or very basic housing provided by employers, and worked excessively long hours often in conditions which were at best potentially detrimental to health and at worst downright dangerous. Circumstances have now improved for many Korean workers. The question of how a nation can achieve economic growth without initially, or even subsequently, exploiting its workers is one that exercises politicians, planners and academics worldwide.

14.4 The environment and pollution

South Korea's remarkable industrial growth has been achieved at considerable expense, not least to the environment. The decision, taken in 1961, to create rapid economic growth was made despite the potential ecological consequences, which at the time were little appreciated even among the world's developed nations.

One example of this was the encouragement of nuclear power. In its efforts to minimise the nation's dependency on imported fuel, especially oil, the government decided to invest in a programme to build a number of nuclear reactors, with the technical assistance of nations such as France. The intention was to boost the ROK's electricity supplies. By comparison with coal-powered generators, nuclear power appeared to be a clean alternative. However, in the aftermath of the Chernobyl disaster (1986), efforts to find an acceptable substitute for nuclear power have increased. It seems likely that, as both natural and city gas replace coal for domestic use—thus reducing air pollution in urban areas—so it will be used in power stations in the future.

The continued used of *yŏnt'an*—a very poor grade of cheap coal with a high sulphur content—as both domestic and industrial fuel throughout the 1980s was a major cause of air pollution. However, stricter standards of enforcement in this respect, together with the more widespread use of gas, have reduced the amount of sulphur dioxide and carbon monoxide in air samples, as has the use of cleaner fuels for automobiles. This latter improvement has, however, probably been offset by the growing number of vehicles on the road.

The bulk of household waste is placed in landfills, some of which until recently were actually inhabited by the nation's poorest people, literally scrounging their living from leftovers and rubbish. Nanji-do, west of Seoul, the largest such landfill, has recently been landscaped and replaced by another larger site near Kimp'o Airport, which is due to last until the mid-21st century. Koreans are now being encouraged to recycle their household waste, with collection points for glass, paper and aluminium located throughout major cities such as Seoul and a 'pay as you throw away' policy introduced for the removal of other domestic rubbish.

Smog, however, continues to be a major problem within the basin in which Seoul is situated. So do other forms of pollution, such as noise levels and water contamination. In 1991, the noise levels in all of South Korea's major cities exceeded acceptable limits in both urban and industrial areas. Industries are major offenders with regard to water pollution. In March 1991, 30 tons of phenol resin were dumped untreated into the Naktong river, a source of drinking water for several million South Koreans living in Taegu and Pusan. As a result of this and other incidents, the government has become increasingly active in its efforts to limit pollution. The 1990s have seen a series of regulations to protect the environment. In 1992, over 400 firms were blacklisted for violations of environmental regulations. The first four-year plan to reduce pollution levels ends in 1996.

Korea has been no slower than other nations (relative to its industrial timescale) in implementing anti-pollution measures. Again, the question of how developing nations can achieve industrialisation without large-scale environmental damage needs to be addressed.

Conclusion

The economic, social and environmental problems currently facing South Korea in the wake of its rapid industrialisation need to be seen in the context of its present industrial strength, its vastly improved infrastructure and its ever-rising living standards. Obviously there is a price to pay for all this. However, the ROK has been transformed within just one generation from a poverty-stricken agricultural backwoods in desperate need of considerable overseas aid to one of the healthiest industrial economies in the world. Its chances of sustained economic growth into the 21st century would have appeared inconceivable in the 1950s and are now considerably better than those in many other countries, including some developed nations. The 'sting in the tail' which all this has incurred has not yet reached the point of being incurable.

Reading

(In addition to those readings listed in chapters 11 and 12)

E. S. Mason *et al.*, 1980. *The Economic and Social Modernization of the Republic of Korea*. Cambridge, MA: Harvard University Press [see especially ch. 11, 'Population, urbanization, and health']

15

THE KOREAN PENINSULA AND BEYOND

15.1 Comparing North and South: Notes on the Constitutions

Both the Republic of Korea and the Democratic People's Republic of Korea date their foundation to 1948. In that year the division of the peninsula into capitalist and Communist states was confirmed. The two constitutions that were promulgated, in the South on 17 July and in the North on 8 September, enshrined the guiding principles of the new states. Successive amendments to each constitution have reflected the political and economic history of both South and North in the decades since their establishment.

South Korea

The constitution of the Republic of Korea has been amended nine times since its introduction in 1948. The most recent amendment, adopted on 8 September 1987, defines at some length the powers and obligations of the president of the ROK, the relationship between the president and the legislative, executive and judicial branches of the government, the status of the constitution and the management of elections, as well as the rights and duties of citizens. If these issues are dealt with so comprehensively—they occupy 119 out of a total of 130 articles—it is because they have loomed so large in the political development of South Korea. The background to the establishment of the ROK was not auspicious: a hostile regime in the north, liberation only a few years earlier from war and colonial suppression and, within living memory, a tradition of conservative and autocratic administration. Founded as a democracy, the ROK has not proved it easy in the past to achieve a proper balance between the authoritarian instincts of its leaders and the implications of a democratic form of government. The threat from the North was always available as justification for strong measures. Rights promised by the constitution were often restricted or withdrawn. On occasion, as when Park Chung Hee amended the constitution in October 1972 to enhance his own powers (see chapter 3.5), the constitution itself has been used by the leadership as a controlling tool. Even the present version allows the president in exceptional circumstances to issue unilateral orders or declare martial law. That notwithstanding, some balance has now been achieved between citizens' needs and those of the state. It has been judged necessary, however, to spell out in detail the limits to presidential and government authority.

The present constitution of the ROK opens with a preamble, establishing the Republic's legitimacy as the successor of the Provisional Government of 1919 (see chapter 2.4) and of the democratic ideals of the April 1960 uprising (see chapter 3.5) and laying upon the country the "mission of democratic reform and peaceful unification of our homeland". The preamble, written in the name of "the people of Korea", leads into a set of general provisions (articles 1-9), which describe the ROK as a "democratic republic", with all state authority emanating "from the people". Its territory is given as consisting of "the Korean peninsula and its adjacent islands". (Here the constitution establishes the ROK's claim to represent the whole of the peninsula.) All "aggressive wars" are renounced. A plural party system is guaranteed, as is the establishment of political parties, provided the latter follow democratic objectives. (The way is thus open to challenge in the Constitution Court the formation of, say, a Communist party.) The country's cultural heritage and national culture are to be cherished. "Citizens residing abroad" are offered state protection.

The second chapter (articles 10-39) enunciates the rights and duties of citizens. Chief among their rights are personal liberty, arrest only under law and freedom from torture and self-incrimination. Confession may not be extracted from a defendant or used as sole evidence against him. (These provisions indicate the sometimes arbitrary nature of legal proceedings in the past.) Basic freedoms of residence, movement, privacy, speech, assembly and association, etc, are guaranteed, as is freedom of conscience and religion. The separation of church and state is stipulated. Civilians may not be tried by court martial except in prescribed conditions.

Parents are required to have their children educated, though the period of compulsory education is free. Women are not to be subject to discrimination. Marriage is to be based on equality of the sexes. The environment is to be protected. Work is a duty enjoined on citizens, with the state undertaking to enforce a minimum wage system and permitting rights of "independent association, collective bargaining and collective action", except for defined categories of workers. All citizens have the duty of "national defence". An important stipulation (article 37) is that "the freedoms and rights of citizens may be restricted by law only when necessary for national security, the maintenance of law and order or for public welfare. Even when such restriction is imposed, no essential aspect of the freedom or right shall be violated."

Chapters 3, 4 and 5 (articles 40-110) set out the manner in which the legislature, in the form of the National Assembly, the executive, functioning through the president, the prime minister, State Council and state ministries, and the judiciary, operating through a system of courts and judges, should work. The National Assembly is composed of a minimum of 200 members elected by universal ballot, whose term of office is for four years. During sessions of the National Assembly, members cannot be arrested (except in case of *flagrante delicto*); at the same time they should not use their positions for personal advantage. Decisions of the Assembly require the attendance of a majority of members and a majority vote. Sessions should normally be open to the public. The president has limited scope to delay the promulgation of bills passed by the National Assembly; and the Assembly is authorised to request the prime minister and government officials to attend to answer questions. Among the most important of the National Assembly's powers are those of recommending the removal of the prime minister and of impeaching the president, prime minister and other officials in cases of violations of the constitution or other laws in execution of official duties.

The authority of the president is made clear. He is head of state, commander-in-chief of the armed forces and chairman of the State Council and is empowered to appoint the prime minister, the chief justice of the Supreme Court and the chairman of the Board of Audit and Inspection with the consent of the National Assembly. He is elected by direct and universal ballot for a single term of five years (this stipulation is intended to prevent arbitrary extensions of office by a president). As already seen, he retains the authority to issue orders with the effect of law in the case of major hostilities, "internal turmoil, external menace, natural calamity or a grave financial or economic crisis".

The executive is headed by the president, who is assisted by the prime minister, the State Council, executive ministries and the Board of Audit and Inspection. (The ROK's system is in effect a combination of a presidential and a cabinet style of government.) Neither the prime minister nor any member of the State Council may be an active member of the armed forces. (The trend in the ROK is towards diminution of military involvement in politics.)

The judiciary functions through courts composed of judges, who are required to rule "independently according to their conscience". The chief justice is appointed for a single term of six years. Trials should generally be open to the public. Issues touching on the constitution itself, such as impeachment, the dissolution of a political party or the constitutionality of a law, are to be referred to the Constitution Court (chapter 6). Chapter 7, on the management of elections, requires the establishment of committees for that purpose and for the management of national referendums.

A short chapter deals with the issue of local autonomy (chapter 8). Local governments, the types of which shall be "determined by law", are entrusted with "administrative matters pertaining to the welfare of local residents", the management of properties and the enactment of provisions "relating to local autonomy". A local government is required to have a council, the organisation and powers of which, as well as the election of members, shall also be determined by law. (South Korea is governed along heavily central lines. The issue of regional autonomy has long been a sensitive one. The imprecision of the wording of chapter 8 would seem to reflect this uncertainty of approach.)

Chapter 9 handles the economy, endorsing the generally free nature of economic activity in South Korea. Nonetheless, while pledging respect for the "freedom and creative initiative of enterprises and individuals in economic affairs" (article 119), the constitution allows the state a regulatory and coordinating role in such affairs, in the interests of balanced growth and stability, a proper distribution of income, the good management of the market and the promotion of "harmony among the economic agents". The state is also permitted to regulate and coordinate foreign trade. The exploitation of natural resources may be carried out under licence, and the land and its resources are to be protected by the state. The state is also committed to support the farming and fishing sectors of the economy through stabilisation of prices of agricultural and fishery products and through development of regional economies. (From being the mainstay of the majority of the population immediately after liberation, these sectors are now much reduced and under pressure from urbanisation and industrialisation.) The basic principle that the producer should own the land he cultivates, put into effect through a land reform law passed in 1949 and put into place in 1956-58, is still honoured in the constitution (article 121, which prohibits tenant farming). However, the leasing of land for agricultural purposes is permitted.

A final chapter (chapter 10) on amendments to the constitution stipulates that such amendments may be introduced by a majority of all members of the National Assembly or by the president, but that amendments for an extension of the term of office of the president or for a change allowing for his re-election "may not be effective" for the president in office at the time of the proposal for such an amendment (article 128). Thus a further check is placed on the ambitions of a serving president.

North Korea

The constitution of the Democratic People's Republic of Korea, by contrast with the evolutions of the South Korean constitution, reflects an almost static political scene. It has been revised twice, in 1972 and in 1992. The 1972 revision introduced important changes in the administrative organs of state, in particular establishing the office of president of the republic and creating the Central People's Committee and the Administration Council, and acknowledging P'yŏngyang as the capital, where the 1948 constitution still claimed Seoul as capital. Six amendments to the first constitution dealt largely with smaller administrative changes.

Such alterations to the administrative fabric of the DPRK have not changed the leading role of the Korean Workers' Party (KWP) or diminished the party's strength and the leadership's control over all aspects of life in North Korea. These basic relationships were made clear at the founding of the DPRK in 1948. Revisions of the constitution have confirmed the political system and the economic and cultural policies that support it. In greater measure than the constitution of the Republic of Korea and all its amendments, the North Korean constitution is a paper exercise, since all the activities of the DPRK are carried out under the leadership of the KWP (article 11), which by implication must take precedence over any provision of the constitution. Nonetheless, some changes in the 1992 constitution do indicate shifts in policy, such as a new readiness to encourage joint operation and joint venture enterprises (article 37).

The other important thing to remember about the North Korean constitution is that it is a classic document of Communism, sharing many features with the constitutions of other present and former Communist states such as the Chinese People's Republic and the former Soviet Union. These features are: a commitment to Marxist-Leninist ideology (though Marxism-Leninism has been ousted in the present North Korean constitution in favour of homegrown ideology); insistence on a socialist economic system incorporating state control and an absence of private ownership; enforcement of the dictatorship of the proletariat over class enemies and hostile elements; the principle of democratic centralism in the operation of all state organs, that is, the exercise of power from the centre, though on the basis of popular suffrage; the leadership of the party; and the conduct of foreign policy on strictly controlled lines.

The theoretical and ideological basis of the DPRK is reflected in the order of themes in the constitution: chapter 1 (articles 1-18) deals with politics; chapter 2 (articles 19-38) with the economy; chapter 3 (articles 39-57) with culture; chapter 4 (articles 58-61) with national defence; chapter 5 (articles 62-86) with the fundamental rights and duties of citizens. Chapter 6 (articles 87-167) sets out in eight sections the varying state institutions. The final chapter (articles 168-171) describes the national emblem, flag and capital of the DPRK. The validity of this order of priorities is supported by the importance given in article 9 to the "three revolutions of ideology, technology and culture" as means of achieving the "complete victory of socialism in the northern half" of the peninsula.

Chapter 1, on politics, opens with a description of the DPRK as "an independent socialist state" representing the interests of "all the Korean people". (North Korea thereby claims the loyalty of all the inhabitants of the peninsula.) The role of *juche* ideology, rather than Marxism-Leninism, is staked out as the guiding principle of the DPRK; that is, the principle of self-reliance and independence developed extensively by Kim Il Sung. As with the South Korean constitution, sovereignty rests with the people, though they are defined in the North Korean constitution as "the workers, peasants, working intelligentsia, and all working people". They exercise such sovereignty through their representative organs, the Supreme People's Assembly (SPA) and local People's Committees, which are elected through universal and direct ballot. The role of mass movements, such as the Ch'ŏngsan-ri method (see chapter 11.2 above), is acknowledged. The DPRK undertakes to defend the national rights of overseas Koreans. In common with other Communist states (such as China), North Korea bases its foreign policy on the five principles of equality, independence, mutual respect, non-interference in each other's internal affairs, and mutual benefit.

In its detailed prescriptions for the economy (chapter 2), the North Korean constitution differs most sharply from its South Korean counterpart. Economic independence is stressed. The means of production are owned "solely by the state and co-operative organisations"—there is no place for private ownership. State property belongs to the whole people, and there is "no limit" to the properties the state may own. All natural resources, major enterprises, banks and transport infrastructure are owned by the state. Those engaged in the co-operative economy, i.e. at a level below state operation, own collectively the land they work, together with livestock, farm implements and fishing boats and smaller enterprises. Personal property, derived from "distribution according to work done", is "property for personal use by the working people for the purpose of consumption".

People's living needs are met through state provision. There are no taxes and no unemployment. The working day is set at eight hours. The minimum age for work is 16, and no child under that age may work (there is no similar provision in the South Korean constitution, which instead undertakes to accord "special protection" to working children). The North Korean economy is described as operating through a series of state plans and on the basis of strict financial control. External trade is conducted either by the state or under its supervision. As already seen, joint operation and joint venture enterprises are now tolerated.(A few such schemes have already been initiated.)

Chapter 3 takes a wide view of socialist culture as "enhancing the working people's creative ability" and "meeting their sound cultural and mental demands". Cultural infiltration by "imperialists" is to be resisted; "national cultural inheritances" are to be preserved; remnants of the old society are to be eliminated, and a "new socialist way of life" established. In North Korea, as in the South, education is accorded a high priority. A mandatory, 11-year school system includes one year of pre-school education, all at no cost to students. All pre-school children are brought up free of charge in nurseries and kindergartens. Literature and art are to be "national in form and socialist in content". The North Korean constitution, unlike that in the South, calls for protection for the Korean language "from all forms of stratagem aimed at destroying" it; this may be a reference to the policy of eliminating Chinese characters from the written language, together with words of foreign origin. Universal free medical care is promised; and the state undertakes to protect the environment.

Chapter 4 introduces a new subject, that of national defence, which was absent from the earlier versions of the constitution. The emphasis is on self-reliance, arming of the populace (as militia), ideological and political readiness of military and people and modernisation of the army.

In support of the communal ethos of North Korean society, the chapter on rights and duties of citizens endorses the collectivist principle of "one for all and all for one" and promises equality of rights in all spheres of social life. The right to vote in elections and to stand for election is accorded to all over 17, including members of the armed forces. Freedom of speech, publishing, assembly, demonstration and association, of religious belief, appeal and petition is indicated. (Practice suggests, however, that only officially directed manifestations of protest are acceptable.) The guarantee in article 67 to "democratic political parties and social organisations" of freedom of action is of paper value only. Two other parties do exist in North Korea besides the Korean Workers' Party: the Ch'ŏndogye Ch'ŏngu Party (Ch'ŏndogye Young Friends Party) and the Korean Social Democratic Party, but it appears they do not contest elections. Freedom of religious belief is promised, including the freedom to erect buildings for religious purposes and to conduct ceremonies, but religion may not be used to bring in foreigners or to disturb social order (article 68; see also chapter 8.7 above). The right to work, to education and to social benefits is balanced by the duty to respect "socialist norms of life", to work, to care for state and communal property and to participate in national defence. Women are accorded equal status and rights as men. Marriage is protected, and the family respected as the "most basic and underlying unit of society", a sentiment that no Confucian could quarrel with.

Chapter 6 details the structure of state organs, from the Supreme People's Assembly, which with its permanent Standing Committee exercises legislative power, through a number of committees and councils holding executive functions, to People's Assemblies at local level. Deputies to the SPA are elected directly for a term of five years. Two-thirds attendance is required for a quorum of the SPA, and laws are passed on the vote of over half the deputies. The president of the DPRK is the head of state. The chairman of the National Defence Committee is commander of the armed forces. Local People's Assemblies are elected directly for a term of four years as local organs of power and are supported by local administrative and economic committees. The judiciary operates through a system of courts headed by the Central Court. A network of assessors assist judges in their hearings.

Readings

Constitution of the Republic of Korea, 1987. Seoul: Korean Overseas Information Service

Chin-wee Chung, 1983. 'The evolution of a constitutional structure in North Korea', in *North Korea Today: Strategic and Domestic Issues*, Robert A. Scalapino and Jun-yop Kim (eds). Berkeley, CA: Center for Korean Studies

Dae-Sook Suh, 1981. *Korean Communism 1945-1980: A Reference Guide to the Political System.* Honolulu: University Press of Hawaii

Sung Chul Yang, 1994: *The North and South Korean Political Systems: A Comparative Analysis*. Boulder, CO: Westview Press/Seoul: Seoul Press [contains text of the 1992 constitution of the DPRK]

15.2 Reunification

In the decades following the end of the Korean War neither Korea formally abandoned the call for unification, but the North was too weak and the South was held in check by the United States. The political conference called for in the Armistice Agreement (see chapter 4.3) convened in early 1954 at Geneva. Both Koreas put forward plans for unification to be brought about by all-Korea elections and the withdrawal of all foreign troops. There was no agreement, however, on how these things might be achieved, and the conference broke up without reaching a settlement in Korea.

It was to be nearly twenty years before the matter was discussed again between the two Koreas. The Korean issue was regularly debated at the United Nations, but until the mid-1970s, the US dominance of the UN meant that pro-North Korean resolutions were easily stopped. In the meantime, North Korea made a rapid economic recovery from the effects of the war, aided by support from China, Eastern Europe and the Soviet Union. By 1957, it was able to stand on its own, and Chinese forces withdrew in 1958. South Korea seemed less successful. Syngman Rhee was not interested in economic matters, seeing reunification as the cure for all ills, and was content to rely on the United States to keep the country going. Rhee's overthrow in 1960 eventually brought to power a group of military men, led by Park Chung Hee, who had a different view of how South Korea should develop. Park began a process of economic reconstruction, which was to bring the South's economy up to that of the North by the early 1970s and then to race ahead of it.

North and South sheltered behind their respective patrons, the Chinese and the Russians for the North, the United States for the South. Reunification became less important as the separate states pursued their development goals and new political elites emerged. Neither side wanted to abandon a formal commitment to unification but each had other priorities. However, the North tried to exploit the political uncertainty in the South in 1960 by putting forward proposals for a confederate state. It drew little response but has remained the basis of the North's proposals ever since. The North also tried unsuccessfully to undermine the South by direct subversion, sending commando teams deep into the country.

Then in 1971, the two Koreas suffered a shock. China and the United States, the major supporters of each side, were talking to each other. Worried that a deal would be concluded without them, the two Koreas began talking. In July 1972, they signed a joint communiqué declaring three principals of reunification—peace, self-reliance and grand national integration. A North-South Co-ordinating Committee was also established.

Hopes were high for a short time, but by mid-1973, they had begun to fade. The talks dragged on at low levels for some years, but neither side seemed interested in pursuing them once it was clear that improved US-China relations were not going to lead to a general upheaval. Park used the 'threat from the North' to tighten political control in the South. The North denounced this as proof that Park was not serious about unification. Among suggestions for international attempts to bring the two Koreas together was one for 'cross-recognition': Japan and the United States would recognise the North and the Soviet Union and China the South. In the face of Chinese and Soviet hostility to the South, nothing came of it (see following section 15.3).

In the mid-1970s, the South Koreans discovered a series of tunnels under the Demilitarized Zone (the DMZ), which they claim had been dug by the North. The North denied this, but it showed the old suspicions remained. Alleged North Korean involvement in an assassination attempt on President Park, in which his wife was killed, and the killing of two Americans in an incident at P'anmunjŏm in 1976 did nothing to improve the atmosphere.

This stalemate continued during the 1980s. The North made overtures to a wide range of people in the South in the uncertainty which followed the death of Park Chung Hee in 1979 but there was little response. When another general, Chun Doo Hwan, seized power in 1980, such overtures came to an end. The North reverted to probing South Korean defences and to terrorism. This culminated in a bomb attack on President Chun and his party in Rangoon in October 1983. Chun escaped but 18 senior South Koreans were killed. The North Koreans denied that they were involved but two North Koreans were captured and tried by the Burmese authorities, who broke off diplomatic relations. There was widespread international condemnation of the attack.

Perhaps in an attempt to undo some of the damage to their international position, in September 1984 the North Koreans offered assistance to the South following massive flood damage. After some hesitation, the South accepted and the relief goods were delivered that autumn. In this improved atmosphere talks opened on economic links and North Korean participation in the 1988 Seoul Olympic games. Red Cross talks on family reunions, which had dragged on for some time, were given new life. In 1985, the first-ever family exchanges between North and South since 1953 took place. In another development, the South Koreans found that East European countries, the Soviet Union and China were willing to open trade, sport and similar contacts. The Chinese also made it clear that they would attend the 1986 Asian Games in Seoul.

Once again, the contacts faded out. The North Koreans used the excuse of the annual South Korea-US military exercise to halt most talks in January 1986. They may have thought that political change was coming in the South, and that it was worth waiting. After a period of quietness between 1980 and 1985, the South Korean political scene became active following the return of veteran opposition leader Kim Dae Jung to Seoul in February 1985. Faced with growing opposition, the government responded with increasing firmness until Chun Doo Hwan was forced to back down in mid-1987 and agree to stand in direct presidential elections.

Talks over the Olympics got nowhere. When the closing date for applications was reached in January 1988, the North Koreans announced that they would not attend. Relations between the two sides were already soured by a further terrorist attack. In November 1987, in a move apparently designed to discourage those going to Seoul for the Olympic Games, North Korean agents planted a bomb on a Korean Airlines airliner on a flight from the Middle East. Again the North denied involvement, but one of those responsible was captured and confessed.

By the time of the Olympics, there was a new government in the South and a new approach to the North. President Roh Tae Woo announced in July 1988 that the South would co-operate with the North on international matters and would help it establish links with Japan and the United States. Proposals for economic and political co-operation followed. This reflected the South's increasingly confident position in the world. Roh had been democratically elected. The Soviet Union and China were now trading with South Korea and formal diplomatic relations were not far off. All this was built on a strong economic base. The North, by contrast, was in economic difficulties and had lost the competition for international support. When the Berlin Wall fell and the Soviet Union collapsed, the contrasting positions of the two Koreas seemed even more glaring.

The North was already talking to the Americans and the Japanese, one of its rewards for not disrupting the Seoul Olympics, and its initial response to Roh's proposals was to dismiss them. But as dramatic changes in the Communist world left it more and more isolated, there were signs of interest in re-opening discussions. This led in September 1990 to the first formal meeting between Prime Ministers of the two sides. After many ups and downs, agreements on conciliation and non-aggression, followed by a joint declaration on the denuclearisation of the Korean peninsula, were signed in December 1991-January 1992.

These conciliatory moves brought immediate benefits to both sides. The South gained security assurances. The North also gained in security terms, with the cancellation of the 'Team Spirit' exercise and signs of interest in economic development from South Korean companies. Yet this new breakthrough was to be as shortlived as all the others. New problems arose over the North's nuclear programme (see following section 15.3). Many in South Korea were unhappy with the pace of Roh's approach to the North. They feared that his wish to crown his presidency with a successful policy towards the North was blinding him to the realities of the situation. By the end of 1992, the high hopes of late 1991 had gone. The nuclear issue, and the uncertainties resulting from the death of Kim Il Sung in July 1994, make it improbable that they will return in the near future.

Outlook

Both Koreas remain pledged to reunification, and each still puts forward proposals from time to time. A strong emotional commitment to unification exists among many ordinary Koreans, at least in the South where such things can be tested. Those with family ties broken by separation are particularly affected, but given the long history of a unified Korea, and the constant teaching in North and South about unification, few can escape its pull.

For most people, however, unification remains a distant dream. The elites who run the two states on the peninsula have no wish to give up their political power or to dismantle the states they have helped create. The North, with the German experience in mind, is fearful of absorption by the South. Because of the greater wealth and population of the South, any merging of the two states would inevitably mean that this would be on the South's terms. Given that the two Koreas fought a savage war and that the North has periodically attacked the South using terrorist methods, few in the North would expect much generosity from a victorious South.

The South too has reservations. After the first flush of enthusiasm after German reunification, a more cautious mood developed, partly because of the enormous costs involved, also on consideration of the social costs of trying to reintegrate two societies that have grown far apart. There is concern that the appeal of 'socialism' might be strong especially among students and other dissident groups dissatisfied with the highly conservative nature of South Korean society. The South expects that unification will come one day but would prefer this to be a managed and slow process, with the two societies coming closer together.

Beyond the two Koreas, there is no open opposition to the idea of a unified Korea. The states traditionally interested in Korea, China, Japan, the USA and Russia, say that the question is one for the Koreans to settle themselves, but that it should be done peacefully, with as little upheaval as possible.

Much will depend on the North's capacity for survival. There have been those who have predicted its imminent collapse since the earliest days of its existence. The North's initial success in carrying through the succession from Kim Il Sung to his son, Kim Jong Il, has shown, however, that it is still a state which can surprise. But it faces formidable difficulties in economic and social terms as it struggles with the consequences of the end of the Soviet Union and the Communist world. It is hard to see how it can survive as an independent state, even with major modifications in its current policies, unless others, including South Korea, help it to do so.

Readings

Hakjoon Kim, 1992. *Unification Policies of South and North Korea, 1945-1991: A Comparative Study.* Seoul: Seoul National University Press

Byung Chul Koh, 1983. 'Unification policy and North-South relations', in *North Korea Today: Strategic and Domestic Issues,* Robert A. Scalapino and Jun-yop Kim (eds). Berkeley: Center for Korean Studies: 264-308

15.3 Strategic and defence issues

The Korean peninsula is roughly the size of mainland Britain. In this area are packed some 1.7 million military, including a contingent of United States forces, large numbers of tanks, aircraft and other military equipment. The North Korean armed forces are estimated to total over one million; the South Korean about 650,000, with some 40,000 US forces in addition. The Demilitarized Zone (DMZ), which has divided the peninsula into two since 1953 and which roughly follows the line of the 1945 division along the 38th parallel, is a tragic misnomer. Few regions in the world are so heavily armed or marked by such hostility as the DMZ.

Historically, among Korea's immediate neighbours, ceremonial and trade links were strong with China, though the Koreans preferred a distant relationship. The Chinese were generally content with this, provided Korea was neither hostile itself nor aided the hostility of others. Relations with Japan were more complex. Japanese ships visited

Korea, trading or raiding by turns. Japanese attacks reached a peak in the great invasions of the 1590s, the scars from which remain today. Yet in times of peace, Korea and Japan were major trading partners. The Japanese were also ambivalent towards Korea. Although no invasion from the Asian mainland had been successful in historic times, the Japanese perceived a threat from that direction. Strong unifying dynasties in China worried them no less than they did the Koreans. Korea therefore appeared to the Japanese as a threat, but also a corridor to the mainland.

Korea's relative isolation changed in the mid-19th century under outside pressure. Korea was forced open and became a strategic concern. The major Western power in Asia, Britain, saw Russia in Korea as threatening its interests. For Britain, Japan balanced Russia and was an ally in the defence of its interests in China, and so the 1902 Anglo-Japanese Alliance left the Japanese a free hand in Korea. Japan fought China in 1894-95 for control of the peninsula. Japan then saw Russia, a strong continental power, as a security threat. The Russo-Japanese War of 1904-5 was followed by the annexation of Korea.

The Korean war and its consequences

Korea was largely forgotten until August 1945. Then Soviet and US forces arrived to accept the surrender of Japanese forces. Faced with the need to decide on where to draw the line, US officers remembered the strategic concerns of fifty years before and concentrated on limiting the area of Soviet occupation. The line drawn at the 38th parallel put the capital and the main west coast port under US control.

The immediate US concern was to prevent the Soviet Union from establishing too strong a position in East Asia. It soon became the more specific task of containing a Soviet threat to Japan. The United States thus slipped into viewing Korea as the Japanese had done, wishing to prevent any strong continental power from controlling the peninsula in its entirety. The Soviet Union, and China after 1949, for their part, had no wish to see a strong outside power in the peninsula, threatening Manchuria and Siberia. For both sides, Korea was not the major concern. When North Korea attempted reunification by force in 1950, conflict was not allowed to spread beyond Korea.

After the Korean war, the Korean states settled down behind their respective defenders. Chinese troops remained in North Korea until 1957. US troops are still in South Korea, though in reduced numbers. (Such troops have also provided a check on any further military adventures by North or South.) The US and South Korea signed a Mutual Defence Treaty in 1954, one of the series of US bilateral treaties with Asian allies. In modified form, it remains in place today. In 1961, China and the Soviet Union signed defensive treaties with North Korea. They remain in force but it is now hard to see any circumstances in which they would be activated.

The 1953 Armistice Agreement established a Military Armistice Commission (MAC), with (North) Korean People's Army and Chinese People's Volunteers on one side, and the United Nations (UN) 'Unified Command' (UNC) on the other. With its attendant systems of liaison officers and the armistice monitoring teams of the Neutral Nations Supervisory Commission (NNSC; Czechoslovakia and Poland, nominated by North Korea and China, and Sweden and Switzerland, nominated by the UNC), the MAC functioned as a point of contact until 1991. There were occasional clashes at P'anmunjŏm, the 'truce village', including the killing of two US officers in 1976. In such cases the two sides quickly defused tension.

The North Koreans have put the established MAC system under pressure since 1991, following the appointment of a South Korean general as the UNC chief representative. The North Korean/Chinese side refuse to attend full MAC meetings. North Korea announced in 1994 that it regarded the Armistice Agreement as at an end, and the Chinese withdrew from P'anmunjŏm. The North Koreans have also undermined the NNSC arrangements. When Czechoslovakia split in 1993, the North refused to accept the Czech Republic's claim to nominate officers to the NNSC. In 1995, the North announced that it would no longer accept the Poles. The MAC has now lost any real importance as a means of settling Korean issues.

Both Koreas engaged in competition for international recognition. By the late 1960s, friends and allies of the Soviet Union had recognised the North, while the United States' allies and friends recognised the South The US dominance of the UN was not sufficient to gain admission for the South, but was strong enough until the late 1960s to prevent successful attacks on South Korea's position.

Changes came after the two Koreas began to talk in 1971. The South abandoned its exclusive recognition policy and its objection to both Koreas entering the UN. The North argued that joint entry to the UN would perpetuate division. In 1973, the UN wound up the United Nations Commission for the Unification and Rehabilitation of Korea (UNCURK), thus removing any bar on recognition of North Korea. In 1975 the UN General Assembly passed contradictory resolutions. One favoured the status quo, the other proposed winding down the Armistice Commission and the UN structure in Korea. The issue might have been tested again in 1976, but the matter was not raised after the killing at P'anmunjŏm.

South Korea found friends in the developed world and the pro-Western Third World. North Korea was more widely accepted among Third World and 'non-aligned' countries, and by all Communist states. North Korea's success in the Third World reflected interest in North Korea's claimed economic and political independence, anti-American stand, and ability to manoeuvre between the Soviet Union and China. After 1973, the division was less clearcut. Countries such as Portugal and Denmark established relations with the North following UNCURK's dissolution. South Korea's US links were viewed more negatively in the Third World than North Korea's treaties with the Soviet Union and China. North Korea joined the non-aligned movement in 1975 while blocking the South's application.

South Korea courts China and the Soviet Union

The South Korean quest for links with North Korea's friends paid little dividend in the 1970s. The Chinese remained aloof. The Soviet Union and Eastern Europe allowed only low-key non-official contacts. Nevertheless, there were tentative moves in small matters such as postal and telephone contacts. After ignoring the Third World until the early 1970s, the South Koreans began to cultivate more Third World countries, partly with an eye to UN recognition.

The 1980s brought several unfavourable developments for the North. Sino-US and Sino-Japanese rapprochement during the 1970s changed Chinese perceptions of the Korean peninsula. The continued growth in South Korea's economy, which after a dip in 1979-80, took off again spectacularly until the end of the decade, aroused interest as both China and the Soviet Union realised that there might be benefits in trading with South Korea.

Today, the formal Chinese position is that the solution to the problems of the Korean peninsula is a matter for the Koreans themselves. Chinese experts express support for North Korean proposals on unification, but they have become less critical of South Korean proposals on the issue. Since the 1991 North-South agreements, and the normalisation of relations with South Korea in 1992, the Chinese speak of a new era on the Korean peninsula. This optimism did not abate in the face of the nuclear issue and the stalling of the North-South dialogue. The Chinese are well aware of current discussions of Korean unification and that this will probably be achieved only on South Korean terms, but they appear to accept this, providing that reunification is peacefully achieved.

Changes in the Soviet position were slower at first, hampered by continued Soviet-US and Soviet-Japanese hostility. The shooting down of a Korean Airlines' Boeing 747 in 1983 set back developing Soviet links with the South, while tensions in Sino-Soviet relations led the Soviet Union to continue courting the North Koreans. There was a substantial revival in military links with the North after 1984, including the supply of MiG 23 aircraft and missiles. Yet the contacts with South Korea revived after the first shock of the KAL incident had faded. As the decade moved on, the Soviet Union became more critical of the North and less of the South.

The late 1980s saw the rapid expansion of South Korean contacts, first with East Europe and then with the Soviet Union. South Korea's development, with its mix of free market and state intervention, offered useful lessons to countries moving away from state-controlled systems. Where economics led, politics followed. The normalisation of Sino-Soviet relations in 1989 was one factor in downgrading Soviet interest in North Korea. Another was the Soviet Union's own economic situation. North Korea had nothing to offer economically; rather, it was a drain on the Soviet economy. The North, which as late as 1990 conducted 52% of all its trade with the Soviet Union, enjoyed 'friendship prices' but failed even to pay these. The South, by contrast, had much to offer and was eager. By the end of 1990, the USSR had ended 'friendship' prices for the North and had established diplomatic relations with the South; it was hard to think of a fuller rejection of the past relationship with North Korea.

By 1992, therefore, South Korea had achieved the goal of recognition by the North's principal security backers. In the process, it had also entered the United Nations, dragging a reluctant North Korea along with it. Once China and the Soviet Union (now Russia) had accepted that South Korea was not a hostile force, their position on the question of unification was likely to be modified.

The North: crossness without cross-recognition

Advocates of cross-recognition had suggested that moves by the Soviet Union and China towards the South would be matched by US and Japanese moves towards the North. The Korean peninsula would thus have remained in balance. But as the South Koreans steadily achieved their goal of winning recognition from the North's allies, the North's attempts to develop links with the South's allies made nothing like the same progress.

There were obvious reasons in the case of the United States. South Korea is one of its oldest allies in Asia. American interest in pre-colonial Korea had been stronger than that of any other Western power and it was kept alive by American missionaries during Japanese rule. Liberation and the Korean War sealed the bond. Whatever private reservations Americans had about Syngman Rhee, the first president in the South, in public he was a great, American-educated, anti-Communist leader. Relations were at first less close under Park Chung Hee, but the initial frostiness soon wore off. South Korean support in Vietnam confirmed it as a staunch anti-Communist ally.

To North Korea, the United States had been its main enemy. The North saw its attempts at unification defeated by the United States, which in the process almost destroyed North Korea itself. The enemy had remained in the South, posing a continued threat to the North. The United States has viewed North Korea in a more hostile fashion than any other country. It is perhaps not surprising. As well as the hard-fought Korean war, and the sour armistice negotiations, intense anti-North Korean feeling has been reinforced since 1953 by the confrontation between the two sides at P'anmunjŏm and by incidents such as the capture of the USS *Pueblo* in 1968 and the killings at P'anmunjŏm in 1976.

The North's approach since the 1970s has been to seek direct high-level talks with the US, but only after Roh Tae Woo (president from 1988 to 1993) had ended ROK objections to such talks and the 1988 Olympics had passed peacefully did the North begin to make any progress. In early 1989, low-level talks began in Beijing and there were other modifications in the US position. For a short time, visits by private citizens in both directions were allowed, as was the export of a limited amount of food and medicines. Various distinguished Americans visited North Korea and were received by Kim Il Sung. They included Billy Graham, academics and members of Congress. Most were stuck by the oddness of North Korea and the reasonableness of Kim Il Sung. The US government's formal position remained that the solution for Korea's problems must lie with the Koreans themselves.

But by then there were new US concerns about the North. US military analysts reported an increasingly forward deployment by North Korean forces. There were frequent reports of North Korea's alleged links with international terrorism and arms sales to the Middle East. But most important was the nuclear issue.

Nuclear programmes in the Korean peninsula

The US introduced nuclear weapons into the Korean peninsula in 1957. Thereafter, the North Koreans demanded the de-nuclearisation of the peninsula. From at least the early 1960s, the North Koreans began a small nuclear programme dependent on the North joining the Nuclear Non-Proliferation Treaty (NPT). However, the North declined to sign the required safeguards agreement with the International Atomic Energy Authority (IAEA) until 1992. South Korea too developed a nuclear energy programme from the 1970s under IAEA auspices.

In the mid-1970s, the South Korean government dropped hints that it might acquire nuclear weapons. The US moved swiftly to stop this. No similar concerns arose about North Korea until the late 1980s, when international suspicions were aroused by satellite photographs of a site at Yŏngbyŏn where the North Koreans had at least one Soviet reactor. The picture showed buildings which seemed unrelated to a civilian nuclear programme and which resembled those associated with the extraction of weapons-grade plutonium. Concern was somewhat alleviated by the North-South nuclear agreement of December 1991 and the North's willingness to sign a safeguards agreement with the IAEA. Neither of these provided assurance for long. Almost as soon as the North-South agreement was signed, the North refused to co-operate. There was a similar story with the IAEA, with early co-operation replaced by obstruction. Eventually, the North announced in March 1993 that it was withdrawing from the NPT.

US concern at North Korea's possible acquisition of nuclear weapons and its failure to abide by its NPT commitments was so great that despite all past US refusals, in June 1993 the United States and North Korea held substantive talks at a senior level in New York. The result was a formal joint statement made on 12 June 1993. This was mainly concerned with the nuclear issue. It recorded the North's decision to "temporarily suspend" its withdrawal from the NPT, but the US agreed to continue the dialogue "based on equality and fairness". The US indicated that political and economic relations might improve if the nuclear issue was resolved.

A year of tension followed as the US and the IAEA tried to keep the North Koreans to the agreement. Threats and promises alternated, but by May 1994, another crisis loomed as the North Koreans began to defuel an experimental reactor. There were US threats of sanctions and North Korean threats of war. Only the intervention of former US president Jimmy Carter in May prevented the matter getting worse. The US and the North began talking again. After a brief pause following the death of Kim Il Sung in July 1994, an agreement was reached in October. In exchange for North Korea's return to the NPT and abandonment of its programme at Yŏngbyŏn, the US undertook to provide fuel oil as a temporary measure and to arrange for the eventual supply of light water reactors, less able to produce weapons-grade plutonium.

Many aspects of the nuclear issue have yet to be settled, and past experience indicates that there are likely to be difficult negotiations ahead. Yet the North Koreans are now talking directly to the US. The South Korean government has accepted the outcome of the talks, but placed the main emphasis on the hope of a settlement of the nuclear issue. Many in South Korea fear that the wider US agenda on nuclear matters may lead it into links with North Korea that would override the South's interests.

Japan and the Korean peninsula

Japan's historic interest in Korea has left an inheritance which creates difficulties for the Japanese today. North and South Korea harp back to the colonial past and to the wrongs done in Korea as a means of extracting concessions. There are no opinion polls in North Korea, but those in South Korea and Japan regularly indicate the low opinions each country holds of the other. Yet, in working style, social organisation and a whole host of other ways, it is possible to see many Japanese practices in both Koreas.

The Japanese are also ambiguous towards their former colonial people. Despite recent improvements, Koreans in Japan still suffer discrimination and are widely seen as a mainstay of the criminal classes. Yet there are close ties between Japan and South Korean conservative politicians and extensive Japanese involvement in the economic development of South Korea. While there was no formal security link, South Korea and Japan maintained informal contact via the United States' alliance system in East Asia, and shared a commitment to anti-Communism.

Security has nonetheless been a difficult issue. The then Japanese Prime Minister, Eisaku Sato, agreed in 1969 that South Korean security was essential to the security of Japan, but this was more a US perception than a Japanese one. When South Korea demanded in the 1980s that Japan should pay South Korea for the 'security protection' which the latter afforded Japan, the Japanese rejected the link. The Japanese still saw the Soviet Union, not North Korea, as their main threat. In the new atmosphere of 'burden sharing' in the early 1980s, however, the Japanese proved more receptive. Thus the US$4 billion loan agreed during Prime Minister Nakasone's visit to Seoul in 1983 was presented as an acknowledgement that South Korea's security concerns were also those of Japan.

Japan's formal relations with North Korea are non-existent, but the reality is more complicated. A substantial number of Koreans—as many as 260,000—in Japan give their allegiance to North rather than South Korea (see following section 15.4, Japan). Some visit North Korea, bringing with them hard currency, and others remit funds; figures of between 60 to 80 billion yen a year are quoted. The pro-North Korean presence in Japan has led to quasi-official contacts over issues such as repatriation and divided families. Such contacts have developed recently. While there was support for North Korea in Japan's left-wing parties, there was no lobby in wider Japanese political circles. Japanese companies were not attracted by the North Korean market and those involved in trade in the 1970s suffered from the non-payment of their debts.

The changing security environment at the end of the 1980s saw a reassessment. As the Soviet threat receded, Asian issues loomed larger in Japanese thinking. North Korea's joint venture laws and the appointment of technocrats to senior posts offered hope of economic development. North Korean restraint during the Seoul Olympics indicated a new approach to the Korean issue, while Roh Tae Woo's policy encouraged third parties to develop contacts with the North.

The Japanese decided to try. They met a North Korea apparently eager for dialogue. The North Koreans were aware of the importance of Japanese aid in South Korean economic development and hoped to obtain similar assistance for themselves. These hopes received a boost in September 1990 during a Japanese parliamentary visit to North Korea led by Shin Kanemaru, then 'kingmaker' of the ruling Liberal Democratic Party, who signed a communiqué agreeing that the Japanese should compensate North Korea for the colonial period and for undefined losses since 1945. It also appeared to endorse unification on North Korean terms. As far as the Japanese government was concerned, this party-to-party agreement committed it to nothing. The North Koreans thought otherwise.

Reactions in South Korea were hostile. Japan was seen as undermining the North-South talks and preventing unification of the peninsula by offering support to the North. There was criticism of Kanemaru's failure to raise the question of North Korea's refusal to sign an agreement on IAEA safeguards. Criticism increased when talks between Japanese and North Korean officials began in January 1991. These continued until November 1992. The Japanese raised the nuclear question and the implementation of the 1990-91 North-South agreements, to the fury of the North Koreans. The talks broke down over links between the bombing of a South Korean airline and a woman travelling on a Japanese passport, who had been trained as a terrorist in North Korea. Meanwhile, Kanemaru had been driven from public life, depriving the North Koreans of one of their few friends in Japanese political circles. Contacts only resumed in spring 1995.

South Korean suspicions of Japan's Korean policies remain strong. The Japanese agree that unification is a matter for the Koreans and they will not hinder the process, but they argue that talking to North Korea improves the atmosphere on the peninsula. Many in South Korea, however, suspect a Japanese wish to keep Korea divided. To them, the Japanese plan to gain an independent foothold in North Korea is seen as an attempt to enable them to play North against South for political and economic gains. Lack of evidence and Japanese denials does not stop such claims.

Outlook

The end of the cold war has left the tensions of the Korean peninsula something of an anomaly. The political and economic disparity between the two Koreas probably means that any reunification will be on the South's terms. The complications involved, however, are such that most in the South would prefer that the issue be postponed to some distant day.

The major powers involved in the Korean peninsula will not oppose reunification. Their concern too is that whatever happens should happen peacefully. None see advantage from disturbances which would have immediate consequences for neighbouring states. Conflict would spill over land borders and there would be many refugees. The United States is more remote, but its treaty commitments and past history would make it difficult to avoid involvement if there was conflict. It is, then, the manner in which unification comes about which will matter. The hope is that the eventual takeover by the South is done with as little disruption as possible.

Readings

Youngnok Koo and Sung-joo Han (eds), 1985. *The Foreign Policy of the Republic of Korea*. New York: Columbia University Press

Hong Yung Lee and Chung Chongwook (eds), 1993. *Korean Options in a Changing International Order*. Berkeley: Center for Korean Studies

Jonathan D. Pollack and Young Koo Cha, 1996. *A New Alliance for the Next Century: The Future of U. S.-Korean Security Cooperation*. Santa Monica, CA: Rand

Sang-Woo Rhee, 1983. 'North Korean ideology, social change, and policy toward the South', in *North Korea Today: Strategic and Domestic Issues,* Robert A. Scalapino and Jun-yop Kim (eds). Berkeley: Center for Korean Studies: 230-263

William J. Taylor jr *et al.* (eds), 1990. *The Korean Peninsula: Prospects for Arms Reduction Under Global Detente*. Boulder, CO: Westview Press

15.4 Korean communities overseas

In contrast to its earlier reputation of an enclosed and inward-looking country, Korea now sends its citizens round the globe. Some go as tourists, now that formerly enforced restrictions on travel have been lifted; other are sent to represent their government or their company abroad and take their families with them; yet others travel for study and research. Britain has its own Korean community, numbering a little over 10,000, of whom the majority are temporary residents, though a few have settled permanently. For reasons of work most live in London or northeast England. Within London itself the southwest suburbs of New Malden and Wimbledon are most popular with Koreans (who may have chosen these areas because they were close to their ambassador's first residence beside Wimbledon Common). Now the district supports shops, churches, restaurants and estate agents catering to the needs of the Korean community.

In some parts of the world, such as Europe and the Middle East, few Koreans expect to stay once their assignment is completed. In other areas, notably China and parts of the former Soviet Union, in Japan and in North and South America, permanent Korean communities have emerged. The total number of Koreans settled in such communities is estimated at four to four and a half million. Their presence in such different parts of the world is an outcome of the complicated and sometimes painful history of Korea over the past 140 years.

China

The largest group of Koreans outside the peninsula is also that nearest to it. These are the members of the Korean national minority living in China. The 1985 Chinese census put their number at 1,765,204, a figure that must by now have increased. The majority of Koreans are settled in the three northeast provinces of Liaoning, Jilin and Heilongjiang, immediately to the north of Korea. (This region constitutes the area known historically as Manchuria or Manchuguo.) Over one million live in Jilin Province, which together with Liaoning Province directly borders North Korea. The strongest concentration of Koreans—40% of the community—is in Yanbian Korean Autonomous Prefecture, Jilin Province, an area of 41,500 sq km just north of the Tuman river. Both there and in the smaller Changbei Korean Autonomous County, Koreans are able to exercise a degree of self-administration and use their own language in accordance with the rights granted to all minority nationalities in China. Korean is in addition recognised as one of the six official languages of the Chinese People's Republic. Outside of the autonomous areas Koreans live in other parts of the northeast, in Inner Mongolia and Hebei Province and in the largest Chinese cities. Some 4000 live in the capital, Beijing.

Koreans are generally esteemed by the Chinese for their good educational standards and are recognised as having double the national rate for students in college education. The first Korean school was established in Yanbian in 1906. In 1949, Yanbian University was founded as the first minority nationality comprehensive university in China (i.e. one offering a general range of subjects). The Korean minority's high educational attainment may partly explain its readiness to participate in politics at regional and national level.

The other important achievement of the Chinese Koreans is in the cultivation of rice in the cold northeast of the country. They were pioneers in opening up the Manchurian region and in particular in introducing wet-field or paddy rice farming, the techniques of which they taught to the surrounding Chinese and spread to other northerly parts of China. Rice was first grown in Yanbian in 1877. In 1933 Korean farmers succeeded in growing rice in the Heilongjiang basin at a latitude of $50^{\circ}15'$. They are still responsible for producing much of the rice crop in Heilongjiang Province.

Korean emigration from the north of the peninsula into the Chinese northeast started in the 1860s, driven by famine and poverty, and was at first clandestine. By 1870, Koreans were living in villages north of the Yalu and Tuman rivers (which between them form much of the border between China and Korea). During the 1880s, as the northeast provinces were opened up, Korean immigrants were permitted to settle as tenant farmers with a degree of self-administration and their position was legalised through the granting of land deeds and the payment of land tax. Yanbian soon emerged as a centre of Korean activity. By 1894 it had a population of 20,846. After the annexation of Korea by Japan in 1910, increasing numbers of Koreans fled across the border into the region, which served as a base for guerrilla raids into Korea. The Japanese occupation of Manchuria in 1931 brought a further flow, which in 1937 became a forced migration as the Japanese drafted in Korean labour. By 1945 the Korean population of Manchuria stood at 2,163,115. Repatriation after the end of the Pacific War brought the number down to between 700,000 and 800,000.

Shortly after the Japanese annexation of the peninsula a number of Korean political exiles fled to Shanghai, which they used as the base for a diplomatic campaign for Korean independence. They sent a representative to lobby, unsuccessfully, at the 1919 Peace Conference in Paris and in the same year formed a provisional government in exile. More direct resistance was mounted from Manchuria, where in the early 1930s Yanbian became a base for anti-Japanese struggle. Close links formed between Koreans in the region and Chinese Communist elements, and in the Chinese civil war (1947-1949), Koreans sided with the Communists against the Nationalists. A contingent of 62,942 Korean youths from the three northeast provinces—5% of the Korean population— fought in the Communist army and helped to secure victory in the northeast. In the Korean War, Chinese Koreans supported the North. Some youths enlisted in the North Korean army, while about 5000 more from Yanbian joined the Chinese People's Volunteers, with a similar number going as auxiliaries.

In 1952, the Korean minority in Yanbian assumed its official status in the new People's Republic of China as the Yanbian Korean Autonomous Prefecture, one of the first such autonomous units in the country. Chinese agreement in the early 1950s with North Korea on the nationality of Koreans in China led to a policy of recognising all those living in the northeast as Chinese citizens, while allowing those living elsewhere in China the choice between Chinese and North Korean citizenship. Several thousand are said to have chosen the second option.

Two bad periods during the Rectification Movement of 1957-1959 and the Cultural Revolution (which the Chinese describe as lasting from 1966-1976) threatened the well-being of the Korean community. In common with all national minorities, the Koreans in Yanbian suffered as the use of their language was discredited and local leaders attacked in attempts to assert Han Chinese superiority. Since the death of Mao Zedong in 1976 the situation has improved. Within the confines of the rigid Chinese state the Koreans enjoy a measure of self-assertion and prosperity. Yanbian has its own Korean-language radio and press, while other centres in the northeast support Korean-language newspapers and publications. Cultural material from both North and South Korea reaches the Chinese Koreans, who are now permitted contact with relatives in the South.

Yanbian prefecture is rich in natural resources and mineral deposits. From an agricultural economy its inhabitants are moving into industry. It is now free to carry on its own foreign trade, private investment is permitted, and it can develop its resources jointly with foreigners and other overseas Koreans. The way is clear for South Korean co-operation.

The former Soviet Union

Korean communities are found in the Central Asian republics of Kazakhstan and Uzbekistan and on the island of Sakhalin off the east coast of Siberia. The Soviet census of 1979 recorded 388,926 Koreans, but unofficial estimates range up to 750,000. The presence of these communities in Central Asia is one of the most unexpected consequences of great power manoeuvring in East Asia during the first half of the 20th century.

Early Korean immigration into Russia started from the same region—the northeast of the peninsula—and for the same reasons—famine and unstable conditions—as the early movement from Korea into China. Russia and Korea had become neighbours following the 1860 Treaty of Peking between China and Russia, which obliged China to cede the territory between the Ussuri river and the Pacific coast to Russia. Even before 1860, Korean farmers had been crossing illegally into this largely uninhabited region, but from that year they were permitted to settle. In 1870, some 8400 Koreans were said to be living in the Maritime Region of the Russian Empire. Some had entered via China across the Russian-Manchurian border. Their numbers grew so rapidly that by the mid-1880s attempts were made to control immigration by requiring passports. In 1884, Russian citizenship was offered to those Koreans who had entered before that year. The new immigrants crowded into the Pos'yet Bay area west of Vladivostok, just across the border from Korea. Vladivostok itself had a Korean quarter, Shinhanch'on ('New Korea Village'). By the beginning of the 20th century, Koreans in the Maritime Region numbered 32,000. They had established schools and churches and had their own newspapers.

From 1905, as Japan steadily extended its control over Korea, the Maritime Region became a base for Korean guerrilla raids across the border. After the 1917 October Revolution Korean resistance groups took on a socialist or Communist flavour and began to receive economic aid and arms from the newly founded Soviet Union through its international front organisation, the Comintern. Between 1918 and 1922 the intervention of Russian White Guards, Western Allied forces and Japanese troops in the far east of Russia brought the Korean resistance under Japanese assault and forced radical groups to relocate in China. The various invading forces were expelled and in 1922 the former Maritime Region was incorporated into the Soviet Union as the Soviet Far East.

Soviet policy towards Korean immigrants was to encourage naturalisation, and by the time of the 1926 census most of the 168,000 Koreans recorded in the Far East Region had acquired Soviet citizenship. Soviet willingness to improve links with Japan after Japan had recognised the new regime in 1925 led to a falling off in Soviet support for Korean independence groups. Towards the end of the 1920s a Korean proposal for an autonomous Korean republic in the area was rejected by the Soviet side. In the following decade, as the political atmosphere in the Soviet Union became increasingly permeated with mistrust and intimidation as Stalin sought to liquidate his opponents, the Korean community itself came under renewed suspicion. As early as 1905 fears had been expressed that it might provide cover for Japanese espionage. Japanese insistence that Koreans in the Soviet Far East were Japanese citizens, coupled with Japanese aggression in Manchuria, revived these fears. In 1937 the decision was taken to relocate the entire Korean community away from the Korean border into Central Asia. By the end of that year the operation appears to have been completed. Those who did not want to go were apparently taken to the Korean border area and urged to make for Manchuria. Compensation was to be offered for houses abandoned and new land and homes were promised in Kazakhstan, a region to which, it appears, some Koreans had already gone in the 1920s to cultivate rice. In all, 180,000 Koreans are said to have been forced to migrate.

For several decades little was known outside of the Soviet Union about the Korean communities in Central Asia, and the details of their forced relocation are still obscure. Since the late 1980s, however, far more has emerged on their life.

As in China, Korean immigrants have won recognition as rice producers. From 1905 they introduced rice cultivation into the Ussuri river basin south of Khabarovsk. In Central Asia they expanded the area on which rice was grown and also produced cotton. Now they appear to be moving steadily towards an urban life, and a professional class is emerging. Nonetheless, they have never been permitted to form a distinct administrative unit, and their language has no official status. Whereas in the Far East Region Korean was the medium of education in their schools and a unified Korean spelling was developed for textbooks, after 1937 education in Korean in the Central Asian republics appears to have fluctuated. It is taught in local primary schools and as a subject for academic research. Russian, particularly among younger people, is now widely spoken and indeed for some is the mother tongue. Assimilation appears to be the way forward for the younger generation.

A Korean-language newspaper, *Lenin Kichi* ('Flag of Lenin'), founded in 1938, is published in Almaty, the capital of Kazakhstan, and serves as a point of contact. Kazakh Radio has since 1984 been providing a weekly service in Korean. A third focus of Korean culture is the Korean Theatre, inaugurated in 1932 in Vladivostok, which moved in 1937 to Central Asia and is now based in Almaty. Korean themes have persisted in the theatre offered, but more traditional Korean types of drama, such as the masked dance and *p'ansori,* have not and plays are now largely performed in Russian. Song and dance groups preserve some Korean music and dance. Korean literature, starved for half a century of contacts with its roots, has been much overshadowed in its development by Soviet literature. The material elements of Korean culture have survived more strongly, such as the use of *ondol* underfloor heating and a traditional arrangement of rooms in the home. Korean dress may be worn on family occasions, and rice and *kimch'i* are still important elements of diet. Given names are often Russian in form, but family names survive, and the prohibition on marriage between two members of the same clan remains in place.

The experiences of the small Korean community living on Sakhalin island are still largely unknown. This group is thought to number between 40,000 and 60,000. Towards the end of the Japanese colonial period Koreans were brought mainly from the south of the peninsula to exploit the southern part of Sakhalin, then in Japanese possession. When the whole of the island came under Soviet control at the end of the Pacific War, these Koreans were obliged to remain. They were offered a choice between Soviet citizenship, which many of them took, and North Korean citizenship. A smaller number, who regarded South Korea as their birthplace, were treated as stateless. Some of the Sakhalin group have joined the larger community in Central Asia.

Japan

The Korean community in Japan is about 700,000 strong. As such it forms the largest element—over 85%—of the foreign population. Despite their status in colonial times as citizens of the Japanese empire, and despite the fact that three-quarters of the present community have been born and reared in Japan, the majority of Koreans are classed as aliens. They are consequently ineligible for certain types of work, such as in the public sector and as teachers in Japanese schools, and for social benefits. Their jobs tend to be in the lower end of the market, and they suffer more subtle forms of discrimination, such as rejection as suitable marriage partners for Japanese. In the main they live in heavily populated urban areas.

The present uneasy relationship between Japan and its Korean residents has its roots in past mutual animosity between the colonisers and the colonised. Koreans had emigrated to Japan in small numbers in earlier centuries, some voluntarily, others unwillingly (such as the craftsmen taken to Japan in the wake of the Japanese invasions of the peninsula at the end of the 16th century). With the enforcement of colonial administration in Korea after 1910, Koreans were drawn increasingly to Japan. Most of the new immigrants were farmers from the southern end of the peninsula—South Kyŏngsang and South Chŏlla provinces—and from Cheju island. Colonial policies of land ownership had left them impoverished and landless. At the same time industrial production in Japan was booming, boosted by the needs of World War I. Japan's demands for labour could not be wholly met from indigenous sources, but employers found they could recruit Koreans, who were attracted by the wages. From about 1917 the flow of Korean immigrants into Japanese factories was stepped up. The newcomers tended to congregate in the industrial regions around Osaka and Fukuoka .

The jobs offered the new immigrants were largely in textile production, glassmaking, mining and construction, areas of employment where recruitment had traditionally been difficult or where conditions were bad. Such work was regarded as suitable for Koreans, who were judged incapable of the more skilled jobs undertaken by Japanese workers. The gap in employment between Japanese and Koreans was reflected in a wage differential of about one-third for all occupations. The Korean workforce was generally badly housed and cared for and treated with suspicion. Nonetheless, labour demands were such that in 1922 restrictions on Korean entrants into Japan were abolished and the numbers of immigrants rose from 40,755 in 1920 to 410,009 in 1930. During the 1930s the immigrant labour force was directed increasingly towards the growing war industries. From 1940, when the number of Koreans in Japan stood at 1,241,315, Koreans were virtually conscripted as contract labourers into Japanese war work, to release Japanese workers for war service. Their numbers peaked during the Pacific War at around two million.

Students formed a smaller group of Koreans living in Japan. They started to arrive in the 1880s, when Korea made its first tentative steps towards modernisation. They viewed themselves as potential reformers of the old system and felt they were drawing support from Japanese liberals. In the various episodes of the reform movement in the 1880s and 1890s, Korean students who had studied in Japan played conspicuous roles. Even after the annexation of Korea, when Japanese intentions could no longer be seen as benevolent, young Koreans continued to travel to Japan, particularly Tokyo, to study. The majority of them financed their own studies, which were often in the social sciences. From 500 in 1910 their numbers rose to nearly 8000 by 1930.

As Japan tightened its grip on Korean affairs, Korean students in Japan came under increasing surveillance. From reform their preoccupations turned to national independence. On 8 February 1919, several weeks before the 1 March Declaration of

Independence in Seoul, some of them prepared their own declaration in Tokyo. From then onwards, left-wing and radical policies spread among Korean students in Japan.

After 1945, extensive repatriation of Koreans from Japan took place, and by 1950 only 544,903 Koreans remained. In 1947, these were obliged to register under the new Alien Registration Law, and their status as foreigners was confirmed in the 1952 San Francisco peace treaty. An agreement negotiated in 1959 through the Red Cross led to the repatriation over the following eight years of about 100,000 Japanese Koreans to North Korea. Agreement on the legal standing of at least some of the Korean minority in Japan was reached with South Korea only in 1965, when diplomatic relations were established. As a result, permanent resident status was offered to those Koreans who had lived in Japan from before the Pacific War. In the event, such status has been granted only to those willing to take citizenship of the Republic of Korea.

The ambiguity surrounding the Korean community is intensified by divisions within it between supporters of North Korea, united in the Ch'ongnyŏn organisation, and of South Korea, grouped in the Mindan organisation. The Ch'ongnyŏn faction runs its own educational institutions and has channelled investment into North Korea. It has also been used by the Japanese authorities as an unofficial means of communication with North Korea. The South Korean government, mindful that in 1974 President Park's wife was killed by a North Korean gunman who had travelled from Japan, has long been wary of the possibilities of North Korean infiltration into its territory through Japan.

North America

In contrast to the formation of Korean communities in other parts of East and Central Asia, Korean emigration to North America has largely followed standard patterns of Asian emigration to the United States and Canada. Korean preference has been for the United States; immigration into Canada has involved much smaller numbers.

The volume of Korean emigration to the United States has been controlled primarily by US legislation. The status of Koreans as citizens of the Japanese Empire during the colonial period was a subsidiary factor in preventing any large-scale movement. In the 1880s and 1890s, individual Koreans had travelled to the United States to study or to escape political difficulties in Korea. Emigration proper began in the early years of the 20th century when, between 1903 and 1905, a group of 7226 Koreans—settlers and their families—were permitted to move to Hawaii to work in the sugar plantations. Such emigration stopped after 1905, mainly under Japanese pressure. Many of the Korean settlers abandoned the plantations to become shopkeepers, and about 2000 moved to the US mainland, generally to California. Between 1910 and 1924, Korean immigrants to the United States comprised women arriving for marriage, political exiles and students.

The Oriental Exclusion Act of 1924 applied a quota system aimed against East European and Asian immigration. It had the effect of reducing Korean immigration to a trickle. At the end of World War II there were some 10,000 Koreans in the United States: approximately 3000 in mainland US and about 7000 in Hawaii. Numbers rose somewhat after 1945 as students and some professional and business people, together with the brides of US servicemen, began to arrive. About 15,000 Koreans entered between 1945 and 1965, when the Immigration and Naturalization Act abolished the former discriminatory quota systems. In 1962, the South Korean government had eased emigration for its own nationals. After 1965, Korean immigration began to gather in momentum, in line with immigration from other Asian countries. Now Asian Americans constitute the fastest-growing minority in the United States.

The Korean rate of entry has been put at around 30,000 in recent years. From a figure of 70,598 in the US 1970 census, the Korean community rose to 357,393 in the 1980 census. Immigration accounted for the greatest part of that increase, with many Koreans arriving to join family members already settled in the United States. Over a passage of time most immigrants have taken US citizenship. The exact present size of the community is not known, but is probably around one million. Two features that distinguish the Korean population are the number of Korean women married to American men and the presence of Korean children adopted into American homes. The continuous stationing of US troops in Korea since 1951 has led to a flow of Korean spouses. By 1981 a total of 53,629 Korean wives had entered the United States.

Around half of the Korean community is estimated to be living in the western states of the United States. In common with other Asian Americans many have chosen California, which is said to be home to around a third of Koreans. New York State is the next choice, with about 10%. The Korean population is predominantly urban, with the largest concentrations in Los Angeles, New York and Chicago. It is on the whole a young population. Reflecting the priorities of the mother society, many Koreans arrive well educated and continue to aspire to good education in the United States. Though some immigrants may have to accept employment inferior to their educational achievement for a while after their arrival, they tend eventually to find more appropriate work. About 20% have professional or technical jobs. Many are self-employed in the retail and service sectors, owning small groceries and running garages and dry-cleaning shops. Social needs are met through a network of family contacts, clubs and churches. A 1985 survey found 1500 Korean churches throughout the United States, one for every 450 immigrants. A Korean-language press and radio stations further serve the community.

The greatest setback to Korean prospects came in 1992 when Korean-owned businesses in the south central district of Los Angeles were the target of looting and vandalising in riots in the city in May of that year. The estimate of the number of Korean stores damaged or destroyed ranges from 1560 to 2500. About 80% of the Korean American economy in the riot area is said to have been devastated. Most of the businesses affected were small ventures run as self-employed concerns, operating in areas of Los Angeles with high proportions of Afro-American and Hispanic residents. Their Korean owners, however, lived mainly elsewhere. Various reasons have been suggested for this singling out of Korean stores: resentment at high prices, anger over what was seen as Korean disdain for the surrounding population, eagerness to get back at apparently prosperous shopkeepers. The riots were the culmination of around a decade of tension between Korean-Americans and Afro-Americans and Latinos in Los Angeles and were preceded by a year-long boycott of Korean grocery stores in the Flatbush district of Brooklyn in 1991, following the shooting by a shopkeeper of an Afro-American. The Korean reaction to such intercommunal violence has been one of anger and dismay, but also of reflection and realisation that the Korean community has to study its relations with other sections of American society.

Readings

China

F. Hoffmann, 1986. 'The Korean minority in China: Education and publishing', *Korea Journal* 26, no.12: 13-26

Chae-Jin Lee, 1986. *China's Korean Minority*. Boulder, CO: Westview Press

'The Koreans' , 1989. *China's Minority Nationalities*, Ma Yin (ed.). Beijing: Foreign Languages Press: 54-58.

Dae-Sook Suh and E. J. Shultz (eds), 1990. *Koreans in China*. Honolulu: Center for Korean Studies

Former Soviet Union

Songmoo Kho, 1987. *Koreans in Soviet Central Asia*. Helsinki: Finnish Oriental Society

Dae-Sook Suh (ed.), 1987. *Koreans in the Soviet Union*. Honolulu: Center for Korean Studies

Japan

M. Weiner, 1989. *Origins of the Korean Community in Japan*. Manchester: Manchester University Press

United States

H. R. Barringer and Sung-Nam Cho, 1989. *Koreans in the United States*. Honolulu: Center for Korean Studies

H. H. Koh *et al.*, 1994. 'Realities and visions of Korean Americans', *Korean and Korean American Studies* 5, no. 1 (Spring/Summer)

D. McEvoy and I. G. Cook, 1993. *Transpacific Migration: Asians in North America*. Second British Pacific Rim Seminar, Liverpool John Moores University, September 1993

Ed. G. O. Totten III and H. E. Schockman, 1994. *Community in Crisis*. Los Angeles: University of California

Eui-Young Yu, 1993. ' The Korean American community', in *Korea Briefing, 1993*, D. N. Clark (ed.). Boulder, CO: Westview Press: 139-162

RESOURCES

EDUCATION MATERIALS

Audio Learning (Series on Korea), 1983. London and New York: Audio Learning
Limited

A series of cassette tapes, basically containing talks and discussions by established
scholars in the field of Korean studies. Five topics are dealt with: *Korea in the 1980s*
(HMA013; H. S. Ferns and K. W. Watkins), *South Korean Economic Affairs*
(HMA014; Lawrence B. Krause and Kim Ki-hwan), *The Problems of Division and
Unification in Korea* (HMA015; Robert Scalapino, Donald S. Zagoria and Han Sung-
zoo), *Korean Music and Art* (HMA016; Hesung C. Koh, Jan Fontein, William P. Malm,
Robert F. Thompson), *Korean Art and Culture* (HMA017; Hesung C. Koh, Robert F.
Thompson, Jonathan D. Spence, George DeVos). A couple of pages of text summarise
the discussions on each tape. The set is now very dated, and we doubt it can be put to
use in contemporary classroom situations.

Discover Korea: a Teacher's Manual for Geography and Industry, 1989. New York:
The Asia Society

Designed for junior high school students (ages 15-16) in the USA, this manual and
accompanying video forms part of a series covering aspects of Korean geography,
history and culture. It draws on the output of several contributors who have worked in
the field to paint a picture of Korea's geography and people and of South Korean
industry. On the whole it is well produced and written, although not directed
sufficiently towards the British National Curriculum to be very useful.

Tom Hewitt, Hazel Johnson and Dave Wield (eds), 1992. ***Industrialization and
Development***. Oxford: Oxford University Press

Designed primarily with Open University students in mind, this textbook is likely to be
used by a number of sixth form teachers. Green headings throughout the book
accompany black and white photographs and what is generally a very well researched
text. Brazil and Korea provide specific case studies, each being allocated separate
chapters and then large chunks of issue-related chapters. Chapter 4, by Chris Edwards,
is devoted to industrialisation in South Korea. The text relies on 1988 data, already out-
of-date by 1992, and now substantially incorrect. Much use is made of other authors,
who are liberally cited, particularly for curious statements, such as Bello's assertion that
South Korea received $6 billion in aid from America over a twenty-year period, almost
as much as the aid provided for the whole of Africa. The conclusion refers to an Alice
Amsden statement, to suggest "the age of paternalism may be over."

F. Czarra, T. Kaltsounis, Shin Se Ho, Kim Doo Jung (eds), 1988. ***The Social Studies,
79/4. The United States and the Pacific Rim: Focus on South Korea***

Another publication from the US with the specific aim of increasing the knowledge and
understanding of Korea among elementary and high school students. Written
principally by Koreans, it covers topics in geography, economic development, life in
South Korea today, as well as the arts and literature. It outlines activities for the
classroom as well as including a comprehensive list of further reading, resources and
useful organisations. Again, it includes some useful information but this is poorly

produced and presented and would not stimulate the interest of teachers or students in the mid-1990s.

Patricia M.Bartz, 1972. *South Korea*. Oxford: Oxford University Press

Published over twenty years ago, and long since remaindered, this text may still be found in school libraries. Generally, the text is sound, but it presents a picture of Korea before the impact of modernisation and industrialisation. It is, consequently, of little classroom use.

R. Beddis, 1989. *The Third World: Development and Interdependence*. Oxford: Oxford University Press

Designed specifically for GCSE Key Stage 4 in British schools. Eight pages are devoted to South Korea (pp.124-131), plus a map (p.116). The book has been reprinted twice (1992 and 1993) and is glossy, with coloured maps and diagrams. Korea appears in Part II, under the general title, 'The Third World: Case studies in development', and if this appears inappropriate then the inclusion of Saudi Arabia is ludicrous. Marred by outdated information (a Hyundai advert is from the early 1980s, per capita GNP is given as $2150, and the population is underestimated at 41.1 million), and a number of significant errors. There are no diacritics in the text, and the map is extremely simple, marking only Kimp'o as an 'international airport'.

R. Buckley (ed.), 1993. *Understanding Global Issues: The Pacific Rim Powerhouse of the 21st Century*. Cheltenham: European Schoolbooks

This forms part of a series of briefing sheets on topical issues which either stand alone or as part of an 'education pack' containing the briefing sheet and a large wall chart in a plastic folder. The target market is Sixth Form and beyond. The series is well researched and produced and contains a wealth of background information, up-to-date statistical data together with additional notes and sources. This issue deals with the rise in importance of the Pacific Rim countries, Japan, China and the four 'little tigers' as well as SE Asia. The focus is on economics, trade and industrial issues. Page 11 offers a section devoted to South Korea that presents concise but useful data and information, marred only marginally by a few loose details.

GENERAL BOOKS

Judith Cherry, 1993. *Republic of Korea. Cassell Business Briefings*. London: Cassell.

Donald N. Clark, 1991, 1992, 1993. *Korea Briefing*. Boulder, CO: Westview

Susan Crowder Han, 1995. *Notes on Things Korean*. Elizabeth, NJ, and Seoul: Hollym

Carter Eckert *et al*, 1990. *Korea Old and New: A History*. Seoul: Ilchokak/Cambridge, MA: Harvard University Press

James Hoare & Susan Pares, 1988. *Korea: An Introduction*. London: KPI

Hagen Koo (ed.), 1993. *State and Society in Contemporary Korea*. Ithaca, NY: Cornell University Press

Peter H. Lee (ed.), 1993. *Sourcebook of Korean Civilisation*. New York: Columbia University Press

Stewart Lone & Gavan McCormack, 1994. *Korea Since 1850*. New York: St Martin's Press

Colin Mackerras (ed.), 1992. *Eastern Asia: An Introductory History*. Melbourne: Longman

Beth McKillop, 1992. *Korean Art and Design: The Samsung Gallery of Korean Art*. London: Victoria and Albert Museum

(readings specific to subject, issues and topics are listed within each chapter of this book)

JOURNALS

Koreana. Concise articles, well illustrated with colour photography. From: The Korea Foundation, 526 Namdaemunno 5-ga, Chung-gu, Seoul 100-095

Korea Focus. Bimonthly publication on politics, economics, and current affairs which mainly translates the writings of Korean journalists. From: The Korea Foundation, 526 Namdaemunno 5-ga, Chung-gu, Seoul 100-095

Korea Journal. Academic articles. From: Korea National Commission for UNESCO, CPO Box 64, Seoul 100-022

Korea Newsreview. Weekly news digest from South Korea, published by Korea Herald, 1-12, 3-ga, Hoehyon-dong, Chung-gu, Seoul 100-771

Morning Calm. Monthly inflight magazine (which routinely includes articles on Korean culture, and on the urban and rural landscape) from Korean Airlines, 11/12 Hanover Street, London W1

Papers of the British Association for Korean Studies. From the editor: Keith Howard, Centre of Korean Studies, School of Oriental & African Studies, Thornhaugh Street, London WC1H 0XG. Six volumes (1991-6)

(More scholarly US journals include *Journal of Korean Studies* and *Korean Studies*)

MUSEUMS

The British Museum, Great Russell Street, London (Korea Foundation Gallery opens in 1998)

The Samsung Gallery of Korean Art, Victoria and Albert Museum, Cromwell Road, London

USEFUL ADDRESSES

Anglo-Korean Cultural Centre, 240 Burlington Road, New Malden, KT3 4NN (organises Korean and Anglo-Korean events, including festivals, lectures and classes)

The British Association for Korean Studies. Prof. Gina Barnes, President, School of East Asian Studies, University of Durham, Elvet Hill, Durham DH1

Centre of Korean Studies, School of Oriental & African Studies, Thornhaugh Street, London WC1H 0XG

Embassy of the Republic of Korea, 4 Palace Gate, London W8 5NF. (maps, films, videos, books; distributes *Korea Newsreview* and a monthly cultural photo-digest, *Seoul*)

Korea National Tourism Corporation, 20 St George Street, London W1R 9RE (posters, maps, booklets)

Korea Trade Centre, Vincent House, Vincent Square, London SW1 (information on Korean business and Korean companies in the UK)